Spring Persistence with Hibernate

PAUL TEPPER FISHER
BRIAN D. MURPHY

Apress®

Spring Persistence with Hibernate

ISBN-13 (pbk): 978-1-4302-2632-1

ISBN-13 (electronic): 978-1-4302-2633-8

Printed and bound in the United States of America 9 8 7 6 5 4 3 2 1

President and Publisher: Paul Manning
Lead Editors: Steve Anglin, Tom Welsh
Technical Reviewer: Sia Cyrus
Editorial Board: Steve Anglin, Mark Beckner, Ewan Buckingham, Gary Cornell, Jonathan Gennick, Jonathan Hassell, Michelle Lowman, Matthew Moodie, Duncan Parkes, Jeffrey Pepper, Frank Pohlmann, Douglas Pundick, Ben Renow-Clarke, Dominic Shakeshaft, Matt Wade, Tom Welsh
Coordinating Editor: Mary Tobin
Copy Editor: Marilyn Smith
Compositor: Kimberly Burton
Indexer: Julie Grady
Artist: April Milne
Cover Designer: Anna Ishchenko

Distributed to the book trade worldwide by Springer Science+Business Media, LLC., 233 Spring Street, 6th Floor, New York, NY 10013. Phone 1-800-SPRINGER, fax (201) 348-4505, e-mail orders-ny@springer-sbm.com, or visit www.springeronline.com.

For information on translations, please e-mail rights@apress.com, or visit www.apress.com.

Apress and friends of ED books may be purchased in bulk for academic, corporate, or promotional use. eBook versions and licenses are also available for most titles. For more information, reference our Special Bulk Sales–eBook Licensing web page at www.apress.com/info/bulksales.

The source code for this book is available to readers at www.apress.com. You will need to answer questions pertaining to this book in order to successfully download the code.

To Melanie, for making it all worthwhile

—Paul

I would like to dedicate this, my first print book, to my mom. I miss you always

—Brian

Contents at a Glance

Contents

About the Authors

 **Paul Tepper Fisher** first began working in technology at Johns Hopkins University, where he spent several years developing a distance-learning application for neuroscience, while completing graduate school there. He has founded two technology start-ups: SmartPants Media, Inc., a software development company specializing in interactive multimedia technology; and dialmercury.com, which develops telephony applications using VOIP and Java.

Paul was also Manager of Technology at Wired.com, where he led the software development team for the online publications of Wired.com, webmonkey.com, and howto.wired.com, using Spring, Grails, and Java technology.

Currently, Paul is Director of Engineering for a new Music Service at Lime Wire, where he manages several development teams using agile methodologies. Comprised of client-side and distributed server-side components, the Music Service is designed for horizontal scalability with a goal of supporting millions of end-users and terabytes of data.

You can read Paul's blog at: `http://paultepperfisher.com`.

 **Brian D. Murphy** is the Chief Architect and Director of Engineering at Condé Nast. He was an early adopter of Spring and Hibernate and uses both technologies to power all of Condé's brands online, including wired.com, newyorker.com, epicurious.com, and vanityfair.com, drawing tens of millions of unique visitors each month. Brian deals with the challenges of building scalable, distributed systems every single day. He has a B.S. in Computer Science from Rutgers University. You can follow Brian on Twitter at `http://twitter.com/@brimurph` or read his blog at `http://turmoildrivendevelopment.com`.

About the Technical Reviewer

■ **Sia Cyrus**'s experience in computing spans many decades and areas of software development. During the 1980s, he specialized in database development in Europe. In the 1990s, he moved to the US where he focused on client-server applications. Since 2000, he has architected a number of middle-tier business processes incorporating Spring and Hibernate. Most recently, he has been specializing in Web 2.0, Ajax, GWT, and Android.

Sia is an independent software consultant who is an expert in Java and development of Java enterprise-class applications. He has been responsible for innovative and generic software, holding a US Patent in database-driven user interfaces. Sia created a very successful configuration-based framework for the telecommunications industry, which he later converted to Spring Framework. His passion could be entitled "Enterprise Architecture in Open Source".

When not experimenting with new technologies, he enjoys playing ice hockey especially with his two boys, Jason and Brandon. He can be reached at sia.cyrus@comcast.net.

Acknowledgments

Writing a book always ends up being more difficult than you initially imagined. Although the absurdly late nights and lost weekends prove difficult to the authors, it is often the people around them that end up suffering the most. To that end, I'd like to thank Melanie Colton for her endless patience and perseverance. She deserves more than a medal for putting up with the many 4am nights and my noisy typing. This book would not have been possible without her support, understanding, and muse.

I would also like to acknowledge my colleagues at Lime Company, for their continued trust and support. It is a rare experience to work with such a talented and committed group of people, and I am grateful for the opportunity to be a part of such an important adventure.

I'd also like to thank Solomon Duskis for starting this journey, and for his unwavering enthusiasm for technology—especially Java and Spring.

I would be remiss if I didn't offer my appreciation and gratitude to my parents, who have inspired me through their relentless trust, support, and faith in everything I set out to do.

Finally, my sincere appreciation goes to Brian Murphy for joining the project and keeping things rolling along. If it hadn't been for Brian's tenacity and motivation, this book would never have seen the light of day. It's been an honor and privilege working with you again.

—Paul Tepper Fisher

We'd like to thank Apress for the opportunity to write this book. Special thanks to Steve Anglin for believing in us and letting us stretch the schedule to cover advanced topics in depth. We owe Mary Tobin a special debt of gratitude for shepherding us through this process and ultimately dragging us across the finish line. Thanks to Tom Welsh, Marilyn Smith, and Sia Cyrus, who provided invaluable feedback, suggestions and encouragement along the way. This is a much better book as a result of their wisdom and patience. Any issues or errors in this text are ours alone.

I would like to thank my wife, Dania, without whom this book wouldn't be possible. She graciously took on the role of super mom while I devoted nights and weekends to writing for far longer than bargained for. I'd like to thank my son Liam for being the most terrific little kid. You provide me with more joy and a new appreciation for the world than you'll ever know. I'd also like to acknowledge our second son, who is due shortly after this book will be published. I can't wait to meet you!

Lastly, I'd like to thank Paul Fisher for sharing this experience with me. This book was Paul's brainchild and I'm glad he invited me along for the ride. Writing this book has been both rewarding and challenging. I learned a ton and it's been great to work with you again.

—Brian D. Murphy

Preface

Since its inception, the Spring Framework has gradually changed the rules of application development in the Java community. This book is the ideal guide and teaching companion for developers interested in learning about the Spring Framework and how it can be leveraged to build persistence-driven applications using Hibernate, one of the most popular Java persistence frameworks today. *Spring Persistence with Hibernate* gets you rolling with fundamental Spring concepts, as well as proven design patterns for integrating persistence into your applications.

Many of the lessons illustrated in this book were culled from years of practical experience building scalable, high-volume web applications using Spring and Hibernate. One of the details that stands out in our joint experience is the importance and benefit of learning through hands-on experience. To this end, we will build a real-world application that utilizes Spring 3, Hibernate 3.5, JPA 2.0, Hibernate-Search, Grails, Spring Roo, and Dozer. We firmly believe that learning about Spring and Hibernate implies far more than simply understanding the respective APIs of each framework. To be able to effectively develop with these two amazing technologies, it is necessary to understand the design patterns and best practices for getting the best from these frameworks, and building on them in a consistent, proven manner. We hope this book will teach you more than just how to use Spring and Hibernate together. Our goal is to channel the development experience, lessons, and best practices we've seen work successfully in our experience, so that you can apply these skills and tools in your own applications.

Throughout these pages, we will introduce core Hibernate fundamentals, demonstrating how the framework can be best utilized within a Spring context. We will start with foundational concepts, such as strategies for developing an effective domain model and DAO layer, and then move into querying techniques using HQL, JPQL, and the Criteria API. After fundamental concepts are introduced, we will move on to more advanced topics, such as fetching and caching strategies. We will also illustrate several approaches for architecting a transactional service facade. Both programmatic and declarative transactions will be examined, showcasing the benefits of using Spring for expressing transactional semantics.

Spring Persistence with Hibernate will also introduce JPA, covering its history and the ways in which Hibernate influenced its development. We will discuss the benefits of following the JPA standard, as well as when it makes sense to utilize Hibernate-specific features. The book will also introduce Grails and GORM, illustrating the differences between the DAO and Active Record patterns. We will port our sample application (which will be developed in the course of the book) into both Grails and Spring Roo, highlighting the benefits and differences of using a rapid-development, convention-over-configuration platform. In these sections, we will explore topics related to concurrency/optimistic locking, Hibernate Session state, caching approaches, and transaction management.

The last part of the book will introduce several advanced techniques, important for working with enterprise Spring/Hibernate applications. We will illustrate some of the pitfalls with integrating legacy databases, as well as best practices for developing REST web services, handling Hibernate proxies and lazy collections, as well as building search functionality using Hibernate-Search.

Here are some of the main topics we will discuss in this book:

- Basic Spring Framework features such as IoC and AOP
- Core concepts for architecting a well-layered persistence tier
- JPA concepts and steps for integrating JPA
- Foundational and advanced concepts for working with Hibernate
- Hibernate querying techniques
- DAO and Service Facade layer development
- Grails, along with the introduction of Active-Record Pattern
- Introduction of Spring Roo
- Building a REST web service
- Translating between a domain model and a DTO using Dozer
- Leveraging other frameworks and technologies, such as Hibernate-Search
- Advanced Caching and Integration strategies

Application with
, and Patterns

...tion, providing the long-term memory that software ...ocations. Despite its importance, the architecture of a ...eration during the design or implementation stages of ...planning can be far-reaching and devastating to an

...ou with the best practices, tools, and strategies required ...persistence tier. Many of the concepts found on these ...perience designing and building web applications ...bjective is to illustrate the patterns and approaches that ...tion details for using Spring and Hibernate in your own

...he years is that it's often best to learn by example. To ...tion over the course of the book: an Image Gallery web ...ws and exhibitions curated by administrators. To ...nitectural patterns for building scalable and ...us on a different aspect of application development, in ...samples and discussion, we will trace the design, ...ing application. Starting with the foundation, each ...one, adding new layers, features, and tests. And of ...ill do significant refactoring as we discover new ...lternative strategies and frameworks. In fact, the last two ...lication entirely, as we examine two new frameworks founded on the concept of "convention over configuration." Intended for a more rapid style of development, Grails and Roo offer a more holistic and consistent development environment with powerful features popularized by frameworks from dynamic languages, such as Ruby on Rails and Django.

The Benefit of a Consistent Approach

As you will learn throughout this book, the manner in which data is saved and queried is an integral part of every application. In fact, the persistence layer often serves as the foundation upon which an application is built. Building on top of this foundation are the three core components of a standard Spring-based persistence tier: the domain model, the Data Access Object layer, and the service facade.

Don't worry if some of these terms are unfamiliar to you. In the following chapters, we will explain the purpose and function of each of these components, demonstrating the role each plays in an application.

While we don't suggest that there is only one correct approach to architecting an application, we do want to emphasize the benefit of using key design patterns and best practices. This is a theme that you will see cropping up over and over again.

The Significance of Dependency Injection

The Spring Framework has helped to take much of the guesswork out of designing and building an application. It has become the de facto standard for integrating disparate components and frameworks, and has evolved far beyond its dependency injection roots. The purpose of dependency injection is to decouple the work of resolving external software components from your application business logic. Without dependency injection, the details of how a component accesses required services can get muddled in with the component's code. This not only increases the potential for errors, adds code bloat, and magnifies maintenance complexities; it couples components together more closely, making it difficult to modify dependencies when refactoring or testing.

By its very nature, Spring helps to enforce best coding practices and reduce dependency on external frameworks, or even classes within an application. At the simplest level, Spring is a lightweight IoC container, meaning that it will assume the responsibility of wiring your application dependencies. Exactly how this wiring responsibility is handled will be discussed in depth throughout this book. However, a theme you will see replayed throughout these pages is how Spring effortlessly ties components together in a loosely coupled manner. This has far-reaching effects for any application, as it allows code to be more easily refactored and maintained. And in the context of this book, it allows developers to build a persistence tier that is not directly tied to a particular implementation or framework.

Spring owes much of its success to the sheer number of integration points it provides, covering a wide range of frameworks and technologies. As developers realized the benefits gleaned from using Spring for integrating the various components within their own code, many new abstractions appeared that relied on Spring to integrate popular open source frameworks. Using Spring to integrate a particular framework not only simplifies the introduction of the framework, it allows the integration to be performed in a consistent manner—no different than the way collaborating components are wired within the context of an application. Additionally, using Spring's dependency injection to wire in a key framework ensures the integration is done in a decoupled way.

One of the leading catalysts for Spring's adoption was its support for the open source, object-relational mapping (ORM) framework, Hibernate. As the Spring Framework began to grow in popularity, the Java development community was also buzzing about Hibernate. It was a pivotal time for open source frameworks, as both Spring and Hibernate offered revolutionary solutions that would change the way many new applications were architected and implemented. As you will see, Spring and Hibernate complement each other in numerous ways, and each is partially responsible for the other's success and widespread adoption.

A Synergistic Partnership

In this book, we will focus on showing how Spring and Hibernate can be used together most effectively. Nevertheless, we will still emphasize strategies for decoupling Hibernate from your application. This is not because we have any concerns about using Hibernate, but because loose coupling provides a cleaner separation of concerns.

No matter how good a framework might be, it's always better to keep dependencies decoupled. Not only does an agnostic persistence tier lead to better, cleaner, more maintainable code (as well as portability from one persistence technology to another), but it also ensures consistency across your application. Suddenly, your code is supported by a backbone that handles dependency wiring, provides aspect-oriented programming (AOP) capability, and generates cohesive configuration metadata that implicitly documents the way your application's pieces fit together.

Spring encourages design practices that help to keep all of your application's dependencies decoupled. Whether it be an external framework, an application component, or even Spring or Hibernate themselves, ensuring that collaborating components are not directly tied together helps prevent the concerns of one layer from leaking into another. By delegating all your wiring details to Spring, you not only simplify your code base by relieving the need to create infrastructural "access code," you also ensure that components are kept distinct. In the next few chapters, you will learn how coding to interfaces and using Spring's ORM abstractions and generic exception hierarchy can help to achieve these goals.

The Story of Spring's and Hibernate's Success

The rise in Spring's popularity stems from more than just its ability to reduce code complexity by helping to wire dependencies together. Much of the early excitement around the Spring Framework was due to its support for other leading open source frameworks, including Hibernate. Hibernate was one of the first open source ORM frameworks that provided an enterprise-level solution for building a persistence tier. Spring's ability to externalize integration details to an XML configuration file or express dependency injection through Java annotations provided a powerful abstraction that greatly simplified and standardized the integration efforts required to bootstrap Hibernate into an application.

ORM frameworks provide an abstraction layer over the actual persistence technology being used (usually a relational database), allowing developers to focus on the object-oriented details of their domain model, rather than lower-level database concerns. There is an inherent *impedance mismatch* between the relational-table world of databases and the object-oriented world of Java, making an effective ORM abstraction difficult to implement. This impedance mismatch is due to the fundamental differences between relational databases and object-oriented languages, such as Java. For example, relational databases don't implement core object-oriented principles such as polymorphism, encapsulation, and accessibility. Furthermore, the notion of equality is vastly different between Java and SQL. We will discuss some of these differences throughout this book, examining approaches to bridging the gap between a SQL database and a Java domain model.

Hibernate represented a significant step in bridging this gap by offering a powerful open source framework for expressing an object-oriented domain model, and defining the ways in which the tables and columns of a database synchronized with the object instances and properties in JavaBeans.

A Better Approach for Integration

Despite the improvements and efficiency with which a persistence tier could now be developed, integrating Hibernate into an application could still be a painstaking endeavor. With no standardized integration approach, developers were left to continuously reinvent the wheel, spending significant resources on the development and maintenance of the infrastructure code required to wedge Hibernate into their applications.

As Hibernate grew in popularity, the Spring Framework started to gain momentum as well. When Spring first came on the scene, its mission was to make the development of server-side Java applications simpler. First and foremost, it offered a better solution to wiring application dependencies together. For this reason, Spring is often referred to as a *container*, meaning that it offers a centralized abstraction for integrating collaborating dependencies via configuration, rather than writing (often repetitive) code to handle this task.

Part of Spring's momentum stems from the way it enables applications to deliver enterprise-level features, such as declarative transactions and security, without requiring the overhead and complexity of an Enterprise JavaBean (EJB) container or forcing developers to grapple with the details of specific technologies or standards. Time has proven EJB, although powerful in theory, to be a victim of overengineering. Spring and Hibernate owe much of their success to the fact that they provide a more reasonable and effective solution than the EJB standard. While Spring offers a simpler approach to declarative transaction management, Hibernate provides a more robust and intuitive ORM abstraction. Both frameworks were built and popularized by the growing need for a solution that was less complex than previous offerings. With the success of Spring and Hibernate came a stronger emphasis on building applications that were simpler and lighter weight, significantly increasing both ease of maintenance and scalability.

Although dependency injection was Spring's core purpose, the framework has evolved far beyond its original IoC foundation. The Spring Framework has expanded into other areas that naturally blend with its IoC roots. Spring now provides a pluggable transactional management layer, AOP support, integration points with persistence frameworks (such as Hibernate), and a flexible web framework, called Spring MVC. The addition of these features was a gradual process, spurred by demand and necessity.

As Hibernate's popularity surged, developers began to rely on Spring's persistence abstractions to simplify the often daunting task of integrating Hibernate into an application. Thanks to Spring, the process of getting up and running with Hibernate became a great deal easier. Developers could start with a Spring configuration file that not only bootstrapped a Hibernate `SessionFactory` (allowing configuration details to be specified via standard XML), but also streamlined the invocation of myriad Hibernate operations through the use of well-crafted abstractions founded on time-tested design patterns, such as `HibernateTemplate` and `OpenSessionInView`. We will discuss these core Spring-Hibernate integration details in the next few chapters. The important point here is that combining Spring and Hibernate affords developers an extremely powerful solution.

Not only does Spring simplify the integration of Hibernate, but it also reduces the coupling of Hibernate to an application. If the need arises to switch to a different ORM or persistence technology, this migration effort becomes much easier because there are few direct dependencies on Hibernate itself. For example, Spring provides a generic exception hierarchy for persistence-related errors. Although not required, it is considered good practice to convert Hibernate exceptions to Spring's generic exception hierarchy, which further decouples your application from Hibernate. Spring includes built-in mechanisms to simplify this conversion, to the point that it is fairly transparent. Additionally, Spring's integration code for other persistence technologies (such as JDBC, JPA, TopLink, etc.) will also handle the translation to Spring's generic exception hierarchy, further simplifying a migration from one persistence technology to another.

Establishing loosely coupled dependency relationships is one of Spring's core purposes. In fact, the framework itself limits direct coupling to itself as much as possible, meaning that your application will rarely be directly tied to Spring classes.

Best Practices for Architecting an Application

The more your code is abstracted away from interfacing directly with a database (and dealing with these lower-level concerns), the easier it is to switch to a different database or persistence technology. Similarly, Hibernate also offers an abstraction over your data model, allowing you to focus on your application's persistence details rather than on the particulars of your database. Through these decouplings, a persistence tier becomes far more portable across disparate databases.

Spring centralizes the wiring of dependencies within your application, making maintenance and configuration easier, and coercing developers to code to interfaces, which brings about cleaner and better code. It also allows you to focus more on your application's business logic, with less concern over how this information is physically stored and retrieved. This concept is often called *layering*. Each layer is focused specifically on accomplishing a particular task (with little knowledge or coupling to other layers within the application).

The Layers of a Persistence Tier

The application tier that deals with persistence is often called the *persistence tier*. Spring helps to enforce a modular architecture in which the persistence tier is divided into several core layers that contain the following:

- The Domain Model

- The Data Access Object (DAO) Layer

- The Service Layer (or Service Façade)

Each of these layers is representative of proven design patterns that are key to building a solid, maintainable architecture. Outside the persistence tier, a typical Spring MVC application also has a controller layer, which handles user interaction, delegating to the service facade and shuttling necessary data back to the view. We will get into these implementation details over the next few chapters. Here, we'll take a brief look at the domain model, DAO, and service layers.

The Domain Model

The domain model represents the key entities within an application, defining the manner in which they relate to one another. Each entity defines a series of properties, which designates its characteristics, as well as its relationships to other entities. Each class within the domain model contains the various properties and associations that correlate to columns and relationships within the database. Typically, there is a domain entity for each table within the database, but this is not always the case.

For example, we might need to define a `Person` domain entity, designed to represent the concept of a *person* within the application and the database. The `Person` class could be represented as follows:

```
@Entity
public class Person implements Serializable {

    private Long id;
    private String firstName;
    private String lastName;
    private String username;
    private String password;
    private Integer roleLevel;

    private Integer version;


    public Person() {
```

```
    }

    @Id
    public final Long getId() {
        return id;
    }

    @Version
    public Integer getVersion() {
        return version;
    }

    . . . Remaining Getters and Setters Omitted
}
```

Part of Hibernate's job is to convert between domain model instances and rows in the database. Developers provide hints to help Hibernate perform these conversions, by specifying mapping rules using XML or annotations. This metadata is used by Hibernate to define the characteristics of the domain model and how the object-oriented properties within a domain model class map to columns and relationships within the database.

Although XML was initially used to define mapping rules, we recommend using annotations as this approach is simpler and more concise. In fact, by applying the @Entity annotation to a class, it is assumed that a class property should be persisted to the database using the property name as the database column name and using the field type as a hint for the database column type. Of course, all these details can be explicitly configured or overridden, but thanks to sensible defaults, your mapping configuration should be relatively terse most of the time.

The Data Access Object (DAO) Layer

The DAO layer defines the means for saving and querying the domain model data. A DAO helps to abstract away those details specific to a particular database or persistence technology, providing an interface for persistence behavior from the perspective of the domain model, while encapsulating explicit features of the persistence technology. The goal of the DAO pattern is to completely abstract the underlying persistence technology and the manner in which it loads, saves, and manipulates the data represented by the domain model. The key benefit of the DAO pattern is separation of concerns—the lower-level details of the persistence technology and datasource are abstracted into a series of methods that provide querying and saving functionality. If the underlying persistence technology changes, most of the necessary changes would be limited to defining a new DAO implementation, following the same interface.

For example, we might create a PersonDAO class to define all the application's persistence needs related to the Person entity. In PersonDao, we would likely have a method like the following:

```
public Person getPersonById(Long id);
```

This method would be responsible for loading a Person entity from the database using its unique identifier.

The following might be another method for our application:

```
void savePerson(Person person);
```

This method would be designed to handle all updates to a given row in the `Person` table (that is, creation or modifications).

When defining a DAO, it is good practice to first write the interface, which delineates all the core persistence-related methods the application will need. We recommend creating separate DAOs for each persistent entity in your domain model, but there are no clear rules in this area. However, defining DAO methods in a separate interface is crucial, as it decouples the purpose and contract of the DAO from the actual implementation, and even allows you to write more than one implementation for a given DAO interface.

It's important to note that such an interface is agnostic to the persistence technology being used behind the scenes. In other words, the interface only depends on the relevant domain model classes, decoupling our application from the persistence details. Of course, the DAO implementation class will use Hibernate, JPA, or whatever persistence technology we have chosen to employ. However, the higher layers of our application are insulated from these details by the DAO interface, giving us portability, consistency, and a well-tiered architecture.

As we mentioned earlier, the Spring Framework also provides a generic data exception hierarchy, suitable for all types of persistence frameworks and usage. Within each persistence framework integration library, Spring does an excellent job of converting each framework-specific exception into an exception that is part of Spring's generic data-access exception hierarchy. All of the exceptions in Spring's generic exception hierarchy are unchecked, meaning your application code is not required to catch them. Spring helps to decouple your application from a particular persistence framework, allowing you to code to a generic and well-defined exception hierarchy that can be used with any persistence technology.

In Chapter 6, we will dive deeper into DAO implementation strategies, exploring the flexible querying and save/update capability afforded by Hibernate and JPA. Querying in particular can require quite a bit of complexity, and to this end, Hibernate and JPA provide two different approaches for searching and accessing your data. HQL and JPQL (Hibernate Query Language and Java Persistence Query Language, respectively) both offer an object-oriented syntax for expressing queries that is very similar to SQL. Although concise and intuitive, HQL and JPQL are interpreted at runtime, which means you cannot use the compiler to verify the correctness and integrity of a query.

To address this limitation, Hibernate also includes a Criteria API, which allows queries to be expressed programmatically. Until recently, JPA did not offer a Criteria API, which meant developers would have to go outside the JPA standard if they required this type of querying facility. However, with the introduction of JPA 2.0, a Criteria API is now available as part of the standard.

Whether to use HQL/JPQL or the Criteria API is sometimes a matter of style. However, there are some cases where the Criteria API is more effective and maintainable. For instance, if you are building a feature that requires dynamic filtering or ordering, being able to dynamically create a query programmatically, based on the user's runtime specifications, is much cleaner than attempting to dynamically generate a JPQL query string via concatenation. We will discuss these types of implementation decisions further in Chapter 6.

The Service Facade

The layer that handles the application business logic is (surprisingly enough) called the *service layer*. The service layer typically defines an application's public-facing API, combining one or more lower-level DAO operations into a single, cohesive transactional unit.

To help you understand how a service layer is built and used, let's take a look at a few examples:

```
Person loginUser(String username, String password);
```

The loginUser() method is intended to authenticate a user (that is, verify that the specified username and password match), and then load important user information into the session (grab user information, such as name, previous login date, role type, and so on). These tasks would likely not be handled by a single DAO method. Instead, we would probably build upon the functionality of two distinct DAO classes, a PersonDAO and a RoleDAO:

```
interface PersonDao {

    Person authenticatUser(String username, String password);

    . . .

}
```

```
interface RoleDao {

    List<Role> getRolesForPerson(Person person);

    . . .

}
```

Together, these DAO methods accomplish a core business goal that is greater than the sum of its parts. In this example, we are using two read-only methods, but imagine a scenario in which we have a business method, such as the following:

```
boolean transferMoney(Long amount, Account fromAccount, Account destAccount)
  throws InvalidPermissionException, NotEnoughFundsException;
```

Now, assume that the preceding service layer method is composed of several DAO methods:

```
boolean validateSufficientFundsInAccount(Long accountId);
```

```
boolean removeFunds(Long accountId, Long amount);
```

```
boolean addFunds(Long accountId, Long amount);
```

It's easy to see what's going on here: we verify that enough cash exists in a particular account, and then pull the funds from one account and transfer them to another. The task is simple enough, but it doesn't take an overactive imagination to visualize the hysteria that might ensue should this business method fail halfway through the process—the funds might be withdrawn but never get deposited into the destination account. That might be good for the bank at first, but after a short while the entire economy collapses, and civilization is left with only a rudimentary barter system based on crazy straws and Star Wars action figures.

Leveraging Declarative Transactions

Service facade methods typically group together multiple DAO methods to accomplish business logic as a single unit of work. This is the concept of a transaction: the entire method (and all of its side effects) completes 100 percent successfully, or the application is rolled back to the state before the method was called. Before Spring persistence came on the scene, transactional requirements often prompted developers to look toward EJBs, which let them declaratively configure transactional semantics for each facade method. When they cannot specify transactional requirements declaratively, developers must instead use a programmatic approach. Not only does this add code complexity and obscure the intentions of the persistence logic, it further couples the persistence technology to the application. Transactional demarcation is often considered a *cross-cutting concern*, meaning it represents functionality that affects many parts of the codebase, but is orthogonal to their other features. Cross-cutting concerns add redundancy to code, since they need to be repetitively interweaved into the fabric of the business logic of an application, reducing code modularity. Aspect-Oriented Programming is aimed at solving this problem by allowing these concerns to be expressed once, and once only, as aspects, and then weaved into business logic as necessary.

In Spring, the service layer typically is intended to accomplish three primary tasks:

- Serve as the core API through which other layers of your application will interface (this is the incarnation of the facade pattern)

- Define the core business logic, usually calling on one or more DAO methods to achieve this goal

- Define transactional details for each facade method

Understanding Aspect Oriented Programming (AOP)

The service layer is where Spring's AOP support is best utilized. Spring ships with transactional support that can be applied to application code through the use of interceptors that enhance your service layer code, by weaving in the transactional goodness. An interceptor is code that can be mixed into the execution flow of a method, usually delegating to the interceptor before and/or after a particular method is invoked. Simply speaking, an interceptor encapsulates the behavior of an aspect at a point in a method's execution.

It's not enough to specify that a method should be transactional. You shouldn't just force each method to occur within the confines of a transaction, rolling back if an error occurs and committing if all goes well. Perhaps certain methods don't attempt to modify any data, and therefore should execute within the context of a read-only transaction. Or more likely, perhaps some exceptions will trigger a rollback, while others will allow the transaction to carry on.

Pointcuts are another important component of Spring AOP. They help to define where a particular aspect (modularized functionality that can be weaved into application logic, such as transactional behavior) should be weaved. With Spring's transactional support, you have fine-grained control over which exceptions may trigger a commit or rollback, as well as the details over the transaction itself, such as determining the isolation level and whether a method should trigger a new transaction or a nested transaction, or execute within the existing transaction.

At a basic level, Spring accomplishes AOP through the use of the proxy design pattern. When you advise your classes by injecting cross-cutting behavior into various methods, you're not actually injecting code throughout your application (although in a way, that is the net effect of using AOP). Rather, you're requesting that Spring create a new proxy class, in which functionality is delegated to your existing class along with the transactional implementation (or whatever aspect you are trying to weave into your code). This explanation is an oversimplification of what actually happens under the hood, but the important thing to remember is that when you weave cross-cutting behavior into your classes via AOP, Spring is not directly inserting code; rather, it is replacing your classes with proxies that contain your existing code intertwined with the transactional code. Under the hood, this is implemented using JDK dynamic proxies or CGLIB bytecode enhancement.

Again, it's easy to see how this is a natural fit for a lightweight, IOC container like Spring. Since you're already entrusting Spring with handling your dependencies, it makes perfect sense to let Spring also take care of proxying these dependencies so you can layer on new cross-cutting behavior.

Although Spring AOP is amazingly powerful when you need to define and introduce new aspects to be weaved into your implementations, key transactional functionality is available out of the box and without the need to learn the details of AOP programming concepts. Still, understanding the basics of what Spring does under the hood is helpful. Keep in mind that AOP is useful for more than just applying transactional behavior—it is helpful for weaving any cross-cutting concern into your application, such as logging or security. We will discuss AOP in more detail later in this book.

Simplifying Transactions

Although applying transactions using Spring used to require a bit of AOP know-how, this process has been greatly simplified in recent versions of the framework. Now, applying transactional behavior to a service layer class is a matter of specifying the `@Transactional` annotation at either the class or method level. This annotation can be parameterized with attributes to customize its behavior, however the most significant detail is whether a transaction is read-only. Many developers don't recognize the importance of using transactions—even within a read-only context. Transactions can be useful for more than just ensuring atomicity. Transactions can also be used to specify a database isolation-level, and to delineate other contextual details that might be ambiguous outside a transactional scope. We strongly recommend that all database operations occur within the scope of some transaction—even if just to gain control over the contextual state of the database. We will discuss some of these details, such as understanding isolation levels and advanced transactional options, in Chapter 8.

The Benefit of Coding to Interfaces

We can rely on Spring to wire DAO dependencies into our service layer classes, ensuring that this integration happens in a consistent way and that the integration point between these two layers is through interfaces rather than specific implementation classes. As we mentioned earlier in this chapter, this is a fundamental concept for leveraging Spring's dependency injection: by coding to interfaces, we get more for our money. We can always rely on Spring to automatically inject required dependencies, but by using interfaces we gain the added benefit of being able to change which implementation should be injected at runtime. Without interfaces, there are no other options—we have hard-coded which dependencies must be injected into our components. Interfaces and Spring's dependency injection capability are a dynamic duo that offer significantly increased flexibility. For instance, without changing any code, you can choose to inject one set of dependencies for unit-testing and another in production deployment. Or you can choose which implementations to use for each environment. These are some of the benefits afforded by adherence to best practices and leveraging the Spring Framework.

Testing your Persistence Tier

As you'll see in later chapters, this separation of concerns helps keep your code clean and ensures that details from one layer don't interfere with the code from another layer. When it comes time for refactoring, this advantage can be significant. Perhaps even more important, these best practices are instrumental for ensuring an effective testing strategy. In Chapter 8, you will learn how Spring greatly simplifies the creation of unit and integration tests. When it comes to testing, it's rather intuitive to see how swapping implementations can really come in handy. Spring 3 includes a powerful TestContext framework that simplifies the creation and management of unit and integration tests—even abstracting away which test framework you happen to be using. Integration tests can often be a tricky matter, especially when you consider the details of instantiating all of a test's dependencies and components. For example, an integration test might require access to a database, as well as test data. Spring can bootstrap the `ApplicationContext` and then automatically inject any required dependencies. In the case of testing persistence-related code, you can choose to have your data occur within the scope of a transaction and then automatically rollback the transaction at the completion of the test to ensure that modifications made by the test are removed.

Advanced Features and Performance Tuning

This book will also cover some more advanced persistence concepts that are indispensable in most applications, such as optimization techniques for loading and managing complex relationships and collections within your domain model. We will discuss performance and optimization strategies, such as eager fetching and caching (at both the domain level and higher abstractions). As we mentioned earlier, Hibernate offers numerous features that can be leveraged to improve application performance. For instance, Hibernate and JPA offer a great deal of flexibility for tuning HQL/JPQL and Criteria API queries. These features enable developers to minimize round-trips to the database, allowing even large data sets to be accessed with minimal SQL queries. Hibernate also provides features such as lazy-loading and powerful caching mechanisms, which can be tuned to control the size and expiration time for cached entities. Understanding how these features work, as well as the myriad options available for controlling them, is critical for maximizing performance.

Caching is an often overlooked feature which can prevent an application from realizing its full potential. In the case of caching, it is either not fully utilized, or not enough time and attention are given to tuning and testing. However, if left untuned, caching can significantly degrade application performance. In Chapter 10, you will learn how Hibernate caching works, strategies for tuning and improving performance, and how to integrate a cache provider, such as ehcache. We will also explore several common pitfalls responsible for performance problems, such as the *N+1 Selects* issue, and how to go about identifying and resolving these issues.

Hibernate-Search

Sometimes, your application will require more than Hibernate or Spring have to offer. So we will discuss some important frameworks that extend Spring and Hibernate, such as Hibernate-Search. Hibernate-Search integrates the popular open source search framework, Lucene, into a Hibernate or JPA application. For features that require true search functionality, a relational database is not able to provide the capability that Lucene is able to offer. Hibernate-Search seamlessly integrates Lucene into your persistence tier, allowing you to execute Lucene queries within the scope of a Hibernate Session or a JPA Persistence Context. In Chapter 10, you will learn how this integration works, as well as the range of functionality afforded by Lucene and Hibernate-Search.

Building a REST Web Service

Since many applications use Spring and Hibernate as part of a web application, we will explore some of the potential issues and work-arounds related to building web applications. We will develop a REST-based web service, to explore some strategies for marshalling domain entities back and forth between Java and JSON or XML. We will examine frameworks, such as Dozer, which help to reduce some of the complexity related to serializing the object graph and dealing with potential `LazyInitializationException`s.

Other Persistence Design Patterns

Spring is based on time-tested design patterns, which go a long way toward simplifying code and reducing maintenance. While we're on the topic of some of the core building blocks of an application, let's look at a few of the more prevalent patterns used in much of the Spring architecture.

■ **Note** You will see many of these patterns in action throughout this book, but it may be useful to take a look at the seminal work that popularized the use of patterns to solve recurring problems in object-oriented programming. This famous book is called *Design Patterns: Elements of Reusable Object-Oriented Software*, by Erich Gamma, Richard Helm, Ralph Johnson, and John Vlissides (Addison-Wesley, 1994). The authors, and by association their patterns, are often jokingly referred to as "The Gang of Four".

The Template Pattern

The Template pattern is one of the most frequently used idioms within Spring's ORM framework integration packages. Spring provides templates for each of the most popular persistence frameworks, making it easy to port your code to a different persistence implementation. The Template Pattern is also used by the Spring framework to more effectively integrate JMS, define transactional behavior, and provide outbound email message capability, among other things.

The Template pattern allows a template to be defined in which a series of standard steps are followed, delegating to a subclass for those operations that are specific to the business logic. For example, when working with Hibernate, it is first necessary to create and initialize a new Hibernate session and optionally begin a transaction, before executing any Hibernate operations. When the operations are completed, it is necessary to close the session, and optionally commit or rollback the transaction. It would be rather redundant to repeat these same steps each time it was necessary to interface with Hibernate. Instead, we can leverage Spring's `HibernateTemplate` or `JpaTemplate` abstractions, which handle these steps for us. Although using these template support classes is an effective approach, we will explore alternative options later in this book.

Typically, a template is defined as an abstract class. To specify the operations to be wrapped within the templated workflow, we extend the template class, providing or extending the implementations for the abstract methods defined in the template parent class.

The Template pattern does exactly what its name implies: it extracts boilerplate and redundant tasks into a template, delegating to your specific implementation for functionality that can't be templated. In most cases, the code that cannot go in a template is your persistence logic itself. Using the Template pattern means you can focus on the database operations, without needing to worry about some of these mundane details:

- Opening a database connection

- Beginning a transaction

- Wrapping your SQL operations in try-catch blocks (to handle unexpected exceptions)

- Committing or rolling back a transaction

- Closing the database connection (and handling any exceptions during this process)

- Catching any exceptions that might occur in the transaction

Without using Spring, much of your code has little to do with your persistence logic, but is the same boilerplate code required by each and every operation.

Spring's HibernateTemplate and JpaTemplate offer a series of convenience methods to streamline much of the common persistence-related functionality. For example, the HibernateTemplate provides some useful methods such as:

- *saveOrUpdate(Object entity)*

- *load(class entityClass, Serializable id)*

- *find(String hqlQuery)*

- *findByCriteria(DetachedCritieria criteria)*

- *delete(Object entity)*

HibernateTemplate offers quite a few more methods, as well as numerous permutations of some of the methods listed above. However, these convenience methods aren't direct examples of the template pattern. Rather, they are more like wrapper methods, which delegate to the core template method found in Spring's `HibernateTemplate` abstraction:

```
public Object execute(HibernateCallback action) throws DataAccessException {
  return doExecute(action, false, false);
}
```

To execute a series of Hibernate operations, ensuring that they occur within the necessary templated steps (such as initializing and closing a Hibernate session), we need to create an anonymous implementation of the `HibernateCallback` interface, which is the single parameter to the preceding *execute* method. For example, to save an entity to the database, we could do the following:

```
public void customSavePerson(Person person) {
  getHibernateTemplate().execute(
    new HibernateCallback() {
      public Object doInHibernate(Session session) throws HibernateException {
        session.saveOrUpdate(person);
      }
    }
  );
}
```

Of course, it would be a lot simpler to just use `HibernateTemplate`'s `save(Object entity)` method. Yet in this contrived example, we define an implementation of the `HibernateCallback` interface, which uses the passed-in `Session` to persist the `Person` entity to the database. Typically, this type of lower-level persistence functionality would be part of a DAO class, which helps to abstract the Hibernate-specific code from the rest of the application.

Although the `HibernateTemplate` and `JpaTemplate` provide an effective construct for streamlining persistence operations, they are no longer as necessary as they once were. Hibernate 3 shipped with a feature called Contextual Sessions, which provides greater flexibility around the scope of a `Session`. Part of what Spring's ORM support provides is the facilitation of a conversation surrounding persistence behavior, allowing Hibernate and JPA operations to be seamlessly integrated into Spring's transactional support. Spring's transactional features couldn't be properly utilized if every Hibernate operation created a new `Session` and a new database connection. To tie multiple lower-level persistence operations into a holistic "conversation," Spring uses the capabilities of `ThreadLocal`, allowing disparate operations to be scoped across a continuous thread. Recent versions of Hibernate provide a pluggable mechanism for defining how accessing the current Session should work. This new capability makes the `HibernateTemplate` and `JpaTemplate` a bit redundant in some circumstances. We will discuss the benefits and drawbacks of Spring's ORM templates in the next few chapters.

■ **Note** Spring can be used for both JTA-managed transactions and local resource transactions. In a JTA environment, transactions are managed by the container, and offer additional behavior, such as distributed transactions. However, there is additional overhead for leveraging JTA transactions, and we recommend going with lighter-weight, local transactions if your application doesn't require the features provided by JTA. One of the advantages of using Spring is that switching between locally-managed transactions and JTA is just a matter of configuration. In the case of JTA, Spring will simply delegate to JTA, rather than manage the contextual state across an application thread.

The Active-Record Pattern

The DAO pattern isn't the only strategy for performing data operations. Another approach that has started to garner more attention recently is the Active-Record pattern. Active-Record is a design pattern popularized by frameworks such as Ruby on Rails and Grails, and takes a different approach than abstracting persistence functionality into a separate layer. Instead, Active-Record attempts to blend a domain object's behavior directly into the domain class itself.

Typically, an instance of a particular domain class represents a single row within the respective database table. To save changes to the instance (and thereby the appropriate row within the database), a `save` instance method is called directly on the instance. To delete an instance, we can simply invoke `delete()` on the instance that needs to be deleted. Query operations are usually invoked as static methods on the domain class itself. For example, in Grails, to find all `Person` entities with a `lastName` property of `Fisher`, we could call `Person.findAllByLastName('Fisher')`.

The benefit of Active-Record is that it provides an intuitive and concise approach for performing persistence operations, and usually reduces code overhead significantly. Active-Record also attempts to combine behavior and properties into a domain object, providing a more object-oriented approach. You will learn more about the Active-Record pattern in Chapter 11, when we discuss Grails.

Summary

Throughout this book, we will demonstrate how Spring integrates with key persistence frameworks and strategies. Along the way, you will learn more about Spring's features and capabilities, and some of the key design patterns it uses to get the job done effectively.

Until several years ago, simple Java Database Connectivity (JDBC) was one of the most popular choices for implementing an application's persistence tier. However, EJB and open source ORM frameworks such as Hibernate have significantly changed the persistence landscape, by allowing developers to focus on a Java-based domain model, maintaining the object-oriented semantics of Java while still working with the relational concepts of a SQL database. ORM offers a level of abstraction that affords increased flexibility by decoupling application code from the lower-level details of a relational database.

However, things aren't always as easy as they seem. ORM is not without its drawbacks and consequences. First, as we mentioned earlier, there is the impedance mismatch between the object-oriented Java world and the relational SQL world. ORM frameworks, such as Hibernate, do their best to address this mismatch by offering extensive options for mapping between SQL and Java. Nevertheless, fundamental differences between these two spheres will always exist, and therefore can't be fully addressed.

Despite some of these limitations, ORM frameworks offer unparalleled benefits by streamlining the way in which developers work with a relational database. For instance, Hibernate introduces ancillary features, such as caching and lazy loading, which can improve the performance of an application dramatically with little or no additional coding effort. Hibernate and JPA also provide tools to seamlessly generate database schemas and even keep them in sync with the Java-based domain model. These features make the integration between application code and database even more seamless—to the point that it is often possible to forget that you are using a database altogether!

With an IoC container at its core, Spring helps to reduce application complexity, as well as coupling between classes, by handling the details necessary to integrate one dependency with another. Spring also provides transactional behavior, AOP capability, and infrastructural classes for numerous persistence frameworks, such as Hibernate and JPA.

Hibernate is an ORM framework intended to translate between relational databases and the realm of object-oriented development. Hibernate provides a querying interface, using Hibernate Query Language (HQL) or the Hibernate Criteria API. Together, Spring and Hibernate are a dynamic duo, capable of simplifying dependency collaboration, reducing coupling, and providing abstractions over persistence operations.

JPA is a Java standard for persistence, the design of which was significantly influenced by the Hibernate developers. Hibernate can be used as an implementation provider for JPA, allowing you to adhere to standards and gain framework portability, while still utilizing the excellent Hibernate implementation. However, there are some useful features that are not available in JPA, but are present only in the Hibernate implementation. With the release of JPA 2.0, many of the limitations of the JPA spec have been addressed, bringing more parity to Hibernate and JPA. For instance, JPA 2.0 now provides a Criteria API for querying in an object-oriented manner, and compile-time checking.

In this chapter, we outlined the foundational layers of a typical persistence tier, which is composed of the domain model, the DAO layer, and the service facade. We also discussed some integral design patterns leveraged by the Spring Framework, such as the Template design pattern. Although adhering to the typical foundational layers for your persistence tier is usually the best approach, some newer frameworks follow slightly different strategies, such as using the Active-Record pattern.

In the next chapter, we will build on the concepts and patterns introduced in this chapter as we incrementally build a Gallery application using Spring and Hibernate. Over the course of this book, it is our aim to illustrate time-tested and pragmatic best practices that we hope you will be able to use in your own applications as well.

Before we start coding, it's important to understand some of the core Spring and Hibernate concepts. So in the next chapter you will learn about Spring's architecture and capabilities, such as dependency injection, AOP, and persistence-related features.

CHAPTER 2

■ ■ ■

Spring Basics

The Spring Framework has its origins in the companion code for Rod Johnson's book, *Expert One-on-One J2EE Design and Development* (Wrox, 2002). The book developed a strong following of developers, who used the Wrox forums to discuss both the book and the corresponding code. Two of those developers, Juergen Hoeller and Yann Caroff, persuaded Rod to turn the code into an open source project. The book referred to the framework as the Interface21 framework, because Rod felt that it represented the future of enterprise Java development—a framework for the twenty-first century. However, when the open source project was formed, they felt they needed a name that could better inspire a community. Yann suggested Spring because of the association with nature, as well as the fact that Spring represented a fresh start after the "winter" of traditional J2EE development. The project went public in 2003, and version 1.0 of the Spring Framework was released in 2004.

Since then, Spring has been widely adopted because it delivers on the promise of simpler development while also tackling some very intricate problems. Another key to Spring's rise to prominence is its exceptional documentation. Many open source projects have faded into oblivion because of the lack of sound documentation. Spring's documentation has been very mature since the very early days of the project.

Despite what some may claim, the Spring Framework is not currently a standard. Standard technologies are great, and Sun deserves a lot of credit for pushing standards-based Java technologies into the mainstream. Standards allow you to do things like develop your web application on Tomcat and then drop it into WebSphere, with little adjustment required (at least theoretically). But even though the Spring Framework is unbelievably popular today, it does not represent a true standard.

Some consider Spring a *de facto standard*, due to the sheer volume of applications that rely on it. Spring provides a means for integrating the various components of your application in a consistent way, and it is deployed far and wide across a variety of application ecosystems. Sometimes, this type of *standard implementation* is a far more valuable proposition than a *standard specification*.

Despite the naysayers that balk at the idea of using any technology that wasn't designed by a giant committee of corporate volunteers, using Spring in your application poses little risk. In fact, the more you utilize Spring for integrating components into your application, the more consistent your integration strategy will be, making maintenance and development easier. That's right—reliance on Spring will often lead to better, cleaner, decoupled code.

Because Spring is such a large framework, and because the documentation is so good, we have no intention of covering it all. Instead, this chapter will serve as a quick overview of the most important concepts that we build on in the rest of this book.

Exploring Spring's Architecture

Spring is composed of a series of modules. The beauty of this design is that you can pick and choose the components that you would like to use. There's no monolithic JAR file. Instead, you explicitly add the components that you want to your project dependencies.

As they say, a picture is worth a thousand words. Figure 2-1 is a depiction of the Spring components. The three primary groupings are the core, web, and data access modules.

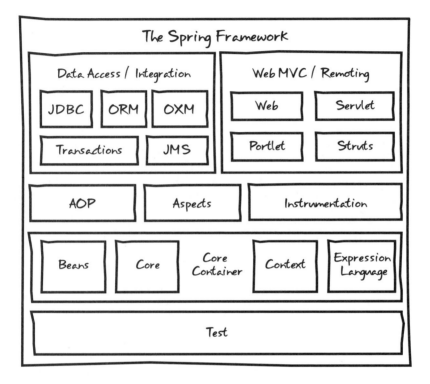

Figure 2-1. *The Spring Framework modules*

We'll be tackling many of these modules in this book. This chapter will take you through the core container and AOP.

The Application Context

Spring's job is to parse your configuration files and then instantiate your managed classes, resolving their interdependencies. Spring is often called a *container*, since it is designed to create and manage all the dependencies within your application, serving as a foundation and context through which beans may also be looked up. This core engine is represented by a base interface called `BeanFactory`.

The `BeanFactory` interface defines the core Spring engine that conglomerates your beans and wires the collaborating dependencies together. But the Spring container is capable of much more than just dependency injection. It can also be used to publish events, provide AOP functionality, support a resource-loading abstraction, facilitate internationalization, and so on. For many of these advanced capabilities, you will need to use an `ApplicationContext` instance.

The `ApplicationContext` extends the `BeanFactory` interface, providing a set of more robust features. The separation can come in handy if you are building a very lightweight application and don't need some of these more advanced features. But for most applications (especially server-side software), you will want to use an `ApplicationContext` implementation. In the case of web applications, you will use a `WebApplicationContext`. Spring ships with a listener that you can throw into your `web.xml` file to automatically bootstrap the Spring `ApplicationContext` and load your configuration file. It's as easy as adding the following lines into your `web.xml`:

```
<listener>
    <listener-class>
        org.springframework.web.context.request.RequestContextListener
    </listener-class>
</listener>
```

These lines will ensure that Spring is loaded when your application first starts up and will parse the configuration file located at `WEB-INF/applicationcontext.xml`.

If you're not building a web application, it's just as easy to load the Spring container. In this case, we recommend going with the `ClassPathXmlApplicationContext` implementation, which is designed to load the Spring configuration files from the classpath. It is invoked in the following way:

```
ApplicationContext context =
    new ClassPathXmlApplicationContext(new String[]{"configfile1.xml", "configfile2.xml"});
```

You can see just how easy it is to get a Spring container instantiated. Once you have a reference to the `ApplicationContext`, you can use it however you wish. The reference that is returned to you is the loaded `ApplicationContext`, with all the beans that you defined instantiated and dependencies resolved.

If you felt so inclined, you could access a bean by name, simply by invoking the following:

```
UsefulClass usefulClass =  (UsefulClass) context.getBean("myBeanName");
```

Assuming that your bean is defined somewhere in your Spring configuration files (referenced by the ID or name attribute), Spring will hand you your class instance, ready to go (meaning all of its dependencies will have been injected). However, we strongly recommend that you try to avoid issuing calls to `getBean()`.

The whole point of Spring is automatic dependency injection, which means not looking up your beans when you need them. That's dependency lookup, which is so 1995. While this approach does decouple and defer your class dependencies, it still requires an explicit lookup step. As a rule of thumb, if you need a reference to a particular dependency, specify these details in the configuration, not in your code.

Some developers will rely on `getBean()` only in circumstances in which they *always* need a new instance of their class (each time they make the call). A better solution to this problem is using the `lookup-method` property in your XML configuration. This property coerces Spring to override or implement the specified method with code that will always return a new instance of a designated bean.

An alternate strategy for accessing beans from the `ApplicationContext` is to implement the `ApplicationContextAware` interface. This interface has the following method:

```
void setApplicationContext(ApplicationContext context);
```

With access to Spring's `ApplicationContext`, your class has the flexibility to look up beans by name or type, without you needing to write code to acquire an `ApplicationContext` from the classpath directly. In practice, there shouldn't be many cases where you need to integrate Spring's API so deeply into your code. The more common approach is to let Spring manage the relationships between beans dynamically through dependency injection.

Beans, Beans, the Magical Fruit

A big part of the secret sauce for the Spring Framework is the use of Plain Old Java Objects, or POJOs. Martin Fowler, Rebecca Persons, and Josh MacKenzie originally coined the term POJO in 2000. POJOs are objects that have no contracts imposed on them; that is, they don't implement interfaces or extend specified classes.

There is often quite a bit of confusion about the differences between JavaBeans and POJOs. The terms tend to be used interchangeably, but that's not always accurate. JavaBeans are best characterized as a special kind of POJO. Put simply, a JavaBean is a POJO that follows three simple conventions:

- It is serializable.

- It has a public, default, and nullary constructor.

- It contains public getters and setters for each property that is to be read or written, respectively (write permissions can be obscured simply by defining a getter, without defining a setter).

An object in Java may be a POJO but not a JavaBean. For instance, it may implement an interface or extend specified classes, but because it refers to objects that are stateful and/or exist outside the scope of the Java Virtual Machine (JVM)—for example, HTTP or database connections—it cannot reasonably be serialized to disk and then restored.

The concept of JavaBeans was originally devised for Swing to facilitate the development of stand-alone GUI components, but the pattern has been repurposed for the land of Spring beans and back-end persistence with Hibernate.

The Spring Life Cycle

Spring not only instantiates objects and wires up dependencies, but it also handles each managed object's *life cycle*.

For example, what if you need to do some initialization in your class, after the Spring-injected properties have been set? One way to accomplish this is through constructor injection (so that you can capture the moment all of a bean's properties are injected). But a cleaner approach is to use the `init-method` feature. By defining an `init-method` attribute on your bean, you can specify an arbitrary method that will be called after all of the Spring properties have been set (that is, after all of your setters have been invoked). Here is an example of using the `init-method` feature of Spring:

```
<bean id="initTest" class="com.prospringhibernate.gallery.InitTest" init-method="init">
    <property name="testString"  value="Let me out of this computer!"/>
</bean>
```

Simple, right? Next, we need to define a class with the `init-method` we specified in the preceding configuration:

```
package com.prospringhibernate.gallery;

import org.springframework.util.Assert;

class InitTest {

    private String testString;

    public void init() {
        // let's do some initialization stuff!
        Assert.notNull(this.testString,
                                "You forgot to set the testString property! What were
you thinking???");
    }

    public Foo doBizLogic() {
        ...
    }

    public void setTestString(String testString) {
        this.testString = testString;
    }

    public String getTestString() {
        return this.testString;
    }

}
```

If you're using Java 5 or later, you can also tap into Spring's annotation support for initialization events. Using this approach, you simply annotate a class's methods with the **@postConstruct** annotation, without needing to specify initialization hints in the Spring configuration. For example, we could refactor our earlier example as follows:

```
package com.prospringhibernate.gallery;

import org.springframework.util.Assert;

class InitTest {

    private String testString;

    @PostConstruct()
    public void init() {
        // let's do some initialization stuff!
        Assert.notNull(this.testString,
                                "You forgot to set the testString property! What were
you thinking???");
    }

}
```

As with everything in Spring, there's actually more than one way to skin a cat. Instead of specifying `init-method` in the configuration or using the `@postConstruct` annotation, you could have your class implement the `InitializingBean` interface. To a certain extent, using this interface makes things a bit easier, since you don't even need to change your configuration. The interface just requires you to implement an `afterPropertiesSet()` method, which will automatically be detected and called for you once Spring has finished setting all the configured properties. The downside with this approach is that you sacrifice your simple POJOs and tightly couple your beans to Spring. While coupling to Spring isn't terrible, the cleaner approach is to keep initialization details entirely within configuration and out of the code. So let this be your mantra: *keep it in the configuration.*

Similar to acting on bean creation, you may also trigger custom logic when beans are destroyed. You can accomplish this in several ways:

- By implementing the `DisposableBean` interface, which is essentially the inverse of `InitializingBean`

- By applying a `@preDestroy` annotation to the method in question

- By configuring the `destroy-method` parameter in your Spring XML configuration, which is what we recommend to minimize tight coupling

Now that you know how to tap into the creation and destruction life-cycle events in Spring, there's another aspect of bean management that's crucial to understand when building enterprise applications: bean scoping.

Understanding Bean Scopes

By default, beans defined in Spring are all scoped as singletons. A *singleton* is a class that is guaranteed to have only a single instance in the JVM. Singletons are great for storing application state, or for any case where you want to be assured that there is only ever one reference in your application. Normally, you would need to write code to achieve this assurance.

The typical singleton meets the following criteria:

- Has a static method to return the single instance of the class (stored as a static reference within the class)

- Has a private constructor, ensuring that only the singleton itself can ever create a new instance (which is your assurance that you won't accidentally create more than once instance simply by invoking `new Singleton()`)

A singleton in your application might look like this:

```
public class Singleton {

    private static final Singleton INSTANCE = new Singleton();

    private Singleton() {
    }
    public static Singleton getInstance() {
        return INSTANCE;
    }

}
```

Although the preceding sample illustrates a useful design pattern, Spring obviates the need to write this boilerplate code, once again allowing you to move these details into the configuration. By default, all Spring beans are singletons. If this is not your intention, you need to specify a different scope for your bean.

In Spring 1.*x*, beans were either prototype beans or singletons. *Prototype* means that each new call to getBean() will return a brand-new instance of your bean. Singleton beans guarantee that there can only ever be a single instance of your class in the entire Spring ApplicationContext. Spring 2.*x* introduced several new standard scopes, as well as the ability to define custom scopes. Spring 3.*x* added a thread scope, though it's not registered by default. Table 2-1 lists the bean scopes that are provided by Spring out of the box.

Table 2-1. Spring Bean Scopes

Scope	Description
Singleton	Scopes a single bean definition to a single object instance per Spring IoC container. This is the default scope.
Prototype	Scopes a single bean definition to any number of object instances.
Request	Scopes a single bean definition to the life cycle of a single HTTP request; that is, each HTTP request has its own instance of a bean created off the back of a single bean definition. This scope is valid only in the context of a web-aware Spring ApplicationContext.
Session	Scopes a single bean definition to the life cycle of an HTTP session. This scope is valid only in the context of a web-aware Spring ApplicationContext.
Global session	Scopes a single bean definition to the life cycle of a global HTTP session. This scope is valid only in the context of a web-aware Spring ApplicationContext, and typically only in a portlet context.
Simple thread	If for some reason, the request, session, or global session scopes don't satisfy your needs, you may enable the simple thread scope to bind a bean definition to an instance of ThreadLocal.

So now you know how to create beans in the Spring ApplicationContext and manage their scope and life cycle. The next piece of the puzzle is how to retrieve those beans from the Spring container within your application.

Dependency Injection and Inversion of Control

Enterprise applications are composed of many objects that provide behavior to emulate business processes. Two very important design patterns have emerged to manage the relationships between objects in an object-oriented application:

> *Dependency injection (DI)*: Classes that employ dependency injection specify the objects that they interact with through constructor arguments, factory method parameters, or public mutators (aka *setters*). With a dependency-injection container or framework like Spring, the ability to externalize simple class properties is just the beginning. Developers can create a complex tree of dependencies, leaving the work of figuring out how each dependency is created and set (also called *injected* or *wired*) to the Spring lightweight container.

> *Inversion of Control (IoC)*: When object location or instantiation is removed as a responsibility for a given bean and instead left to the framework, control has been *inverted*. This inversion of control is a very powerful concept and represents the foundation on which the Spring Framework is based.

Dependency injection and IoC lead you down a path toward clean code that embodies high cohesion and loose coupling.

Setter-Based Dependency Injection

Although frighteningly simple, Spring's use of POJOs as a means of configuration and integration is quite powerful. Consider the example of a fictitious `User` bean, which could be used in an application to specify user credential information:

```xml
<?xml version="1.0" encoding="UTF-8"?>
<beans xmlns=http://www.springframework.org/schema/beans
    xmlns:xsi=http://www.w3.org/2001/XMLSchema-instance
    xsi:schemaLocation="http://www.springframework.org/schema/beans
        http://www.springframework.org/schema/beans/spring-beans-3.0.xsd">

  <bean id="userBean" class="com.prospringhibernate.gallery.User">
      <property name="username" value="admin" />
      <property name="password" value="password" />
  </bean>

</beans>
```

You can take away several things from the preceding example. The first is that we use horribly insecure passwords. But it does demonstrate how a simple Spring bean is configured via XML.

To make this work on the Java side, we need a valid JavaBean class that looks like the following:

```
package com.prospringhibernate.gallery;

public class User implements Serializable {

    private String username;
    private String password;

    public User() {
    }

    public String getUsername() {
        return this.username;
    }

    public void setUsername(String name) {
        this.username = name;
    }

    public String getPassword() {
        return this.password;
    }

    public void setPassword(password) {
        this.password = password;
    }

}
```

Notice that, for each property entity in the Spring XML configuration, we have a corresponding getter and setter defined in the Java class. In Spring terms, this is called *setter injection*, since the property values are configured by invoking the JavaBean's setter methods.

Constructor-Based Dependency Injection

An alternate approach is to use *constructor injection*, which allows the property values to be injected via the constructor of the class. To use constructor injection, we refactor our code and Spring configuration as follows:

```
<?xml version="1.0" encoding="UTF-8"?>
<beans xmlns=http://www.springframework.org/schema/beans
       xmlns:xsi=http://www.w3.org/2001/XMLSchema-instance
       xsi:schemaLocation="http://www.springframework.org/schema/beans
           http://www.springframework.org/schema/beans/spring-beans-3.0.xsd">

    <bean id="userBean" class="com.prospringhibernate.gallery.User">
        <constructor-arg index="0" value="admin" />
        <constructor-arg index="1" value="password" />
    </bean>

</beans>
```

And here's the corresponding code for the updated User bean:

```
package com.prospringhibernate.gallery;

public class User implements Serializable {

    private String username;
    private String password;

    public User(String username, String password) {
        this.username = username;
        this.password = password;
    }

    public String getUsername() {
        return this.username;
    }

    public String getPassword() {
        return this.password;
    }

}
```

Although either approach is valid, we recommend the setter-based approach, as this better conforms to the conventions of JavaBeans and makes your code easier to test later.

Instance Collaboration

In the preceding examples, we injected two string values, which are specified directly within the configuration file. This is a useful shortcut to abstract basic configuration details away from your code and into a more readily changeable file. However, the same concept can be taken a step further for satisfying dependencies between collaborating instances within your application.

For example, let's assume that authentication was implemented in a separate class. In our Spring configuration file, we might have the following:

```
<?xml version="1.0" encoding="UTF-8"?>
<beans xmlns=http://www.springframework.org/schema/beans
       xmlns:xsi=http://www.w3.org/2001/XMLSchema-instance
       xsi:schemaLocation="http://www.springframework.org/schema/beans
           http://www.springframework.org/schema/beans/spring-beans-3.0.xsd">

    <bean id="userBean" class="com.prospringhibernate.gallery.User">
        <property name="authHandler" ref="authService" />
    </bean>

    <bean id="authService" class="com.prospringhibernate.gallery.AuthService"/>

</beans>
```

And here's the corresponding code for the updated **User** bean:

```
package com.prospringhibernate.gallery;

public class User implements Serializable {

    private AuthenticationService authHandler;

    public User() {
    }

    public AuthenticationService getAuthHandler() {
        return this.authHandler;
    }

    public void setAuthHandler(AuthenticationService authHandler) {
        this.authHandler = authHandler;
    }

}
```

Simple, isn't it? We just wired up critical parts of our application with a few configuration lines. It's easy to imagine defining code for an alternate authentication service and then simply modifying the bean reference in your Spring configuration to manipulate the behavior of your application.

Coding to Interfaces

Earlier, we mentioned that Spring has the tendency to lead developers to write better, cleaner, and more loosely coupled code. You might be starting to pick up on why this is the case. Not only are your classes free of application wiring code, but you'll also find that applications based on Spring are usually more interface-based, meaning that your code is dependent on interfaces rather than specific implementations. This strategy is often called *coding to interfaces,* and it allows you to easily swap out one implementation for another, simply by altering the class attribute within a Spring bean. As long as your code is written to rely on an interface, and the interface isn't changing, no changes to your class files will be necessary.

For instance, notice that in the preceding example, the **User** bean depends on an **AuthenticationService** bean. In your code, a good practice is to define an **AuthenticationService** interface that specifies core methods related to user access and security. Your code would then reference the **AuthenticationService** interface, and your Spring configuration would map the concrete implementation class to your **User** object.

As an oversimplified example, our **AuthenticationService** interface might look like the following:

```
package com.prospringhibernate.gallery;

public interface AuthenticationService {
    public User authenticateUser(String username, String password)
      throws AuthenticationException;
}
```

And our concrete implementation would be something like this:

```
package com.prospringhibernate.gallery;

public class AuthenticationServiceImpl implements AuthenticationService {

    public User authenticateUser(String username, String password)
      throws AuthenticationException {
        // authentication logic goes here
    }

}
```

Finally, bringing everything together in our Spring configuration, the `userBean` then points to a particular implementation of the `AuthenticationService` interface by using the `ref` property.

```
<?xml version="1.0" encoding="UTF-8"?>
<beans xmlns=http://www.springframework.org/schema/beans
       xmlns:xsi=http://www.w3.org/2001/XMLSchema-instance
       xsi:schemaLocation="http://www.springframework.org/schema/beans
           http://www.springframework.org/schema/beans/spring-beans-3.0.xsd">

    <bean id="userBean" class="com.prospringhibernate.gallery.User">
        <property name="authHandler" ref="authService" />
    </bean>

    <bean id="authService" class="com.prospringhibernate.gallery.AuthServiceImpl"/>

</beans>
```

The key point here is that the `User` class does not depend directly on the `AuthenticationServiceImpl` implementation, but rather on the `AuthenticationService` interface. Although the difference may appear subtle, expressing dependencies on interfaces is an effective means of ensuring your application is loosely coupled. If your code doesn't express any direct coupling to a particular implementation, you will gain the flexibility of defining these details in the Spring configuration, and only in that configuration. In this way, you can easily swap implementations without needing to refactor your code.

No matter what type of library, class, or framework you need to integrate into your application, Spring will allow you to work with these internal and external components cleanly and with a shallow learning curve. This integration without direct coupling is the greatest benefit of IoC. Essentially, the hooks into third-party libraries (or even in-house frameworks and classes) are moved outside the source code and into configuration files (or annotation-based metadata within your classes). This type of configuration lets developers worry less about how the various components of code fit together and focus more on coding the core functionality itself.

Dependency Injection via Autowiring

Another type of injection is what Spring calls *autowiring*. This method allows you to simply define getters and setters of a particular type or name, putting on the Spring container the onus of figuring out which class to inject. This very powerful feature comes with some risk as well: should there be some ambiguity as to which instance to inject, you may run into problems. For instance, if you have a class that depends on the `AuthenticationService` interface and you have a `BasicAuthenticationServiceImpl` and a `RemoteAuthenticationServiceImpl` defined in your application (both of which implement the `AuthenticationService` interface), Spring may get confused as to which implementation you intend to inject.

@Annotation-Based Dependency Injection

Up to this point, we've shown how to specify how objects depend on one another in XML configuration files. Over time, XML configurations for enterprise applications grew massive and unwieldy. Beginning with Spring 2.5 and JDK 1.5, another configuration strategy was introduced. Utilizing annotation-based metadata, you can now specify dependency wiring directly within your classes. The advantage of this approach is that a class's dependencies can be expressed directly within the code. The downside is that you don't benefit from having a centralized collection of configuration files that illustrate and document how your application's components are wired.

Which path you take is up to you. Certainly, using annotations does simplify the configuration process. Furthermore, you can mix and match both XML configuration and annotations, allowing some dependencies to be configured within the Spring XML, while other dependencies are detected via annotations.

Here's our `User` object, revised to use an annotation-based approach.

```
package com.prospringhibernate.gallery;

import org.springframework.beans.factory.annotation.Autowired;

public class User implements Serializable {

    @Autowired
    private AuthenticationService authHandler;

    public User() {
    }

    public AuthenticationService getAuthHandler() {
        return this.authHandler;
    }

    public void setAuthHandler(AuthenticationService authHandler) {
        this.authHandler = authHandler;
    }

}
```

Notice the `@Autowired` annotation above the `authHandler` member variable. This tells Spring to inject (using the autowiring strategy we discussed earlier) an implementation of the `AuthenticationService` interface.

In cases where ambiguity could be an issue, Spring provides a means for providing clues to the container by using qualifiers. *Qualifiers* can be inserted as a separate annotation on an `@Autowired` field, or within an XML configuration to provide specific hints to the Spring container in order to help disambiguate a situation in which multiple instances of a particular type or interface are present. For instance, we might indicate which `AuthenticationService` was needed by adding the following annotation:

```
@Autowired
@Qualifier("basicAuthHandler")
public void setAuthHandler(AuthenticationService authHandler) {
    this.authHandler = authHandler;
}
```

Now that we have disambiguated which implementation of our `AuthenticationService` should be injected into the `setAuthHandler` method listed above, we need to "tag" this dependency so that Spring is able to select the correct instance. In Spring XML, we can provide this hint by including the qualifier element:

```
<bean id="authHandler" class="com.prospringhibernate.gallery.BasicAuthServiceImpl"/>
    <qualifier value="basicAuthHandler"/>
</bean>
```

It is also possible to provide disambiguating hints on dependencies by applying the `@Qualifier` annotation to a class annotated for Spring's component-scanning capability. We will demonstrate these features later in this book. The `@Autowired` annotation may be applied to more than just member variables. It can also be applied to methods and constructors. Furthermore, the `@Qualifier` annotation may be applied directly to method parameters to target qualification to a specific parameter or to apply different qualifying hints to different parameters within a method or constructor.

Set It and Forget It!

All this externalization doesn't seem like a big deal at first, but it really is, and you'll notice that when you begin development. You can simply focus on the implementation without worrying about how a reference from one class can get to another. You learn to simply define setters and getters for the dependencies each class requires, and then leave the wiring to Spring. Imagine some of the alternatives.

Many applications rely on singletons to centralize and hand out references to needed dependencies. This type of strategy will certainly work, but inevitably, your code becomes more about wiring classes together than about your application's core functionality.

Spring and IOC allow you to focus on the application design and business logic, and forget about the wiring. Ron "Ronco" Popeil used the tagline "Set it, and forget it!" in some infomercial. You may find this slogan floating through your head each time you start developing with Spring.

Slick configuration and life-cycle management are really only a small portion of the overall Spring package. Spring also provides powerful integration points to most major frameworks in the Java ecosystem, including many persistence frameworks. This greatly simplifies integrating these frameworks into an application and makes maintenance and development easier overall. Beyond these integration points, Spring also provides a powerful set of AOP and proxying features, which are instrumental for configuring declarative transactions, logging, and remoting. These capabilities make Spring a viable replacement for the enterprise-level features offered by EJB and Java EE application servers.

Injecting Code Using AOP and Interceptors

AOP is often a hard pill for developers to swallow. In truth, it can be a somewhat confusing topic, as it is a fairly new development paradigm. For those experienced in object-oriented methodologies, AOP can seem a bit unconventional.

AOP is a strategy that allows behavior to be injected into code in places across an application. In much the same way that Spring provides a means to inject values and instance references into a bean, AOP allows developers to weave code from one class directly into another. Why on Earth would you ever want to do this? Well, sometimes, you want to apply functionality across a whole slew of classes, but extending from a base class to accomplish this goal doesn't make sense, as the functionality you wish to inject may be orthogonal to the destination class. This notion is often called *cross-cutting concerns*, because the intention with AOP is to apply functionality across a series of classes that has little to do with the main purposes of those classes.

For example, say you have a few classes that are designed to store and retrieve data to and from a relational database. As part of this implementation, you may wish to do some auditing (for example, to track details of each successive write operation). Extending from a base auditing class isn't a viable or proper way to accomplish this task. If you extend from any class at all, you probably want to inherit behavior that relates more to manipulating your domain model and saving data (you don't want to inherit auditing behavior). In this example, we might say that auditing functionality is *orthogonal* to the core persistence functionality (that is, completely independent of it). Furthermore, the auditing aspects of the code can be applied in a reasonably similar and standard fashion across all the application code. This is the perfect scenario for AOP. You can apply aspects of the unrelated auditing functionality across all of the classes that aim to handle image gallery logic.

The way AOP works in practice is fairly simple: a class's methods can be altered so that new functionality can be injected before, after, or around (essentially, before *and* after) a method is called. So, in the case of an auditing aspect, you could inject a block of code that writes a row in a database (constituting a piece of an overall auditing trail) each time a method within a category of methods is called.

A similar scenario concerns security. A security check can be inserted into your core data-access code to ensure appropriate permissions or roles are verified each time certain methods are called. The interesting part of this approach is that you can keep the security code entirely separate from your core implementation (which no longer needs to worry about the implementation details of security). This leads to cleaner code, as your core application need not get bogged down with details of your security implementation.

Furthermore, it is often useful to have distinct teams manage features that are disparate. AOP makes this feasible, as security-related code can be crafted by experts in this domain, while the application business logic is developed and maintained by a different team. By ensuring these two facets don't intermingle (from a code standpoint), specialization becomes more attainable. These two distinct pieces of functionality can be developed and maintained entirely separately, leading to cleaner and more loosely coupled code.

This ability to intercept method calls and introduce, or *inject*, new functionality is the secret sauce behind Spring's support for declarative transactions. Using Spring's declarative transaction support, you can advise your persistence facade layer with transactional semantics. We'll cover transactions in detail in Chapter 7, but to illustrate the separation of concerns offered by AOP, we'll leave you with this snippet of code as a teaser:

```
public class ServiceFacadeImpl implements ServiceFacade {

    @Transactional(readOnly = false, propagation = Propagation.REQUIRES_NEW)
    public void save(Map map) {
        // business logic goes here
    }

}
```

By simply annotating this method as @Transactional, Spring can enforce the transaction semantics specified, without requiring that you write any code to start and complete a transaction in the body of the save method. Don't worry about the details associated with the annotation for now. Just know that externalizing this logic via AOP enables modifications to the transaction implementation without requiring you to refactor all the portions of the code base that depend on it. Similarly, you can be confident that changes to the core business logic won't break the transaction semantics.

Summary

In this chapter, you've learned about the fundamental concepts that power the Spring Framework. You saw how to bootstrap a Spring ApplicationContext, learned the basics of configuring bean dependencies in Spring XML configuration files, and developed an understanding of bean scopes and life cycles. The benefits of dependency injection are now clear. You can effectively delegate to the Spring container to manage and resolve your application dependencies, and doing so can help keep your application's dependencies loosely coupled. Finally, you were given a glimpse into the power of managing orthogonal coding concerns with AOP.

Throughout the rest of this book, we will build on the Spring concepts introduced in this chapter to define and implement an art gallery application.

CHAPTER 3

■■■

Basic Application Setup

In this chapter, we'll take you on a crash course though setting up a basic project using Spring and Hibernate. The tool we'll use for managing our application is Apache Maven 3. If you're already well versed in Spring, Hibernate, and Maven, you may want to just skim through this chapter, so you can get a feel for structure and conventions we'll be using throughout the book as we flesh out an art gallery application. We're going to cover a lot of ground very quickly and provide references to the chapters where we dive deeper into the various configurations along the way.

Application Management with Maven

Maven was written by Sonatype's Jason van Zyl in 2002 and reached its 1.0 release as a top-level Apache Software Foundation project in 2004. Maven strives to simplify day-to-day development by ensuring an easy, repeatable process for configuring. managing, and interacting with Java-based software projects.

Maven revolves around the concept of a Project Object Model (POM), which represents the configuration for your project or module. In Maven parlance, a module is just a subproject for a given "parent" Maven project. This organizational construct allows you to create a project that is compartmentalized into a collection of smaller modules. Your POM describes many things about your project, including required dependencies, plugin configuration. and the order and operations for compiling and assembling your application.

Maven provides a ton of features out of the box. Also, a tremendous amount of plugins have been developed by its massive community of users. When the time comes to further customize your project's build process, writing Maven plugins on your own is a snap.

Managed Dependencies

Maven's killer feature is its dependency management. Maven downloads all of your project's dependencies from Maven repositories when you build or compile your application. This is a huge win when working in a team. Do you want to upgrade the version of Spring your project uses? Just update the project dependencies, commit to source control, and everyone on the team will automatically have their project upgraded to the newest version of Spring as well! Maven even handles transitive dependencies, meaning that Maven can automatically fetch the dependencies of the libraries your project depends on without you explicitly including them all.

Remember how we told you that there are a huge number of mature plugins available for Maven? One example of a handy plugin that you have at your disposal is the excellent m2eclipse plugin, for integrating Maven with Eclipse. Figure 3-1, which comes courtesy of m2eclipse, shows you everything you need to know about why using a tool like Maven is important for managing enterprise Java applications. The image isn't really legible, and you can't even see all of the dependencies, which extend off to the left and right of the screen, because there are so many components that make up our application.

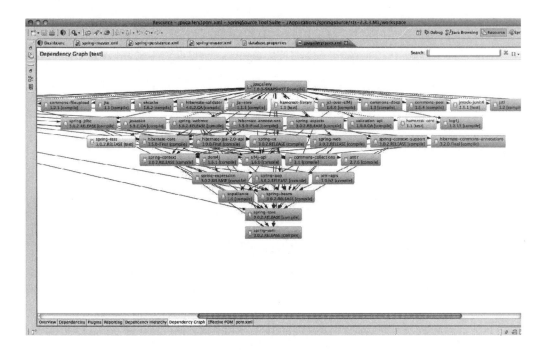

Figure 3-1. *A set of dependencies as displayed by Maven and m2eclipse*

The number of dependencies may seem a bit daunting at first, but when you're using Spring and Hibernate, you are given a lot of granular choice about which JARs to include and when, which to exclude, and so on. This results in many smaller library dependencies. Through your project's dependency configuration, Maven is aware of which JAR files are required for your project and which JARs have dependencies on one another. It knows which libraries are needed only while executing unit tests, as well as which libraries should be bundled into your resulting WAR file to be deployed on an application container like Apache Tomcat.

With all of this power comes a good bit of complexity, and for that reason, Maven also has its fair share of detractors. The fact remains that at the time of this writing, Maven is far and away the most prevalent tool used by shops big and small for managing Java applications. Once you get over some of the jargon, Maven is quite simple to configure and use. Get started by downloading it from `http://maven.apache.org`, and let's see how you can put it to use.

Standard Directory Structure

Let's first create the folder structure required for a standard Maven 3 web application. Though you can define a custom directory structure and modify your Maven settings or graft Maven onto a legacy project with a directory structure that's already defined, your best bet is to stick with the basic folder structure that Maven expects. That will ensure proper interoperability with all of the plugins and tools that are available.

Since we're building a basic art gallery application, start by making a folder called **gallery**:

```
mkdir gallery
```

Within the **gallery** folder, we'll create the folders that are customary for a Java application:

```
mkdir gallery/src
mkdir gallery/src/main
mkdir gallery/src/main/java
mkdir gallery/src/main/resources
mkdir gallery/src/main/resources/META-INF
```

For web applications, we need a **webapp** and **WEB-INF** folder:

```
mkdir gallery/src/main/webapp
mkdir gallery/src/main/webapp/WEB-INF
```

We also need to create the folders that are required for unit testing our application:

```
mkdir gallery/src/test
mkdir gallery/src/test/java
mkdir gallery/src/test/resources
```

And finally, we'll create the two folders where Spring configuration files are ordinarily placed:

```
mkdir gallery/src/main/webapp/WEB-INF/spring
mkdir gallery/src/main/resources/META-INF/spring
```

■ **Note** You can also have maven automatically generate your project's structure by using Maven's archetype feature. Maven archetypes are like project templates that can be used to streamline the creation of a maven project, including setting up your directory structure and a baseline `pom.xml` file.

POM Deconstruction

The primary configuration file for Maven is **pom.xml**. With this configuration file, you can specify important metadata and build details about your project. The **pom.xml** file resides at the root of a given Maven project, so we'll create it within the **gallery** folder. This listing is abridged for the sake of simplicity. We recommend you check out the full listing in the source code that accompanies the book.

```xml
<project xmlns="http://maven.apache.org/POM/4.0.0"
         xmlns:xsi="http://www.w3.org/2001/XMLSchema-instance"
         xsi:schemaLocation="http://maven.apache.org/POM/4.0.0
                             http://maven.apache.org/mavenv4_0_0.xsd">

  <modelVersion>4.0.0</modelVersion>

  <groupId>com.prospinghibernate</groupId>
  <artifactId>gallery</artifactId>
  <version>1.0.0-SNAPSHOT</version>

  <packaging>war</packaging>

  <properties>
    <spring.version>3.0.2.RELEASE</spring.version>
    <hibernate.version>3.5.0-Final</hibernate.version>
  </properties>

  <dependencies>
    <dependency>
      <groupId>org.springframework</groupId>
      <artifactId>spring-core</artifactId>
      <version>${spring.version}</version>
    </dependency>

    <dependency>
      <groupId>org.hibernate</groupId>
      <artifactId>hibernate-core</artifactId>
      <version>${hibernate.version}</version>
    </dependency>

    <!-- Most dependencies omitted for brevity... -->

  </dependencies>

  <build>
    <plugins>
      <plugin>
        <groupId>org.codehaus.mojo</groupId>
        <artifactId>tomcat-maven-plugin</artifactId>
        <version>1.0</version>
      </plugin>
    </plugins>

    <!-- Other plugins omitted for brevity... -->

  </build>

</project>
```

There is a lot happening in this POM configuration file. First, you'll notice the XML namespace that's defined for Maven and its POM schema definition.

modelVersion is used to declare the version of the POM for your project. This protects you from compatibility issues when upgrading the version of Maven you are using.

Next up is a series of fields commonly referred to as the *project coordinates* because they uniquely identify the project. By convention, the groupId uses the reverse domain of the organization that created the project. The artifactId is the unique name within a given groupId, and version is the specific release of a project. No two projects may have the same combination of groupId:artifactId:version.

The packaging element is a special attribute in the project coordinates. It's not used as a part of the unique identifier, but it describes the output of a given project. The default value is jar, to produce a Java archive (JAR file). Since, we're building a web application, we specify war to output a web archive (WAR file).

The properties section offers a convenient place to define variables that you use in the rest of your configuration. In our project, we have ten Spring JAR files outlined as dependencies. Managing them all individually is tedious. Using the properties attributes simplifies the management of upgrading versions of Spring.

Finally, the build attribute offers a place for you to define, among other things, the plugins you require for your project. For our project, the Tomcat Maven plugin provides an excellent mechanism for easily building and running our web application on the Apache Tomcat application server.

With that, we have a very basic application stubbed out. You can execute mvn initialize from your root gallery folder at a command prompt. If you've done everything correctly, Maven will fetch your dependencies and deliver the message BUILD SUCCESS.

Of course, our application doesn't yet *do* anything. Let's start laying down our Spring configuration so we can change that.

Spring Configuration

When building reasonably large Spring applications, you end up with a lot of Spring beans configured in the Spring ApplicationContext. As you saw in Chapter 2, every object that you configure for use in the Spring container is registered in the ApplicationContext, which is a subinterface of Spring's BeanFactory. The ApplicationContext provides you with the tools you need to interact with your configured beans. We recommend creating a root configuration file, and then importing all other configuration files, so that the XML files don't become too large and obtuse.

The following is an extremely basic Spring configuration file (gallery/src/main/resources/META-INF/spring/spring-master.xml).

```xml
<?xml version="1.0" encoding="UTF-8" standalone="no"?>
<beans xmlns="http://www.springframework.org/schema/beans"
       xmlns:context="http://www.springframework.org/schema/context"
       xmlns:xsi="http://www.w3.org/2001/XMLSchema-instance"
       xsi:schemaLocation="http://www.springframework.org/schema/beans
            http://www.springframework.org/schema/beans/spring-beans-3.0.xsd
            http://www.springframework.org/schema/context
            http://www.springframework.org/schema/context/spring-context-3.0.xsd">

  <context:property-placeholder location="classpath*:META-INF/spring/*.properties"/>
```

```
<context:component-scan base-package="com.prospringhibernate">
  <context:exclude-filter type="annotation"
                          expression="org.springframework.stereotype.Controller"/>
</context:component-scan>

<import resource="spring-datasource.xml"/>

</beans>
```

Let's break down the contents of this **spring-master.xml** file in more detail.

Namespace Support

Spring introduced extensive namespace support as of version 2.0 of the framework. Everything is just a bean in the IoC container, but over time, your configuration can become incredibly verbose. The introduction of namespaces is intended to simplify the XML configuration when dealing with integration points like transactions. You can even define your own namespaces if that's required.

Two namespaces are used in our **spring-master.xml** configuration file, marked by the **xmlns** declarations:

- The **beans** namespace is required for defining all basic bean definitions for your application (such as DAOs, service layer beans, and so on).

- The **context** namespace is provided as a convenience for configuring some of the core plumbing of Spring.

Externalizing Property Configurations

This configuration defines a **PropertyPlaceholderConfigurer**, which allows you to externalize some of your settings to a properties file outside the Spring configuration.

```
<context:property-placeholder
    location="classpath*:META-INF/spring/*.properties"/>
```

The **property-placeholder** will automatically locate and parse any property files you have in your classpath under the **META-INF/spring** directory. Any property you want replaced should be indicated in your Spring configuration like so: **${propertyKey}**. You'll see a full example later in this chapter when we configure a datasource for the gallery application.

Component Scanning

The next important piece of configuration is component scanning, which was introduced in Spring 2.5 as a mechanism for further simplifying the way you go about configuring Spring applications.

```
<context:component-scan base-package="com.prospringhibernate">
```

This declaration will cause Spring to locate every **@Component**, **@Repository**, and **@Service** in your application. In practical terms, this allows you to write a POJO, and then simply annotate the new POJO as a @Service. Spring will then automatically detect, instantiate, and dependency inject your service at startup time.

Additionally, component scanning turns on other notable Spring annotations like @Inject, @Named, and @PostConstruct support. These annotations allow you to use common Spring and Java EE annotations in your classes without needing to do any special configuration. The most commonly used annotation is @Inject, which instructs Spring to dependency-inject an object into your class. You can then also have your new service injected into any other class that requires it, simply by declaring a field for your service inside the relying class.

■ **Note** @Inject and @Named are just two of the annotations defined as a part of JSR-330. JSR-330 defines a standard set of annotations to be used in Java EE applications. @Inject and @Named are wholesale replacements for the @Autowired and @Qualifier annotations in Spring that you may already be familiar with. This makes your application more portable in the event that you should decide to change your dependency-injection implementation to something like Google Guice.

The matching rules used by the component scanner can also be customized with filters for including or excluding components. You can control this matching based on type, annotation, AspectJ expression, or regular expressions for name patterns. The default stereotypes can even be disabled. In our configuration, we declared the following exclusion:

```
<context:exclude-filter type="annotation"
expression="org.springframework.stereotype.Controller" />
```

This exclude-filter is declared to avoid instantiating our @Controller classes, as these should be instantiated by a web tier application context. Yes, you read that right: our application will actually have several distinct application contexts. We will talk about this a bit more when we introduce our web application configuration via web.xml later in this chapter.

Import Statements

After the property-placeholder configurer, you'll notice that we specify an import statement:

```
<import resource="spring-datasource.xml"/>
```

Imports allow you to specify an external Spring configuration file to be integrated into your application context. This is a useful construct, especially in our demonstration application, as we can easily externalize the different persistence strategies, keeping each version in its own file. These imports can also reference your application classpath with the following syntax:

```
<import resource="classpath*:spring-config-name.xml"/>
```

Imports are invaluable when you're dealing with large application contexts, as they provide a great deal of flexibility for organizing your bean definitions. You can partition your application in any number of ways to make it more approachable by new developers and to help understand how the project changes over time.

Database Integration

Now that you have a clearer picture of how Spring is bootstrapped within your application, let's get back to integrating your database of choice. You've learned that Spring's adherence to interface-based concepts helps to take implementation choices out of your code and into configuration. So, whether you choose to use a Java Naming and Directory Interface (JNDI) factory bean to pull in a database reference from an external JNDI directory or configure a specific database driver directly, your code won't be affected one bit. In the end, you'll always end up with a JDBC `DataSource`, and that's all your code needs to care about.

JDBC Support

In our example, we'll keep things simple. Let's start off by defining a Spring bean that will create a JDBC `DataSource` instance:

```
<bean id="galleryDataSource"
      class="org.springframework.jdbc.datasource.DriverManagerDataSource">
      p:driverClassName="${jdbc.driverClassName}"
      p:url="${jdbc.url}"
      p:username="${jdbc.username}"
      p:password="${jdbc.password}"/>
</bean>
```

If we wanted to get a bit fancier, we could instead choose a popular database connection pool as our bean implementation. A connection pool is ideal for web applications that require multiple concurrent database operations. A connection pool can be optimized for different usage scenarios, ensuring a more efficient means for handing off new database connections to the application. Again, switching to a database connection pool will give your application more efficiency without requiring any code changes.

■ **Note** Connection pools used to be something that developers had to write on their own. Their use is actually a fun gauge to use to see how long engineers have been writing web applications in Java. If they've written their own connection pools, they've probably been at it for a long while. As a result of needing to roll their own pools, every open source project wound up with a unique implementation of a connection pool. Fortunately, all of the projects that are part of the Apache Software Foundation came together to create the `commons-dbcp` library (`dbcp` is short for database connection pool).

Notice in the configuration that follows how easily we switch to using a connection pool. This is made possible by coding to interfaces, externalizing configuration, and leveraging dependency injection. It's a really rewarding experience to be able to make such large changes so quickly and easily.

```
<bean id="galleryDataSource"
    class="org.apache.commons.dbcp.BasicDataSource">
    p:driverClassName="${jdbc.driverClassName}"
    p:url="${jdbc.url}"
    p:username="${jdbc.username}"
    p:password="${jdbc.password}"/>
</bean>
```

You may have noticed that the `id` for our `DataSource` bean is `galleryDataSource`. In most enterprise applications, you end up with several datasources. As a result, the best approach is to give each one a unique name so you have finer-grained control over which portions of your application use which datasource.

Also notice that we have specified properties for `driverClassName`, `url`, `username`, and `password` for our `datasource` bean. These properties determine how an application connects to a given database. Within the Spring configuration, we can use placeholder references through the ${} notation. These placeholders represent external values stored in our `jdbc.properties` file, injected into our configuration file, courtesy of our `PropertyPlaceholderConfigurer`. This detail isn't necessary, but it makes our configuration more portable. It allows us to easily define different database configurations for different machines and platforms without needing to change our Spring configuration. For instance, here is a snippet of our `src/main/resources/META-INF/spring/jdbc.properties` file:

```
jdbc.url=jdbc\:h2\:mem\:prosh;DB_CLOSE_DELAY\=-1
jdbc.driverClassName=org.h2.Driver
jdbc.username=sa
jdbc.password=
```

The syntax is intuitive. Each line contains a simple expression, in which the left side represents the property name and the right side (after the =) represents the configured value. This externalization makes it easy to swap different database configurations for different environments and better externalizes these details from application-specific configuration.

Different databases will require different JDBC URLs. In this example, we use the popular H2 database. H2 is a Java-based database and is therefore easy to integrate into any Java-based application (it doesn't require a separate database process). You could just as easily use PostgreSQL, MySQL, or any database for which a JDBC driver is available. Just make sure your database is up, running, and configured to listen on the URL specified in the bean's configuration.

It is also critical that you include the appropriate JDBC driver on your classpath when the application is first started. Because H2 is Java-based, simply including the H2 JAR file on your classpath is all that is required to get rolling.

Integration with JNDI

Hibernate almost always implies a relational database, so starting there makes the most sense. Java has evolved into a platform for building enterprise-level applications, so there are many options for connecting it to a standard relational database.

At the simplest level, you can instantiate the database driver for your database of choice, but most applications require more than that. Many application servers offer their own optimized database connection pools to improve performance when multiple clients are using the application concurrently. To simplify administration and integration, many application servers use JNDI to interface with a database.

JNDI is often described as the opposite of Spring's IoC. Instead of having dependencies automatically injected into your application, JNDI allows dependencies to be looked up from a centrally managed directory. There are certainly benefits to both approaches. For example, in the case of JNDI, developers can define logical names for database resources in their application configuration, but allow a system administrator to manage mapping that logical name to the proper database connection pool in the web application container configurations, effectively deferring the specification of database connection details until runtime. When a database migration is required, JNDI can simplify some of these administrative tasks, as no changes to the application configuration will be required.

No matter which approach you decide to take, Spring makes integrating a datasource into your application easy. The key factor is that Spring's persistence templates never require a specific type of datasource implementation. Instead, they depend on the more generic `javax.sql.Datasource` interface. Whether you intend to use a database connection pool or a JNDI-retrieved datasource, the resultant configuration should always produce a standard `javax.sql.Datasource` reference.

This brings us to a key concept in Spring: the `FactoryBean` interface. The `FactoryBean` is Spring's answer to the well-known factory design pattern. The key concept here is that you remove a direct dependency on a specific implementation by delaying the selection or instantiation of the specific implementation until runtime. You define a factory, and it is the factory's job to pick the correct implementation at runtime and instantiate (or look up) that specific class.

The Spring `FactoryBean` concept is quite similar. Normally in Spring, when you define a bean, the class specified by the `classname` attribute is the class that will be instantiated and injected into other beans that have that bean ID wired into them. This isn't the case with a `FactoryBean`. When you use a `FactoryBean`, you are instead instantiating a factory class that will then be responsible for creating the specific implementation used to resolve dependencies in Spring. So essentially, the `classname` attribute in this case just defines a factory implementation, whose job will then be to create the actual target implementation you need.

This concept allows us to use multiple strategies to access a datasource without tying ourselves down to a particular solution. If you use the JNDI `FactoryBean`, you will still end up with a datasource reference, and the same will occur if you choose to use the pooled datasource implementation.

There are other reasons to use a `FactoryBean` in Spring, as well. For instance, a `MapFactoryBean` can be used to create a Java `Map` entirely in your configuration file (which can be quite convenient in certain cases).

A Spring `FactoryBean` implements the `FactoryBean` interface, which defines three methods designed to instantiate the target object (that is, the instance the factory is intended to create), the target object's type, and whether the target object is a singleton or prototype. For our scenario, we would configure our JNDI datasource in the following way:

```
<bean id="galleryDatasource" class="org.springframework.jndi.JndiObjectFactoryBean">
    <property name="jndiName" value="java:comp/env/jdbc/gallery"/>
</bean>
```

Although the preceding example is fairly concise, in some situations, you can make your configuration easier to read and more terse by importing a namespace intended to handle a very specific type of configuration. For example, by importing the `jee` namespace, we can simplify the preceding JNDI lookup further:

```
<jee:jndi-lookup id="galleryDatasource"
        jndi-name="java:comp/env/jdbc/gallery"/>
```

Not only have we reduced the configuration to a single line, but we've also made the intention of our configuration clearer.

Web Application Configuration

Java web applications are deployed as WAR files. A WAR file is a special kind of JAR file that includes things like servlets, JSPs, tag libraries, and static HTML assets.

The key configuration file for a WAR is web.xml, which outlines the structure for an application in accordance with the Java EE specifications. The configuration that follows adheres to the Servlet 2.5 specification, and can be interpreted by all major application server containers, including Tomcat, Resin, Jetty, WebSphere, WebLogic, GlassFish, and so on. The web.xml file should be placed under the WEB-INF directory. For Maven projects, the WEB-INF directory is located under src/main/webapp. Here's a basic src/main/webapp/WEB-INF/web.xml to get our art gallery application started.

```xml
<?xml version="1.0" encoding="UTF-8" standalone="no"?>
<web-app xmlns="http://java.sun.com/xml/ns/javaee"
         xmlns:xsi="http://www.w3.org/2001/XMLSchema-instance"
         xsi:schemaLocation="http://java.sun.com/xml/ns/javaee
                             http://java.sun.com/xml/ns/javaee/web-app_2_5.xsd"
         version="2.5">

    <!-- Listener to create the Spring Container shared by all Servlets and Filters -->
    <context-param>
        <param-name>contextConfigLocation</param-name>
        <param-value>
            classpath*:META-INF/spring/spring-master.xml
        </param-value>
    </context-param>

    <listener>
        <listener-class>
            org.springframework.web.context.ContextLoaderListener
        </listener-class>
    </listener>

    <!-- Spring DispatcherServlet for HTTP requests -->
    <servlet>
        <servlet-name>galleryDispatcher</servlet-name>
        <servlet-class>
            org.springframework.web.servlet.DispatcherServlet
        </servlet-class>
        <init-param>
            <param-name>contextConfigLocation</param-name>
            <param-value>
                WEB-INF/spring/spring-master-web.xml
            </param-value>
        </init-param>
        <load-on-startup>1</load-on-startup>
    </servlet>

    <servlet-mapping>
        <servlet-name>galleryDispatcher</servlet-name>
        <url-pattern>*.art</url-pattern>
    </servlet-mapping>

</web-app>
```

As mentioned earlier, with web-based Spring applications, you ultimately end up with multiple application contexts containing all of your Spring beans. There's a single root application context and potentially many child application contexts.

ContextLoaderListener implements the javax.servlet.ServletContextListener interface. Listeners that implement the ServletContextListener interface receive notifications from the application container whenever the servlet context is initialized or destroyed. It's a convenience mechanism to simplify your application configuration and ease system maintenance. Spring's ContextLoaderListener fires upon receiving such a notification when the servlet context is created during application startup. It expects to find a contextConfigLocation parameter defined in the servlet context, and then uses this parameter to retrieve the bean definitions and instantiates them. The beans outlined by the contextConfigLocation compose what is commonly referred to as the *root application context*.

Servlet Definition

The web.xml file is also where you configure any implementations of the Servlet interface that your application requires. Servlets are configured, along with any initialization parameters the servlet class expects, and then associated with the URL pattern to which you want the servlet to be applied.

For a Spring application, you would take advantage of the framework's DispatcherServlet class. DispatcherServlet is a flexible implementation of the Servlet interface that serves as a central routing mechanism for HTTP requests. With the help of adapter classes offered by Spring, you can specify how each instance of DispatcherServlet handles everything from view resolution to exception handling in a nice, pluggable way.

Each of these instances of DispatcherServlet has its own namespace, commonly referred to as a *child application context*. That means that each DispatcherServlet has its own ApplicationContext, but they all share the root application context. In short, this means that Spring beans defined in the ApplicationContext of a DispatcherServlet may reference the beans from your root ApplicationContext but not vice versa. It also means that separate DispatcherServlet instances may not share their bean definitions.

■ **Note** The ApplicationContext used by each DispatcherServlet is technically an implementation of Spring's WebApplicationContext interface. The WebApplicationContext adds a getServletContext method to the generic ApplicationContext interface. It also defines a well-known application attribute name that the root context must be bound to in the bootstrap process.

Let's take another look at our galleryDispatcher servlet definition. Just as with our datasources, we give each configured DispatcherServlet a unique name, because we expect to end up with several.

```
<servlet>
    <servlet-name>galleryDispatcher</servlet-name>
    <servlet-class>
        org.springframework.web.servlet.DispatcherServlet
    </servlet-class>
    <init-param>
        <param-name>contextConfigLocation</param-name>
```

```
        <param-value>
            WEB-INF/spring/spring-master-web.xml
        </param-value>
    </init-param>
    <load-on-startup>1</load-on-startup>
</servlet>
```

The servlet is defined with an `init-param` named `contextConfigLocation`, which provides the servlet with all the information it needs to acquire and instantiate its Spring bean configuration. And beans in `spring-master-web.xml` may safely reference beans the `ApplicationContext` defined in `spring-master.xml` and its subsequent imports.

However, there's one large exception to this `ApplicationContext` hierarchy: implementations of the `BeanFactoryPostProcessor` interface and its sibling `BeanPostProcessor` just apply to the `BeanFactory` that defines them. The `PropertyPlaceholderConfigurer` class described earlier in this chapter is one such example. This means that you need to define a property placeholder once for each `DispatcherServlet` in addition to the one already defined in the `spring-master.xml` root application context.

Finally, we instruct our application container to map any requests that start with `/art/` to this `galleryDispatcher`:

```
<servlet-mapping>
    <servlet-name>galleryDispatcher</servlet-name>
    <url-pattern>/art/*</url-pattern>
</servlet-mapping>
```

With that configuration in place, a fictitious request to `/art/foo` would be mapped to the `galleryDispatcher`, which would in turn route the request to a proper Spring MVC controller.

Spring MVC

As of Spring 3.0, bootstrapping Spring MVC is incredibly simple. The following are the contents of `src/main/webapp/WEB-INF/spring/spring-master-web.xml`, which is the configuration file behind the `galleryDispatcher` servlet.

```
<?xml version="1.0" encoding="UTF-8" standalone="no"?>
<beans xmlns="http://www.springframework.org/schema/beans"
      xmlns:context="http://www.springframework.org/schema/context"
      xmlns:mvc="http://www.springframework.org/schema/mvc"
      xmlns:xsi="http://www.w3.org/2001/XMLSchema-instance"
      xsi:schemaLocation="http://www.springframework.org/schema/beans
          http://www.springframework.org/schema/beans/spring-beans-3.0.xsd
          http://www.springframework.org/schema/context
          http://www.springframework.org/schema/context/spring-context-3.0.xsd
          http://www.springframework.org/schema/mvc
          http://www.springframework.org/schema/mvc/spring-mvc-3.0.xsd">

    <context:component-scan base-package="com.prospringhibernate"
                            use-defaultfilters="false">
    <context:include-filter type="annotation"
                            expression="org.springframework.stereotype.Controller"/>
    </context:component-scan>
```

```
<mvc:annotation-driven/>

<!-- selects a static view for rendering without the need for an explicit controller -->
<mvc:view-controller path="/index.jsp"/>
```

```
</beans>
```

We're using Spring's component scanning again in this WebApplicationContext. This time around, we're specifying an include-filter to restrict the beans we instantiate to only those POJOs annotated with the @Controller stereotype annotation.

Next, we employ the mvc-namespace declaration to turn on support for mapping requests to Spring MVC @Controller methods.

```
<mvc:annotation-driven/>
```

This convenience configuration syntax also registers default Spring formatters and Spring validators for use across all controllers. This allows us to write controller code like the following:

```
@Controller
@RequestMapping("**/people")
public class PersonController {

    @RequestMapping(value = "/{id}", method = RequestMethod.GET)
    public String show(@PathVariable("id") Long id, ModelMap modelMap) {
        // business logic to retrieve a Person entity
        return "person";
    }

    @RequestMapping(value = "/{id}", method = RequestMethod.DELETE)
    public String delete(@PathVariable("id") Long id) {
        // business logic to delete a Person entity and
        // return the appropriate view goes here
    }

}
```

This abridged code is annotated as a controller. It's also mapped to **/people via the Spring MVC @RequestMapping annotation. We use the @RequestMapping annotation again at the method level to specify that any HTTP GET request to **/people/{id} should trigger the show method. The @PathVariable annotation will take that {id} parameter and set it as Long id for use within the show method. Similarly, when an HTTP DELETE is issued against the URL /art/people/{id}, the request will be routed through the galleryDispatcher to the PersonController's delete method. That's a lot to digest in a short period of time, but suffice it to say that Spring's MVC annotations greatly reduce the amount of code required to build out a full-fledged enterprise web application.

Finally, we demonstrate Spring's mechanism for static view resolution:

```
<mvc:view-controller path="/index.jsp"/>
```

Often, you will want to simply route a request to a view without any logic in a controller. This is where the mvc:view-controller comes in.

Summary

In this chapter, you have gotten a sense for what is involved in setting up a web application using core Spring, Maven, a database, and Spring MVC.

Maven is a great tool that development teams can use to simplify day-to-day development. You can manage your dependencies, ensuring repeatable build processes, and provide a consistent interface for developers on your team to use for interacting with your project.

You've also learned about some of Spring's features, including component scanning, `BeanFactoryPostProcessors` like the `PropertPlaceholderConfigurer`, Spring's namespace support, and more advanced XML configuration management with `import` declarations. Component scanning is likely the most important of these features, since it allows Spring to locate classes within a specified package structure so that it can manage these components and resolve dependencies appropriately.

The component-scanning feature allows developers to use annotations as hints for Spring. It simplifies the work required to wire dependencies together and even reduces the amount of XML configuration required. For instance, the `@Repository` annotation should be used to indicate those classes that compose the DAO layer, the `@Service` annotation can be used to designate those classes that are part of an application's service façade, and the `@Controller` annotation denotes the presence of a POJO that should be used for Spring MVC interactions. These annotations simplify the definition of the respective tiers, imbuing layer classes with metadata that helps describe their purpose.

You also saw what's required to integrate a database into a Spring application using the Apache `commons-dbcp` library for connection pools or via JNDI if you want to use the datasource offerings from your application container.

In the next chapters, we'll build out our domain model and integrate Hibernate into our art gallery application.

■ ■ ■

CHAPTER 4

Persistence with Hibernate

Much like Spring, Hibernate changed the software development landscape when it first appeared on the scene. The timing was ideal. Developers were frustrated by the complexity of J2EE and the overhead associated with using EJB for persistence in particular. Hibernate solves the persistence problem through simplicity and clean, thoughtful design.

Also like Spring, Hibernate relies heavily on POJOs. Other ORM frameworks force developers to muddy their domain model with restrictive and rigid requirements, such as alternate and parent classes, as well as Data Transfer Objects (DTOs). Hibernate enables persistence with little reliance or coupling to Hibernate. Spring helps to decouple Hibernate further through several classes of its own, which serve to simplify and standardize integration and persistence operations. Additionally, Spring provides a framework-agnostic solution for implementing transactional behavior in a standardized, declarative fashion, without requiring Hibernate-specific code.

Looking back, it is easy to see how Spring and Hibernate were instrumental to each other's success. With philosophies that stressed lightweight methodologies, simplicity, and code cleanliness, the Hibernate-Spring duo ushered in a new age for enterprise Java applications and persistence. This mutual success had a dramatic impact on the Java community, and was the catalyst to numerous changes that embraced a lighter-weight approach to application development.

There is often a great deal of confusion about the various persistence options in the Java ecosystem. What's the difference between EJB 3, JPA, JDO, and Hibernate anyway? We'll attempt to demystify these things in this chapter by going over a bit of history and defining some terms. With that out of the way, we'll demonstrate how to integrate Hibernate into a Spring application.

The Evolution of Database Persistence in Java

JDBC was included by Sun Microsystems as part of JDK 1.1 in 1997. JDBC is a low-level API oriented toward relational databases. It provides methods for querying and updating a database. JDBC provides a great set of tools, but all of the heavy lifting is left entirely to the developer, who must write SQL, map query results to domain objects, manage connections and transactions, and so on. Most other persistence frameworks are built as abstractions on top of JDBC to ease this developer burden.

Beginning in 2000, version 3.0 of the JDBC specification was managed as a part of the Java Community Process (JCP). The JCP was created in 1998 as a mechanism for interested parties to participate in shaping the future directions of the Java platform. The JCP revolves around Java Specification Requests (JSRs), which are formal documents outlining proposed additions or changes to the Java platform. Each JSR has one or more individuals playing the role of specification lead and a team of members referred to as the expert group, who collaborate to hammer out the specification. A final JSR also includes a reference implementation.

This distinction between a *specification* and an *implementation* is one of the primary sources of confusion among developers when discussing the various persistence options available. For example, JPA is a *specification*, and Hibernate is just one of many projects that provide an *implementation* of the JPA specification. Other implementations of the JPA specification include OpenJPA, DataNucleus, and the reference implementation, EclipseLink. But we're getting ahead of ourselves. Let's walk through the origins of some of these specifications and implementations.

EJB, JDO, and JPA

In the late 1990s and early 2000s, the leading technology for developing large-scale applications in Java was EJB. Originally conceived by IBM in 1997, the EJB 1.0 and 1.1 specifications were adopted by Sun in 1999. From there, EJB was enhanced through the JCP. JSR 19 served as the incubator for EJB 2.0, which was finalized in 2001. The EJB 2.0 specification became a major component in Sun's Java 2 Platform, Enterprise Edition (a.k.a J2EE) reference implementation.

There's no question that the problems that EJB set out to solve, including enabling transactional integrity over distributed applications, remote procedure calls (RPC), and ORM, are complex, but EJB quickly earned a reputation for being more trouble than it was worth. The EJB 1.0, 1.1, and 2.0 specifications were marred by the complexities of checked exceptions, required interfaces, and heavy use of abstract classes. Most applications just didn't require the heft associated with EJB 1 and 2. Against that backdrop, there was a huge opportunity for competition and innovation.

The first official attempt to create a lightweight abstraction layer on top of JDBC by the JCP was JSR 12: Java Data Objects (JDO). The expert group behind JDO set out in 1999 to define a standard way to store Java objects persistently in transactional datastores. In addition, it defined a means for translating data from a relational database into Java objects and a standard way to define the transactional semantics associated with those objects. By the time the specification was finalized in 2002, JDO had evolved into a POJO-based API that was datastore-agnostic. This meant that you could use JDO with many different datastores, ranging from a relational database management system (RDBMS) to a file system, or even with an object-oriented database (OODB). Interestingly, the major application server vendors did not embrace JDO 1.0, so it never took off.

Between JDO and EJB, there were now two competing standards for managing persistence, neither of which were able to break through and win over developers. That left the door open for commercial players and open source frameworks. Hibernate is usually the ORM framework that people think of as replacing EJB 2.0, but another major player actually came first.

An ORM by the name of TopLink was originally developed by The Object People for the Smalltalk programming language. It was ported to Java and added to the company's product line by 1998. TopLink was eventually acquired by Oracle in 2002. TopLink was an impressive framework, and its features played a major role in shaping the persistence specifications that have since emerged in the Java world. As a fringe commercial project, TopLink never saw the level of adoption enjoyed by EJB, which was heavily backed by the application server vendors like IBM and BEA; nor was it able to really compete with the lightweight open source frameworks that emerged, such as Hibernate.

Gavin King set out to build Hibernate in 2001 to provide an alternative to suffering through the well-known problems associated with EJB 2 entity beans. He felt that he was spending more time thinking about persistence than the business problems of his clients. Hibernate was intended to enhance productivity and enable developers to focus more on object modeling, and to simplify the implementation of persistence logic. Hibernate 1.0 was released in 2002, Hibernate 2.0 was released in 2003, and Hibernate 3.0 was released in 2005. Throughout that entire period, Hibernate gained a huge amount of momentum as a free, POJO-based ORM that was well documented and very approachable for developers. Hibernate was able to deliver a means to develop enterprise applications that was practical, simple, elegant, and open source.

Throughout the first five years of Hibernate's existence, it did not adhere to any specification, and it wasn't a part of any standards process. Hibernate was just an open source project that you could use to solve real problems and get things done. During this time, many key players ,including Gavin King himself, came together to begin working on JSR 220: Enterprise JavaBeans 3.0. Their mission was to create a new standard that remedied the pain points associated with EJBs from a developer's point of view. As the expert group worked through the EJB 3.0 specification, it was determined that the persistence component for interacting with RDBMSs should be broken off into its own API. The Java Persistence API (JPA) was born, building on many of the core concepts that had already been implemented and proven in the field by ORMs like TopLink and Hibernate. As a part of the JSR 220 expert group, Oracle provided the reference implementation of JPA 1.0 with its TopLink product. JSR 220 was finalized in 2006, and EJB 3 played a central role in Sun's definition of Java Enterprise Edition 5, or JEE 5.

■ **Note** Please pay attention to the change in notation from J2EE to JEE. J2EE is now a legacy designation for the Enterprise Edition of Java. It's time to fix your résumé! s/J2EE/JEE/

This evolution played out perfectly for JPA. JPA 1.0 was a huge milestone for persistence in Java. However, many features that were essential for developers already using tools like Hibernate didn't make the cut due to time constraints. JPA 2.0 added many important features, including the Criteria API, cache APIs, and enhancements to the Java Persistence Query Language (JPQL), JPA's object-oriented query language. The JPA 2.0 standard was finalized in December 2009 as a new, stand-alone JSR that was targeted for inclusion in the Java EE 6 specification. Oracle donated the source code and development resources for TopLink to Sun in order to create the EclipseLink project. EclipseLink went on to become the reference implementation for JPA 2.0. Hibernate 3.5 was released in the spring of 2010 with full support for JSR 317: JPA 2.0.

That's a long and sordid history, but things have worked out quite nicely. JPA now encompasses most of the functionality that you need for developing large-scale enterprise Java applications.

HOW ABOUT JDO?

Persistence standards in Java aren't quite as clear as one might like. You see, JDO is still very much alive and well. JSR 243 ushered in JDO 2.0 in 2006 and has seen several minor revisions since. In many ways, JDO is a superset of JPA. As a result, JDO implementers like DataNucleus have been able to incorporate both the JDO specification and the JPA specification into their products. For a variety of reasons, JDO isn't implemented by Hibernate, and it isn't incorporated into the EJB 3 specification at all. Nevertheless, JDO has been enjoying bit of a resurgence in recent years.

Because JDO is datastore-agnostic, while JPA is wholly about relational datastores, there are many interesting use cases that aren't suitable for JPA but hit a sweet spot for JDO. For instance, JDO is a key ingredient for developing Java applications on the Google App Engine (GAE). GAE is a "platform as a service" (PaaS), which is built on top of Google's BigTable custom datastore rather than an RDBMS.

So why not just use JDO and forgo the creation of JPA in the first place? The reasons for competing specifications are numerous—some technical, some ideological, and some political. The largest companies in the industry heavily influence the JCP, and they obviously sometimes have competing motivations.

How Hibernate Fits In

Now that we've talked about the standards, let's look at where Hibernate fits in and dispel a few common misconceptions.

First of all, Hibernate 3 is not EJB 3 and vice versa. EJB 3 is a specification to provide a distributed, container-managed, server-side component architecture. EJB 3 encapsulates several distinct specifications to facilitate many things, including distributed transaction management, concurrency control, messaging, web services, and security—just to name a few. The EJB 3 specification assumes persistence handling can be delegated to a JPA provider.

Secondly, Hibernate is not JPA. Rather, Hibernate is one of many frameworks that provide a standards-compliant implementation of JPA. The first release of Hibernate to support JPA 1.0 was Hibernate 3.2, which became generally available in the fall of 2006.

There are often specialized features provided by frameworks like Hibernate that fall outside the JPA specification. As such, Hibernate can be thought of as a superset of JPA. On one end of the spectrum, Hibernate's architecture allows you to use Hibernate Core without using any parts of the JPA specification at all. On the polar opposite end of the spectrum, you can strictly use only the pieces of Hibernate that adhere to the JPA specification. Strict adherence to the JPA specification ensures true frictionless portability to other JPA implementations like Apache's OpenJPA project.

When using Hibernate, we recommend that developers stick to the JPA specification as closely as possible, but don't drive yourself crazy. Because open source projects tend to evolve at a much more rapid pace than the JCP, frameworks like Hibernate will offer solutions to problems not addressed by the standards process. If these custom offerings ease developer pain, please, please be pragmatic and take advantage of them! This is part of the beauty of the standards process—implementers of the various specifications are free to innovate, and the best, most successful ideas are likely to be incorporated into future revisions of the specification.

The JPA specification defines a set of annotations that can be applied to domain classes in order to map objects to database tables and member variables to columns. JPA also features a SQL-like language called JPQL, which can query the database with an object-oriented flavor. To access your database-mapped domain model, or to execute JPQL queries, you use `javax.persistence.EntityManager`.

Prior to JPA, Hibernate applications revolved around using Hibernate's `SessionFactory` and `Session` interfaces. Simply speaking, Hibernate's `SessionFactory` is aware of global configuration details, while the `Session` scope is limited to the current transaction. The JPA `EntityManager` serves as a cross between Hibernate's `SessionFactory` and `Session`; therefore, it is aware of both your database connection configuration and the transaction context. In this chapter, you'll learn a bit about JPQL, `EntityManager`, and how they interact with Spring, but mostly, you'll learn how to go about setting up an application to use Hibernate's implementation of the JPA 2.0 specification.

JPA Interface Hierarchy

Figure 4-1 outlines the four key interfaces in any JPA application. The `EntityManagerFactory` represents the configuration for a database in your application. You would typically define one `EntityManagerFactory` per datastore. The `EntityManagerFactory` is used to create multiple `EntityManager` instances.

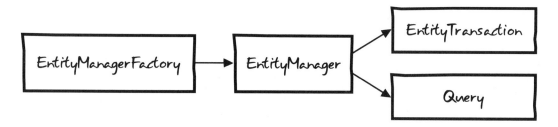

Figure 4-1. *JPA interfaces*

Each `EntityManager` instance is analogous to a database connection. In a multithreaded web application, each thread will have its own `EntityManager`.

■ **Note** By default, all Spring objects are singletons. `EntityManager` is no different, but it is still thread-safe and knows about transactional boundaries. Spring passes in a shared proxy `EntityManager`, which delegates to a thread-bound instance of the `EntityManager` that knows all about the context of the request (including transaction boundaries).

Each `EntityManager` has a single `EntityTransaction`, which is required for persisting changes to the underlying database. Finally, the `EntityManager` serves as a factory for generating `Query` classes. Classes that implement the `Query` interface are needed for executing queries against the database.

The `EntityManagerFactory` is relevant only when starting up an application, and we'll show you how that is configured in a Spring application. Querying will be covered in more depth in Chapter 6, and transaction management will be discussed in Chapter 7. As you'll see in this chapter, the `EntityManager` interface is the interface that you tend to interact with the most.

■ **Note** Since JPA is intended to be used in both heavyweight and lightweight containers, there are many configuration options. For example, you can use an EJB container to configure JPA, and then expose the container's `EntityManager` for Spring to access via JNDI. Alternatively, you can configure JPA directly within Spring using one of the many existing JPA implementations. One significant difference is the need (or lack thereof) of *load-time weaving*, which is the type of bytecode manipulation required for AOP. Load-time weaving is needed for creating transactionally aware JPA `EntityManager` and `Entity` objects that can perform lazy-loading. EJB servers have their own load-time weaving mechanism, and so does Spring. A single `EntityManager` can handle this type of functionality only through the support of the level of indirection that a proxy can provide. The Hibernate JPA implementation is one of the frameworks that doesn't require load-time weaving, so it allows you to get up and running in a JPA environment as quickly as possible.

The Art Gallery Domain Model and DAO Structure

Now it's time to get back to building our art gallery application. The core thing that we must represent in an art gallery application is an entity for the works of art. In the Figure 4-2, you'll see that an ArtEntity class represents the artwork. In our gallery, we will allow gallery curators to associate ArtEntity entities to Category entities and allow the general public to apply Tag and Comment entities. These ArtEntity entities are organized into Exhibition entities for public display, and we're capturing all of the metadata for a given work of art in a polymorphic representation called ArtData. We also define a Person type to represent all users of the application. These Person entities are qualified by an enum representing the possible system roles they may take on.

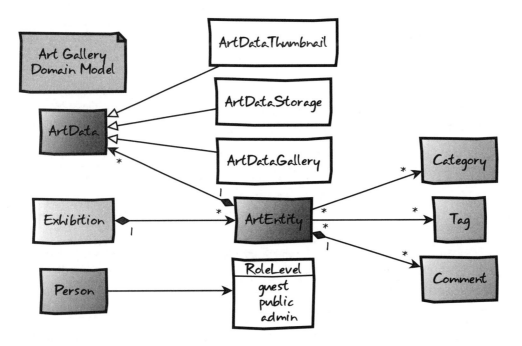

Figure 4-2. The art gallery domain model

JPA allows us to specify how a Java class is mapped to the database via annotations. The most important annotation is the @Entity annotation.

An @Entity-Annotated POJO

Adding a JPA @Entity annotation to a POJO makes it a persistable object! Well not quite—you still need to add an @Id somewhere and, ideally, a @Version field, but it's just that simple.

```
package com.prospringhibernate.gallery.domain;

import javax.persistence.Id;
import javax.persistence.Entity;
import javax.persistence.Version;
import javax.persistence.GeneratedValue;

@Entity
public class Person implements Serializable, DomainObject {

    private Long id;
    private Integer version;

    @Id
    @GeneratedValue
    public final Long getId() {
        return id;
    }

    public void setId(Long id) {
        this.id = id;
    }

    @Version
    public Integer getVersion() {
        return version;
    }

    public void setVersion(Integer version) {
        this.version = version;
    }

    // getters, setters and fields omitted
}
```

■ **Note** We've included all of the requisite import statements in the code listings here to help you see where the various annotations are coming from. Annotations are great for eliminating XML, but as the number of annotations on a given class or method grows, they can become a bit hard to read at times. Anything in the javax.persistence package is explicitly provided by JPA.

Unless told otherwise, the JPA implementation will employ convention over configuration and map this bean to a `Person` table. The `@GeneratedValue` JPA annotation tells Hibernate to use an autogenerated `id` column. Hibernate will choose the best ID-generation strategy for the specific database you're using. Hibernate is also smart enough to determine the right data type for each database column based on the Java primitive type or enumeration used for each member variable. You can customize these field mappings further through the use of the `@Basic`, `@Enumerated`, `@Temporal`, and `@Lob` annotations. Every member of the entity is assumed to be persistent unless it is `static` or annotated as `@Transient`. We'll talk more about the convention over configuration concept and Hibernate annotations in Chapter 5.

The `implements Serializable` that you see in the `Person` class isn't strictly necessary as far as the JPA specification is concerned. However, it is needed if you're going to use caching or EJB remoting, both of which require objects to be `Serializable`. Caching is a key component in achieving optimal performance in any JPA application, as you'll learn in Chapter 9, so implementing the `Serializable` interface is a good habit to adopt.

That's all you need to do from the POJO side, but an `@Entity`-annotated POJO doesn't do anything on its own. We need to, at the very least, provide code for basic CRUD operations. For now, we're going to embrace the DAO pattern. We'll explore coding in a more domain-centric style with the Active Record pattern when we cover Grails and Roo in Chapters 11 and 12, respectively.

Simplified DAO Pattern with Generics

Let's create a DAO that saves and finds a `Person` entity. We're going to get fancy with our class hierarchy using generics so that we can abstract away the boilerplate CRUD operations that would otherwise be repeated over and over again by each DAO in our application.

In the pseudo-UML in Figure 4-3, notice that our `Person` domain object implements an interface called `DomainObject`. That `DomainObject` interface is an empty interface that is used by our `GenericDao` interface as well as our `GenericDaoJpa` concrete class to bind our domain objects in a generic way. This structure enables us to push common methods into the `GenericDaoJpa` class, which in turn, allows us to keep our Hibernate DAOs succinct.

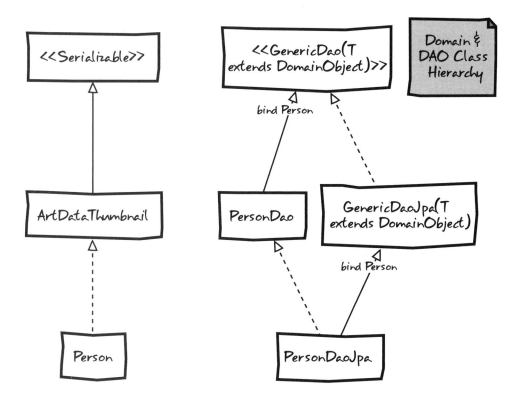

Figure 4-3. Art gallery domain and DAO class hierarchy

In the diagram in Figure 4-3, solid lines represent inheritance, and interface inheritance is depicted with dotted lines. The key usages of Java generics are highlighted by the "bind Person" annotations. Generics in Java allow a type or method to operate on objects of various types while providing compile-time type-safety.

Let's see how this plays out in actual code. The first class we'll tackle is `GenericDao`:

```
package com.prospringhibernate.gallery.dao;

import java.util.List;
import com.prospringhibernate.gallery.domain.DomainObject;

public interface GenericDao<T extends DomainObject> {

    public T get(Long id);
    public List<T> getAll();
    public void save(T object);
    public void delete(T object);

}
```

Each generic type variable is represented as T. As you can see, we've defined four basic methods in this interface that are essential when managing persistent objects. The delete method will remove a given entity from the database. The save method allows us to insert a new row or update an existing row in the database based on the contents of the entity. The two basic getters provide a means for reading in any entity T, which uses our DomainObject interface.

In the code that follows, we implement those methods on our concrete GenericDaoJpa class using JPA's EntityManager.

```java
package com.prospringhibernate.gallery.dao.hibernate;

import java.util.List;

import javax.persistence.EntityManager;
import javax.persistence.PersistenceContext;

import org.springframework.transaction.annotation.Transactional;

import com.prospringhibernate.gallery.dao.GenericDao;
import com.prospringhibernate.gallery.domain.DomainObject;

public class GenericDaoJpa<T extends DomainObject> implements GenericDao<T> {

    private Class<T> type;

    protected EntityManager entityManager;

    @PersistenceContext
    public void setEntityManager(EntityManager entityManager) {
        this.entityManager = entityManager;
    }

    public GenericDaoJpa(Class<T> type) {
        super();
        this.type = type;
    }

    @Transactional(readOnly=true)
    public T get(Long id) {
        if (id == null) {
            return null;
        } else {
            return entityManager.find(type, id);
        }
    }

    @Transactional(readOnly=true)
    public List<T> getAll() {
        return entityManager.createQuery(
            "select o from " + type.getName() + " o"
        ).getResultList();
    }
```

```java
    public void save(T object) {
        entityManager.persist(object);
    }

    public void remove(T object) {
        entityManager.remove(object);
    }

}
```

As we've discussed, `EntityManager` is the core mechanism for interacting with JPA. It performs data-access operations in a transaction-aware manner. With it, the `GenericDaoJpa` class can perform basic CRUD tasks: finding single or multiple instances of the class, as well as saving, updating, and deleting an instance.

You'll notice that the `SELECT` clause looks like it was written in SQL, but it wasn't. It's JPQL, which is specifically geared toward querying for JPA `Entity` objects, rather than tables.

This class uses the `@Transactional` and `@PersistenceContext` annotations. The `@Transactional` annotation is provided by Spring. It lets Spring know that this class requires transaction management, as well as the details of which types of operations are being performed within each method. You can add `@Transactional` at the class level to tell Spring that each and every method requires a transaction. You may also use the `@Transactional` annotation at the method level. If you annotate at both the class level and method level, the method level annotation will take precedence. We'll cover transaction semantics in depth in Chapter 7.

`@PersistenceContext` is a JPA annotation that tells Spring that it needs to inject the proxied `EntityManager` via autowiring. `@PersistenceContext` can be used on member variables, but the preferred approach is to use it on a setter as shown here.

The next interface is `PersonDao`. This interface extends `GenericDao` bound by the type `Person` and declares the methods that are specific to interacting with our `Person` entity in our DAO. Or class hierarchy has allowed us to simplify the following code to the point that we just need to define method signatures that are uniquely applicable to our `Person` entity.

```java
package com.prospringhibernate.gallery.dao;

import com.prospringhibernate.gallery.domain.Person;
import com.prospringhibernate.gallery.exception.AuthenticationException;
import com.prospringhibernate.gallery.exception.EntityNotFoundException;

public interface PersonDao extends GenericDao<Person> {

    public Person getPersonByUsername(String username) throws EntityNotFoundException;

    public Person authenticatePerson(String username, String password)
        throws AuthenticationException;

}
```

And finally, here's the implementation for the `PersonDaoJpa` class, which implements `PersonDao` and extends `GenericDaoJpa` bound with our `Person` entity:

```
package com.prospringhibernate.gallery.dao.hibernate;

import java.util.List;

import javax.persistence.Query;
import javax.persistence.EntityManager;

import org.springframework.dao.DataAccessException;
import org.springframework.stereotype.Repository;

import com.prospringhibernate.gallery.domain.Person;
import com.prospringhibernate.gallery.dao.PersonDao;
import com.prospringhibernate.gallery.exception.AuthenticationException;
import com.prospringhibernate.gallery.exception.EntityNotFoundException;

public class PersonDaoJpa extends GenericDaoJpa<Person> implements PersonDao {

  public PersonDaoJpa () {
    super(Person.class);
  }

  public Person authenticatePerson(String username,   String password)
    throws DataAccessException, AuthenticationException {

    List<Person> results = null;
    Query query = entityManager.createQuery(
      "from Person as p where p.username = :username and p.password = :password"
    );
    query.setParameter("username", username);
    query.setParameter("password", password);
    results = query.getResultList();
    if (results == null || results.size() <= 0) {
        throw new AuthenticationException("No users found");
    } else {
      return results.get(0);
    }
  }

  public Person getPersonByUsername(String username)
    throws DataAccessException, EntityNotFoundException {

    List<Person> results = null;
    Query query = entityManager.createQuery(
      "from Person as p where p.username = :username"
    );
    query.setParameter("username", username);
    results = query.getResultList();
    if (results == null || results.size() <= 0) {
```

```
      throw new EntityNotFoundException(username + " not found");
    } else {
      return results.get(0);
    }
  }

}
```

The Spring `@Repository` annotation has three primary purposes in this example:

- It tells Spring that this class can be imported via classpath scanning.

- It's a marker for Spring to know that this class requires DAO-specific `RuntimeException` handling.

- We specify the name to be used in the Spring context to represent this class. By specifying that the DAO should be recognized as `personDao`, via `@Repository("personDao")`, we can refer to this DAO elsewhere in our Spring configuration simply as `personDao`, rather than `personDaoJpa`. This allows us to change the underlying DAO implementation to something else with far less friction.

Using the `@Repository` annotation allows us to quickly group all DAOs through IDE searching, and it also lets a reader know at a glance that this class is a DAO.

Because of our use of generics, the code that remains in the `PersonDaoJpa` implementation is nice and short, and relevant only to the `Person` domain class. Developers are often intimidated by generics, but they can help you avoid doing a lot of rote, repetitive work that adds no value.

The Life Cycle of a JPA Entity

Let's take a closer look at how JPA actually handles our **Person** entity internally. Figure 4-4 highlights the various states that an entity might be in, some of the key methods involved, and a handful of useful annotations for intercepting calls to modify behavior with cross-cutting aspects.

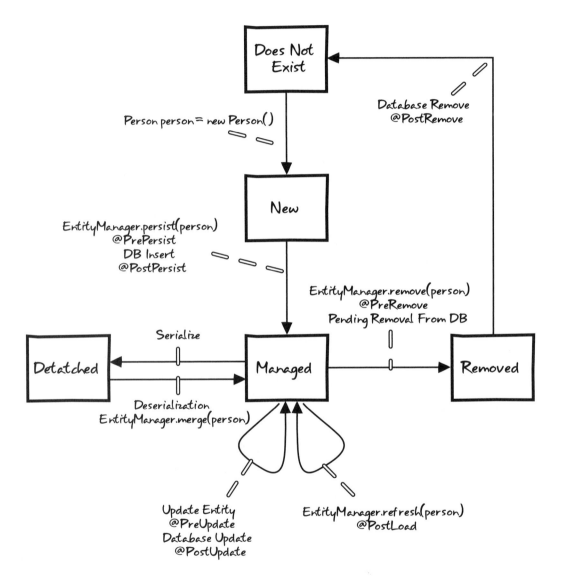

Figure 4-4. *The life cycle of a JPA entity*

There are five key states: Does Not Exist, New, Managed, Removed, and Detached. In addition, there are seven life-cycle callback annotations. The callback annotations, when implemented within your entity class, are referred to as *internal callback methods*. Alternatively, they can be defined outside a given entity class as a listener class. These are referred to as *external callback methods*. You may implement any subset of the callback methods or none at all. You may apply only a specific life-cycle callback to a single method. You may use multiple callbacks on the same method by applying all of the annotations that apply. You can also use both internal callbacks and external callbacks on a single entity. The external callbacks fire first, and then the internal callbacks are executed. There are a ton of options for taking advantage of these callbacks.

■ **Note** Callback methods should not interact with other entity objects or make calls to `EntityManager` or `Query` methods, to avoid conflicts with the original database operation that is still in progress.

Let's walk through a fictitious life cycle for a person through each of the five key states:

- *Does Not Exist*: We start here.

- *New*: A new person object is instantiated via `Person person = new Person()`. At this stage, the `person` object is in the New state. It is not associated with an `EntityManager`. and it has no representation in the database. Also, because we're using an autogenerated strategy for our primary key, the object is in memory but has no ID associated with it. Again, this is something to be wary of when managing objects in collections, as an entity has the potential to break the `equals()` and `hashCode()` contract if an object's equality is based off its identifier and this property suddenly changes from null to a real value upon being persisted via Hibernate. We will discuss this issue in more detail in Chapter 5.

- *Managed*: We persist the `person` entity with a call to `EntityManager.persist()`. If we have a method annotated with `@PrePersist`, that method is executed followed by an insert into the database, optionally followed by the execution of any custom method we've annotated with `@PostPersist`. Now our `person` entity is in the Managed state. In this state, there are many things that could happen to our `person` entity. For instance, we could make a call to `EntityManager.refresh()`, which would discard the object in memory and retrieve a fresh copy from the database, optionally taking advantage of the `@PostLoad` callback. Or we could delete the entity via `EntityManager.remove()` resulting in a call to `@PreRemove`.

- *Remove*: Once the record is deleted from the database, the entity is in a Removed state, pending execution of a method annotated with `@PostRemove` before returning to the Does Not Exist state.

- *Detached*: The Detached state comes into play when the object is no longer associated with an `EntityManager` or persistence context. Detached objects are often returned from a persistence tier to the web layer where they can be displayed to the end-user in some form. Changes can be made to a detached object, but these changes won't be persisted to the database until the entity is reassociated with a persistence context.

JPA Configuration

A few pieces of the puzzle remain. Before we have a fully working system, we need to do the following:

- Set up a JPA environment that knows about our **Person** domain object.

- Configure a database connection.

- Manage the system's transactions.

- Inject all of that into the DAO.

We'll first look at the setup from the JPA side, and then handle the Spring side of the configuration.

Bare-Bones JPA Setup

JPA requires you to create a `META-INF/persistence.xml` file. We're going to set up the easiest possible configuration:

```
<persistence xmlns="http://java.sun.com/xml/ns/persistence"
             xmlns:xsi="http://www.w3.org/2001/XMLSchema-instance"
             xsi:schemaLocation = "http://java.sun.com/xml/ns/persistence
                 http://java.sun.com/xml/ns/persistence/persistence_2_0.xsd"
             version="2.0">

    <persistence-unit name="galleryPersistenceUnit" transaction-type="RESOURCE_LOCAL"/>

</persistence>
```

This creates a persistence unit called **galleryPersistenceUnit**. It's recommended that you name your persistence unit in a way that expresses the relationship to a given database so that you may easily incorporate more datastores later without your bean definitions getting too confusing. By default, all classes marked as **@Entity** will be added to this persistence unit.

Now that we have JPA up and running, the Spring configuration needs to be made aware of the **persistence.xml**. We'll set that up next.

MORE JPA CONFIGURATION OPTIONS

In the persistence.xml file, you can optionally configure which classes you want to include for a given unit, but generally that's necessary only for more complicated scenarios, such as managing multiple databases in a single application. When you do need to map entities to a particular persistence-unit, add <class> elements to the persistence.xml like so:

```
<persistence xmlns="http://java.sun.com/xml/ns/persistence"
            xmlns:xsi="http://www.w3.org/2001/XMLSchema-instance"
            xsi:schemaLocation="http://java.sun.com/xml/ns/persistence
                http://java.sun.com/xml/ns/persistence/persistence_2_0.xsd"
            version="2.0">

    <persistence-unit name="galleryPersistenceUnit" transaction-type="RESOURCE_LOCAL">
        <class>
            com.prospringhibernate.gallery.domain.Person
        </class>
    </persistence-unit>
</persistence>
```

There's also a concept of mapping files. Rather than define classes inline, you can declare a mapping file that's referred to in the persistence.xml file in a <mapping-file> element. That file allows you to declare entity classes, and even override mapping configuration, such as column names and the mechanisms for retrieving IDs. This approach also lets you map classes that don't have any JPA annotations whatsoever.

The persistence.xml can also be used to define implementation-specific properties, such as Hibernate properties. Spring's JPA configuration requires you to configure these properties in persistence.xml in a <properties><property> element. Unfortunately, that means that you won't be able to put your environment-specific configuration details in a Spring property file without getting fancier with your build scripts.

JPA is extremely configurable and feature-rich. For more details on the persistence.xml configuration file, see a book devoted to the topic, such as *Pro JPA 2: Mastering the Java Persistence API* by Mike Keith and Merrick Schincariol (Apress, 2009).

Spring Integration

We need a way to create a usable `EntityManager` in the Spring `ApplicationContext`. In typical Spring fashion, there is more than one way to configure JPA. The following are some of the options:

- A `LocalEntityManagerFactoryBean` uses JPA's Java SE bootstrapping. `LocalEntityManagerFactoryBean` requires the JPA provider (for example, Hibernate or OpenJPA) to set up everything it needs, including database connections and a provider-specific load-time weaving setup. The bean would look something like this:

```
<bean id="entityManagerFactory"
    class="org.springframework.orm.jpa.LocalEntityManagerFactoryBean">
    <property name="persistenceUnitName" value="galleryPersistenceUnit"/>
</bean>
```

- If you have a Java EE container and you want to use EJB 3, you can use Spring's built-in JNDI lookup capabilities:

```
<jee:jndi-lookup id="entityManagerFactory" jndi-name="persistence/galleryPersistenceUnit"/>
```

- The Spring JPA `LocalContainerEntityManagerFactoryBean` requires a bit more Spring configuration than the other two options. However, it also gives you the most Spring capabilities. Setting up a `LocalContainerEntityManagerFactoryBean` requires you to configure a datasource and JPA vendor-specific adapters, so that the generic Spring JPA configuration can set up some of the extras required for each vendor. This is the approach we'll take in this chapter.

We're going to use some of the generic Spring configuration we've touched on earlier. We'll also use component scanning to tell Spring to automatically create DAOs found in specific packages.

Let's create a file called `spring-jpa.xml` under `src/main/resources/META-INF/spring`. This file will have the `LocalContainerEntityManagerFactoryBean`, our datasource, a JPA transaction manager, and annotation-based transactions. We'll start the `spring-jpa.xml` file with the namespace setup for the Spring file. There are a bunch of Spring namespaces that we'll use to configure JPA.

```
<?xml version="1.0" encoding="UTF-8" standalone="no"?>
<beans xmlns="http://www.springframework.org/schema/beans"
       xmlns:p="http://www.springframework.org/schema/p"
       xmlns:tx="http://www.springframework.org/schema/tx"
       xmlns:xsi="http://www.w3.org/2001/XMLSchema-instance"
       xsi:schemaLocation="http://www.springframework.org/schema/beans
                           http://www.springframework.org/schema/beans/spring-beans-3.0.xsd
                           http://www.springframework.org/schema/tx
                           http://www.springframework.org/schema/tx/spring-tx-3.0.xsd">

  <!-- The rest of the config is covered below -->

</beans>
```

This tells the XML parser that we want to use the following schemas as part of our configuration:

- The default Spring beans schema

- The p schema, which reduces the verbosity of setting properties

- The tx schema for transaction management

Because we're using the p namespace, we can configure Spring values more simply. For example, using p:url has the same effect as using the <property name="url" value="…"> XML fragment. You can also use the p namespace to create references.

Next, let's set up an in-memory H2 database datasource:

```
<bean id="dataSource"
      class="org.apache.commons.dbcp.BasicDataSource"
      destroy-method="close"
      p:driverClassName="org.h2.Driver"
      p:url="jdbc:h2:mem:gallery;DB_CLOSE_DELAY=-1"
      p:username="sa"
      p:password=""/>
```

Obviously, you don't need to use an in-memory database. There are plenty of other ways of getting a datasource, including JNDI lookups and connection pooling.

We're using LocalContainerEntityManagerFactoryBean, which creates a JPA EntityManager according to JPA's stand-alone bootstrap contract. This is the way to set up a completely Spring-managed JPA EntityManagerFactory:

```
<bean id="entityManagerFactory"
      class="org.springframework.orm.jpa.LocalContainerEntityManagerFactoryBean"
      p:dataSource-ref="dataSource"/>
```

The LocalContainerEntityManagerFactoryBean can use a Spring-managed datasource and a few Hibernate-specific properties, such as showSql, generateDdl, and databasePlatform.

Our @Repository annotation gets picked up as a result of Spring's component scanning. Recall that we set up component scanning in our spring-master.xml file, like so:

```
<context:component-scan base-package="com.prospringhibernate">
    <context:exclude-filter type="annotation"
                            expression="org.springframework.stereotype.Repository"/>
</context:component-scan>
```

This directive will ensure that Spring loads and manages all of our application's DAO classes. As part of this process, Spring will inject the correct EntityManager instance into the respective DAOs, as expressed by the @PersistenceContext annotation.

The following settings allow our environment to perform JPA transactions. This very basic configuration is required for our JPA application to be able to update data.

```
<bean id="transactionManager"
    class="org.springframework.orm.jpa.JpaTransactionManager"
    p:entityManagerFactory-ref="entityManagerFactory"/>

<tx:annotation-driven mode="aspectj" transaction-manager="transactionManager"/>
```

As you've seen, there is a fair amount involved for JPA configuration, but it's definitely worth the effort for the amount of functionality that is delivered!

Summary

Frameworks like Spring and Hibernate provided a means to solve some complex enterprise challenges. The critical difference between EJB 2.0 and frameworks like Spring and Hibernate is that this complexity is an option that you can elect to utilize, rather than an integral component of the framework architecture that you are forced to embrace.

In this chapter, you took a stroll down memory lane to see how persistence has evolved in the Java ecosystem, and now have a firmer understanding of the terminology as well as the distinctions between specifications and implementations. You've learned that you can have an application that uses many permutations of specifications and implementations. For instance, you can build a single application that uses EJB 3.0 for a distributed component-based architecture, with JPA for persistence powered by Hibernate as the JPA implementation. You also got a feel for the domain model and DAO structure that underpins our art gallery example application. Finally, you learned quite a lot about setting up a JPA application in a Spring environment. You are now armed with enough information to get a JPA application working.

In the next chapter, we'll continue building the domain model for our art gallery application.

■ ■ ■

CHAPTER 5

Domain Model Fundamentals

The domain model is the foundation upon which a persistence tier is constructed. Each domain class defines the properties to be persisted to the database, as well as the relationships between one class and another. This rich object-oriented structure is not easily translated to the relational world of databases. Hibernate provides the required mechanism to help address this impedance mismatch between these two realms.

Mapping is the process through which you provide hints to Hibernate regarding how the properties and references in your domain classes are translated to tables, fields, and associations in your database. When Hibernate first appeared on the scene, developers used XML (called `.hbm.xml` files) to specify a domain model's mapping rules. With the release of the JPA specification came a series of annotations that can be applied to your domain classes, providing similar types of hints to the XML mapping files.

Hibernate's strength is the ease with which developers can begin building a persistence tier. The first step is usually to define your domain model using simple JavaBeans (or POJOs). In the previous chapter, we introduced several core classes that compose the root of our application's domain model. In this chapter, we will build on this foundation, introducing some additional classes.

Understanding Associations

In Chapter 4, we introduced our art gallery domain model and created the `Person` entity. We mentioned that the `ArtEntity` class will represent artwork, images, and photos in our gallery application. We also said that our domain model will include a `Comment` class, which will represent an individual comment about a particular `ArtEntity`.

An `ArtEntity` will naturally contain multiple comments to allow for an unlimited number of site visitors to add their own comments about the particular piece of art they are viewing. Although an `ArtEntity` may contain many `Comment` instances, a given `Comment` can reference only a single `ArtEntity`, as typically a comment is intended to relate to a particular piece of content within the gallery application. The association between an `ArtEntity` and its `Comment` instances is best described as a *one-to-many* relationship. Inversely, the relationship between a `Comment` and its associated `ArtEntity` is known as a *many-to-one* association. Because each entity is able to reference the other, the association is considered to be *bidirectional*. If one entity is able to reference another entity, but the inverse is not true, this is considered a *unidirectional* association.

Whether you should use unidirectional or bidirectional associations depends on your application. However, if you don't have a specific requirement to use bidirectional associations, it can be easier to stick with a unidirectional approach, as bidirectional associations can require circular references and may end up complicating marshaling or serialization implementations.

It's always important to consider the way in which the domain model and its relationships will be translated into a database schema, even when ORM abstractions often handle these details for us. The `ArtEntity` and `Comment` association will require two tables: an `Art_Entity` table and a `Comment` table. An `ArtEntity` instance will then be associated with a `Comment` through a foreign key reference to the `Art_Entity` in the `Comment` table, as illustrated in Figure 5-1.

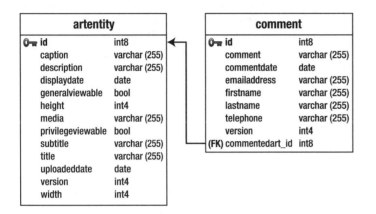

Figure 5-1. The relationship between the ArtEntity and Comment tables

Our gallery application will also require a `Category` class to represent a category into which a particular `ArtEntity` may be placed (to help organize artwork and photos into logical groups). Each `Category` may contain more than one `ArtEntity` instance. Similarly, each `ArtEntity` may be placed into multiple `Category` entities. This type of association is normally referred to as *many-to-many*. The many-to-many association is a bit more complicated than the one-to-many relationship. The best way to model this type of relationship in the database is to use a *join table*. A join table simply contains foreign keys from the two related tables, allowing rows in the two tables to be associated with each other. Figure 5-2 illustrates this relationship.

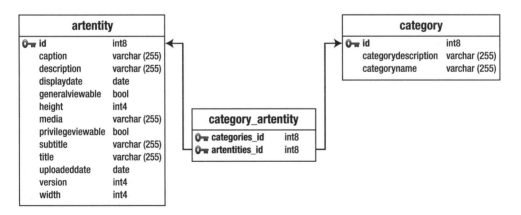

Figure 5-2. The relationship between the ArtEntity and Category tables

Although it is important to have a clear understanding of your domain model's table structure, Hibernate can take care of creating these database-specific details for you. Instead, you need to focus on the definition of the classes and the way they relate to each other from an object-oriented standpoint.

Developers have different philosophies on the best way to go about defining a Hibernate domain model. Some developers believe it is best to define a database schema first, and then create the classes to match the database structure. Obviously, there is no wrong way (provided your application works reliably) to go about this process. However, in our experience, we have achieved the best results by defining the Hibernate mappings first, allowing us to consider the Java classes and the database table structure in tandem.

With JDK 1.5 and Hibernate 3, the definition of Hibernate mapping files in XML is no longer necessary. Of course, you are welcome to continue following this more verbose methodology, and for many developers, externalizing the specifics of the database mapping is very much a good thing. However, it is hard to argue the fact that using Hibernate's new annotation support is easier and far less verbose. But using annotations isn't your only (nor necessarily best) option.

Building the Domain Model

We've already described a few of our sample application's core entities, along with their corresponding associations. Now that we've considered how these entities will be represented in the database, let's start building our Java classes. Let's first define the Comment class:

```
@Entity
public class Comment implements Serializable {

    private Long id;
    private String comment;
    private ArtEntity commentedArt;
    private Date commentDate;
    private String firstName;
    private String lastName;;
    private Integer version;

    @Id
    @GeneratedValue
    public Long getId() {
        return id;
    }

    public void setId(Long id) {
        this.id = id;
    }

    @ManyToOne
    public ArtEntity getCommentedArt() {
        return commentedArt;
    }

    public void setCommentedArt(ArtEntity commentedArt) {
        this.commentedArt = commentedArt;
    }
```

```
@Temporal(TemporalType.TIMESTAMP)
public Date getCommentDate() {
    return commentDate;
}

public void setCommentDate(Date commentDate) {
    this.commentDate = commentDate;
}

@Version
public Integer getVersion() {
    return version;
}

public void setVersion(Integer version) {
    this.version = version;
}

}
```

Next, let's define the `ArtEntity` class:

```
@Entity
public class ArtEntity implements Serializable {

    private Long id;
    private String title;
    private String subTitle;
    private Date uploadedDate;
    private Date displayDate;
    private Integer width;
    private Integer height;
    private String media;
    private String description;
    private String caption;
    private String imagePath;
    private Integer version;
    private Set<Category> categories = new HashSet();
    private Set<Comment> comments = new HashSet();

    public ArtEntity() {
    }

    @Id
    @GeneratedValue
    public Long getId() {
        return id;
    }
```

```java
    public void setId(Long id) {
        this.id = id;
    }

    @Version
    public Integer getVersion() {
        return version;
    }

    public void setVersion(Integer version) {
        this.version = version;
    }

    @ManyToMany(mappedBy = "artEntities")
    public Set<Category> getCategories() {
        return categories;
    }

    public void setCategories(Set<Category> categories){
        this.categories = categories;
    }

    @OneToMany
    public Set<Comment> getComments() {
        return comments;
    }

    public void setComments(Set<Comment> comments) {
        this.comments = comments;
    }

    public boolean addCommentToArt(Comment comment) {
        comment.setCommentedArt(this);
        return this.getComments().add(comment);
    }

}
```

■ **Note** For simplicity, the domain objects in these code listings only implement Serializable. However, as we demonstrated in the previous chapter, our GenericDao assumes that each domain entity implements our DomainObject marker interface. Although our code samples follow this approach, we've kept these listings a bit simpler for illustrative purposes.

We've omitted some of the redundant getters and setters to conserve space. However, you'll immediately recognize that we're essentially defining a JavaBean or POJO. There is no reference to Hibernate dependencies, and no parent class from which to extend.

We have defined the properties that we need to persist in the database along with their respective getters and setters. As well as the appropriate getters and setters, we have also added an `addCommentToArt(Comment comment)` method. This is a convenience method for bidirectional associations, since it is important that references are set on both sides of the association. In the `addCommentToArt(Comment comment)` method, we ensure that the specified `comment` parameter is added to the `ArtEntity`'s comment collection and that the `comment`'s `commentedArt` property properly references the `ArtEntity` instance. We strongly recommend creating this type of "association management" method on one side of the relationship to ensure that both sides of a bidirectional relationship are properly set.

Our `Comment` domain entity also has the `@ManyToOne` annotation. This tells Hibernate that the `commentedArt` property will have a many-to-one association to the `ArtEntity` table. From a database perspective, specifying a `@ManyToOne` annotation on the `Comment` field will add a foreign key field on our `Comment` table to the `ArtEntity` table. This also demonstrates some of the advantages of using Hibernate to architect both your domain model and your database schema. If Hibernate is used to generate your schema, it will also create foreign key constraints for your associations to ensure the referential integrity of your database is not compromised.

Convention over Configuration

The simplicity of Hibernate's annotation support stems from using sensible defaults, as well as Hibernate's ability to infer associations and database field types by considering the Java type of each JavaBean property. When mappings are defined in XML, we must explicitly delineate the details of each property and association. With Hibernate, because annotations are embedded into code, we have the benefit of drawing hints from the code itself, which dramatically simplifies configuration efforts.

As you learned in Chapter 4, the key annotation for Hibernate persistence is `@Entity`. This annotation tells Hibernate that we intend to persist this class. If we were following the XML mapping approach, we would then need to define each field explicitly in the `hbm.xml` mapping file. With Hibernate annotations, it is necessary to define only the details that don't conform to Hibernate's default behavior.

Hibernate will look at each property's Java type and its name, and use this metadata to define a column's field type and field name, respectively. The default behavior is to assume that all POJO properties are persistable, but you can also specify this behavior explicitly by using the `@Basic` annotation. Using `@Basic` also provides you with a way to customize various persistence-related aspects, such as whether a particular property should be lazily loaded. If you don't want certain fields persisted, you need to specify that these properties are transient using the `@Transient` annotation.

■ **Note** Hibernate offers control over fetching associations, allowing related entities to be lazily loaded —that is, only when needed, rather than when the originating object is loaded from the database. This has dramatic performance benefits (if used properly), but can also degrade performance if you're not careful. We'll be covering lazy loading in more detail in Chapter 9.

In addition to the `@Transient` and `@Basic` annotations, you can also use the `@Temporal` annotation for controlling the way date or time-based properties are mapped to the database. In our `Comment` class, we specify the following to declare that a `Date` property be persisted in the database as a timestamp:

```
@Temporal(TemporalType.TIMESTAMP)
public Date getCreatedDate() {
    return this.createdDate;
}
```

This concept of sensible defaults, or *convention over configuration*, really reduces the amount of coding required to get a domain model up and running. And Hibernate's annotation support provides ample flexibility to override any of the default behavior, should you be so inclined. For instance, if we wanted to define a table name for our `Comment` class that is different from the Java class name, we could accomplish this feat by using the `@Table` annotation:

```
@Table(name = "HOGWASH")
class Comment {
    . . . (Methods Omitted)
}
```

Similarly, we can require that the `comment` property maps to the column `commentText` by using the `@Column` annotation:

```
@Column(name = "commentText")
public String getComment() {
    return this.commentText;
}
```

This level of customization is very useful, but most of the time is unnecessary and redundant (unless you are mapping your domain model to a legacy database).

■ **Note** You should have a very good reason before you override any of Hibernate's default behavior. If you feel the need to map a Java property to a column of a different name, you may want to reconsider your naming conventions. Now, it's not wrong to have discrepancies between column names and Java property names, but simplicity of configuration is very important, and we encourage you to limit the overriding of default behavior whenever possible. After all, less code equals less maintenance.

Managing Entity Identifiers

Hibernate annotation support does require that you define a primary key and all of your JavaBean's associations. In our `Comment` class, we have added the `@Id` annotation above the `getId()` method. This annotation tells Hibernate that the `id` property of our `Comment` class is the identifier (or primary key) for our `Comment` entity.

Below the `@Id` annotation is the `@GeneratedValue` annotation, which specifies the way in which a given instance's identifier will be created. The default is `AUTO`, and in our example, this is the identifier-generation strategy Hibernate will use (since we haven't defined a strategy at all). AUTO will look at the underlying database to make the decision as to how identifiers should be created. The options are to use a sequence, an identity column, or to use a special table for generating new IDs. If you wanted to override the default behavior and use a sequence, your @GeneratedValue annotation might look like this:

```
@GeneratedValue(strategy=GenerationType.SEQUENCE, generator="COMMENT_ID_SEQ")
```

This would create a sequence named COMMENT_ID_SEQ to be used for generating new IDs for our Comment table. Hibernate offers many more options for a domain class's identifier, including UUID-based generation, or simply allowing your application to assign identifiers directly.

■ **Note** When using the AUTO mode for ID generation, Hibernate will pick the ideal strategy based on the database you are using. However, for many databases, Hibernate will end up creating a single sequence to use across all your tables. This can get a bit messy, and we have often found that creating explicit sequences for each table is a little cleaner. If your domain model has some complexity to it, we recommend specifying a different sequence for each table or class.

Using Cascading Options to Establish Data Relationships

Associations within a domain model represent how different domain entities relate to one another. Often, these relationships can be expressed in layman's terms as *parent-child relationships*, meaning that one entity owns or encapsulates a collection of another entity. Within the database, associations are represented through table joins, but there is no clear analogue for representing the more hierarchical relationships we have within Java. This is where Hibernate comes in. Cascading options help to establish parent-child relationships, or more precisely, the rules for how operations such as save and delete that are applied to one entity should *cascade* to associated entities. This concept is often referred to as *transitive persistence*.

For example, within our gallery application, we would assert that ArtEntity owns a collection of Comment instances. This is logical since a Comment is *attached* to a particular ArtEntity instance. An end user can post a comment about a particular image, and this comment is typically relevant only to the image about which it was posted. Furthermore, if an ArtEntity instance is deleted, it doesn't make sense to keep its related Comment instances around anymore. In essence, comments are children of an ArtEntity.

Since comments can be considered children of an ArtEntity, we can assert that a save operation invoked on an ArtEntity should also cascade to any added or updated Comment instances associated to that ArtEntity instance. Additionally, should an ArtEntity be deleted, we would want the delete action to cascade to any associated Comment instances. We can represent these cascading rules using the following annotation:

```
@OneToMany(orphanRemoval = true, cascade = { javax.persistence.CascadeType.ALL })
public Set<Comment> getComments() {
    return comments;
}
```

In this case, we are setting orphanRemoval to true, which will also ensure that any dereferenced comments will also be deleted. We also specify a CascadeType of SAVE_UPDATE, which will ensure save and update operations invoked on an `ArtEntity` instance will be passed along to child `Comment` instances as well.

Adding Second-Level Caching

Hibernate allows entities, as well as association collections (a group of comments) to be implicitly cached. With caching enabled, Hibernate will first try to find an entity or collection in the cache before trying to query the database. Since loading data from the cache is far less expensive than performing a database operation, caching is another effective strategy for improving application performance.

Hibernate integrates with several caching frameworks, such as Ehcache, and provides a `CacheManager` interface if you want to add your own caching solution. Once integrated, caching happens implicitly, without requiring any additional coding, other than specifying caching rules for each entity and collection.

To get basic caching enabled on our domain model, we can add the following annotation to each domain entity, as well as its corresponding collections, to ensure they are appropriately cached:

```
@Entity
@Cache(usage = CacheConcurrencyStrategy.NONSTRICT_READ_WRITE)
public class ArtEntity implements Serializable {

    . . . Methods Omitted . . .

    @OneToMany(orphanRemoval = true, cascade = { javax.persistence.CascadeType.ALL })
    @Cache(usage = CacheConcurrencyStrategy.NONSTRICT_READ_WRITE)
    public Set<Comment> getComments() {
        return comments;
    }

    public void setComments(Set<Comment> comments) {
        this.comments = comments;
    }

    . . . Methods Omitted . . .

}
```

Specifying a read-write caching strategy ensures that Hibernate will invalidate the cache whenever a particular domain instance is updated. This prevents stale data from being stored in the cache.

There are three types of caching options for Hibernate: domain, collection, and query. Domain and collection caching are demonstrated in the preceding example, as we have specified the `@Cache` annotation for the top-level domain entity as well as for the comments association.

Caching details should be adjusted using the configuration file appropriate for the caching implementation you have selected. In the case of Ehcache, you can configure specifics, such as the time-to-live and cache size on a domain-by-domain basis within the `ehcache.xml` file.

We will cover caching strategies in more detail in Chapter 9.

Using Polymorphism with Hibernate

For our gallery application, we require a few more classes to help provide the persistence details for all of the gallery's functionality. As a quick recap, here is an overview of our domain model, as it currently stands:

- **Person**: Represents an administrative user or a registered user of our gallery application.

- **Exhibition**: Organizes collections of images into logical groups.

- **ArtEntity**: Represents an image in the application and contains metadata about the image, as well as its location.

- **Comment**: Represents an individual comment that relates to a particular **ArtEntity** instance.

Our **ArtEntity** class represents basic metadata about an image, but what if we need to store an image in different resolutions, such as thumbnails, medium-resolution versions, and high-resolution versions? We could certainly insert additional fields into our **ArtEntity** class, but Hibernate provides a cleaner solution.

ORM solutions like Hibernate go far beyond mapping database fields to domain model instances. Object-oriented concepts, such as polymorphism, are also enabled by Hibernate and are an effective means for establishing a hierarchy of domain objects that share a set of core properties and functionality.

Rather than store an image path directly within our **ArtEntity** class, let's instead refactor this data into a separate base class called **ArtData**. We will then create three subclasses that each extend the **ArtData** class (and therefore share its properties) but are tailored to represent a particular type of image. We will define the following four new domain classes:

- **ArtData**: The bulk of the properties will be stored here, since it is the base class.

- **ArtData_Gallery**: This class will be used to represent the standard view of an image within the gallery listing pages.

- **ArtData_Thumbnail**: This class will be used to represent thumbnails.

- **ArtData_Storage**: This class will persist a high-resolution version of the image, suitable for archival purposes or for zoomed-in views.

■ **Note** We won't include the entire source code for our domain model here. You can download the example code for this chapter if you would like to follow along.

Hibernate provides four different options for implementing polymorphism:

Implicit polymorphism: This option uses the Java inheritance structure without requiring these structural details to affect the database schema. In other words, using implicit polymorphism, you will be able to query a parent class, and Hibernate will issue select queries for all tables within the specified Java class hierarchy. While this strategy allows you to leverage the polymorphic structure inherent in your Java classes without affecting the database, these types of queries can be a bit inefficient, as Hibernate must do a lot more heavy lifting to translate distinct tables into a coherent class hierarchy, without being able to effectively leverage the database. The other polymorphic strategies rely on the database to some degree to delineate the associations between classes in the Java hierarchy.

Table-per-hierarchy: This option combines all the properties of a class hierarchy into a single table, using a *discriminator field* to help determine which Java type is represented by each row in the database. A discriminator is simply a table column, the value of which is used to specify to which class that particular row should be associated. The advantage of this approach is that all the necessary fields for any class within the hierarchy are included in a single table, without requiring the overhead of a database join. The disadvantage is that the design is not very normalized, and for any given type, there will likely be fields that will not be utilized. This can impose limitations on your database schema, such as preventing you from being able to specify not-null constraints. Since field requirements will differ between classes in the hierarchy and they are all shared within a single table, you must simplify the schema down to the lowest common denominator.

Table-per-subclass: Using this option, each Java class in the hierarchy is represented by a different table. Properties related to the parent class are persisted to a single table. The specific properties unique to each subclass are stored within their own database tables. A particular subclass in the hierarchy is then represented through a join between the parent table and the subclass table. The advantage of this approach is that the design is clean and normalized, since shared properties are stored in a single parent table and only subclass-specific attributes are sequestered into their own subclass tables. However, although cleaner from a relational database modeling perspective, you should consider the performance hit incurred by the necessity of joining tables together.

Table-per-concrete-class: This option requires that every Java class that is not declared as abstract be represented by its own table. Subclasses are not implemented as joins between multiple tables. Instead, all the properties of each class—including those properties inherited from a parent class—are persisted to their own table. This obviously requires a bit of redundancy, as the same fields across a class hierarchy will be present in each mapped table. However, Hibernate can implement polymorphic queries more efficiently by leveraging SQL unions across all tables mapped to a particular class hierarchy. The downside is the increased verbosity and redundancy in your database schema. Furthermore, Hibernate imposes limitations on the ID-generation strategy used by tables mapped with this polymorphic approach.

Which option to use really depends on your domain model. If there isn't too much disparity across classes within your class hierarchy, then the table-per-hierarchy option probably makes the most sense. In our case, this is the strategy we will employ.

Let's take a look at the base `ArtData` entity:

```java
@Entity
@Inheritance(strategy=InheritanceType.SINGLE_TABLE)
@DiscriminatorColumn(discriminatorType = DiscriminatorType.STRING)
@DiscriminatorValue("GENERIC")
public class ArtData implements DomainObject {

    private Long id;
    private byte[] picture;
    private Integer version;

    public ArtData() {
    }

    public ArtData(byte[] picture) {
        this.picture = picture;
    }

    @Id
    @GeneratedValue
    public Long getId() {
        return id;
    }

    public void setId(Long id) {
        this.id = id;
    }

    public byte[] getPicture() {
        return picture;
    }

    public void setPicture(byte[] picture) {
        this.picture = picture;
    }

    @Version
    public Integer getVersion() {
        return version;
    }

    public void setVersion(Integer version) {
        this.version = version;
    }

}
```

Much of this class should look familiar. You will notice the standard JavaBean conventions, as well as the core Hibernate annotations. Let's focus on the annotations that enable the inheritance in our model.

The @Inheritance annotation tells Hibernate that we want to use inheritance and that we are defining our base class.

```
@Inheritance(strategy=InheritanceType.SINGLE_TABLE)
```

We are also specifying that we intend to use the table-per-hierarchy strategy (meaning that we want to persist all the fields in the entire hierarchy within a single table).

The @DiscriminatorColumn annotation provides Hibernate with the details about our discriminator. As mentioned earlier, the discriminator provides Hibernate with the clues it needs to infer to which Java type a particular database row corresponds. In our example, we are defining our discriminator column to be a String type. We could also use a char or an Integer.

Last, we define the discriminator value that each type will use through the @DiscriminatorValue annotation. In the case of the ArtData base class, we specify a value of GENERIC. So, for each ArtData instance that is persisted to the database, Hibernate will set the discriminator column to a value of GENERIC.

Next, we must define the classes that extend from our ArtData base class. Each class is fairly similar to one another in our scenario, but inheritance provides a clean way to classify the different types of images within our gallery application. Furthermore, this approach also provides future extension points, should we need to define additional metadata that only relates to a particular image type, such as a thumbnail aspect ratio or archival details for our ArtData_Storage class.

Here's our ArtData_Thumbnail class:

```
@Entity
@DiscriminatorValue("THUMBNAIL")
public class ArtData_Thumbnail extends ArtData {

    public ArtData_Thumbnail(byte[] picture) {
        this.setPicture(picture);
    }

    public ArtData_Thumbnail() {
    }

}
```

This is a fairly straightforward class. Notice, however, that we've set a discriminator value of THUMBNAIL.

Let's look at our ArtEntity class again, now with all of our refactorings applied:

```
@Entity
public class ArtEntity implements DomainObject {

    private Long id;
    private Integer version;
    private ArtData_Gallery galleryPicture;
    private ArtData_Storage storagePicture;
    private ArtData_Thumbnail thumbnailPicture;
    private Set<Category> categories = new HashSet();
    private Set<Comment> comments = new HashSet();

    public ArtEntity() {
    }
```

```java
@Id
@GeneratedValue
public Long getId() {
    return id;
}

public void setId(Long id) {
    this.id = id;
}


@Version
public Integer getVersion() {
    return version;
}

public void setVersion(Integer version) {
    this.version = version;
}

@OneToOne(cascade = CascadeType.ALL)
@JoinColumn()
public ArtData_Gallery getGalleryPicture() {
    return galleryPicture;
}

public void setGalleryPicture(ArtData_Gallery pic) {
    this.galleryPicture = pic;
}

@OneToOne(cascade = CascadeType.ALL)
@JoinColumn()
public ArtData_Storage getStoragePicture() {
    return storagePicture;
}

public void setStoragePicture(ArtData_Storage pic) {
    this.storagePicture = pic;
}

@OneToOne(cascade = CascadeType.ALL)
@JoinColumn()
public ArtData_Thumbnail getThumbnailPicture() {
    return thumbnailPicture;
}

public void setThumbnailPicture(ArtData_Thumbnail pic) {
    this.thumbnailPicture = pic;
}
```

```
@ManyToMany(mappedBy = "artEntities")
    public Set<Category> getCategories() {
        return categories;
    }

    @OneToMany(orphanRemoval = true, cascade = { javax.persistence.CascadeType.ALL })
    @Cache(usage = CacheConcurrencyStrategy.NONSTRICT_READ_WRITE)
    public Set<Comment> getComments() {
        return comments;
    }

    public void setComments(Set<Comment> comments) {
        this.comments = comments;
    }

}
```

Notice that we have now defined a few one-to-one relationships for our `thumbnailPicture`, `galleryPicture`, and `storagePicture` properties. To simplify our code, we defined three separate one-to-one associations. However, we could have also chosen to put all the `ArtData` entities into a single collection, with a generic type of the `ArtData` base class. Since each image type is represented by a different subclass, it would be easy to differentiate between the different image types.

Also, notice that we have defined a many-to-many association to the `Category` class for the `categories` property. We have added the `mappedBy` hint here to indicate that the inverse side of this relationship is referenced by the `artEntities` property in the `Comment` class. For bidirectional many-to-many associations, we need to tell Hibernate which side of the collection is the owner. By adding the `mappedBy` attribute to the `Comment` class, we are asserting that the `Category` class owns the relationship.

OVERRIDING EQUALS AND HASHCODE

In simple scenarios, Hibernate is able to maintain entity equivalence without requiring any special changes to the domain objects themselves. However, if your application requires that you add entities to Java collections, such as `java.util.Set`, or you plan to work with detached entities, you will probably need to override the default `equals()` and `hashCode()` methods for your domain objects.

Hibernate is able to maintain entity equivalence only within a single EntityManager scope. If you attempt to reattach a detached entity, Hibernate is no longer able to make the same guarantees. The way to resolve this problem is to override `equals()` and `hashCode()` for each of your domain objects, providing equality rules that are reflective of its identity within the database.

The simplest approach is to use an entity's identifier to determine equality and generate its hash code. However, if you are planning to use a generated identifier strategy, this can have negative implications. When an object is first created, it will have a default null identifier. If you attempt to add this newly created entity to a `java.util.Set` and then later save this instance, the invocation of `EntityManager.save()` will trigger an identifier to be generated for the entity in question. However, because you have based `equals` and `hashCode` on the object's identifier, you will run into a situation where the `hashCode` for the object suddenly changes. This change breaks the contract for many of the Java collection types, such as `Set`, and could lead to unexpected behavior in your application.

There are two options to get around this problem:

- Don't use a generated identifier strategy (and instead assign an entity identifier when the domain object is first instantiated)

- Base equals() and hashCode() on business equality, rather than row equality

Using an assigned identifier strategy isn't too difficult, but can impose some limitations on your application. Generally, the recommended approach is to generate equals() and hashCode() using the values of key properties of a domain object—specifically, properties that define an object's uniqueness from a business logic perspective.

Here is an example of a customized equals and hashCode for the Category domain object:

```
@Override
public boolean equals(Object o) {
    if (this == o) return true;
    if (!(o instanceof Category)) return false;

    Category category = (Category) o;
    if (categoryName != null ?
        !categoryName.equals(category.categoryName) : category.categoryName != null) {
        return false;
    } else {
        return true;
    }
}

@Override
public int hashCode() {
    return categoryName != null ? categoryName.hashCode() : 0;
}
```

Summary

In this chapter, we've introduced the fundamentals for defining a domain model with Hibernate. You learned about the mapping process and how you can use annotations to provide Hibernate with the appropriate clues to effectively map your object-oriented domain classes to your relational database.

We also examined association mapping, differentiating between the various cardinality options Hibernate provides. These details—such as whether to use many-to-many or one-to-many associations—have a significant impact on your domain model design, as well as the resultant database schema. Furthermore, it is important to think carefully about whether an association should be unidirectional or bidirectional. While bidirectional associations are often necessary to simplify reference walking and access, this option can have consequences in terms of circular dependencies that may complicate marshaling implementations.

Hibernate provides a powerful feature called cascading that allows you to associate the operations applied to one entity with its children entities so that these operations cascade. This feature is useful for ensuring that child entities are kept in sync with the state and life cycle of their parent entities.

■ ■ ■

CHAPTER 6

DAOs and Querying

If the domain model serves as the persistence tier's foundation, then the DAO layer might be considered the engine. As you've learned in previous chapters, the DAO pattern is intended to abstract lower-level persistence functionality, including creating, reading, updating, and deleting entities. But a DAO typically provides more than basic CRUD functionality.

Specialized queries that reflect the core entity-access capability of an application are usually baked into a DAO layer. For example, since our gallery application requires that end users be able to view a series of images within a particular category, the ability to query and load the relevant ArtEntity domain objects by a specified Category should be provided by a DAO class. In other words, you can think of an application's DAO classes as the building blocks utilized by the service layer to provide the necessary persistence-related functionality for the application. We will discuss the service layer in the next chapter, but it is helpful to keep in mind that the service layer typically encapsulates an application's business logic, relying on the DAO layer to get the persistence dirty work done.

One of the reasons that the DAO pattern is considered a best practice is that it helps to abstract the persistence implementation details (and technology) from the DAO interface. This allows application developers to settle on the methods and features of a particular DAO, extracting these specifics into the interface. The DAO interface then becomes the integration hub between the actual persistence implementation and the service layer—the contact for lower-level persistence functionality. This is another area where Spring can help to decouple these components.

In this chapter, we will build some of the DAO classes for our art gallery application and look at how to use the various querying mechanisms afforded to us by Hibernate and JPA, such as Hibernate Query Language (HQL), Java Persistence Query Language (JPQL), and the Criteria API.

A Basic Hibernate DAO Implementation

To begin our first DAO implementation, we will turn to Spring's HibernateTemplate. This support class leverages the Template design pattern, an approach used numerous times throughout the framework.

■ **Note** Although it is one of the more commonly used techniques, building DAO classes on the HibernateTemplate is not the only approach to take. We will examine a few alternative solutions later in this chapter. Since HibernateTemplate has been around for many years, you are bound to run into some legacy code that uses it, even if you opt for an alternative strategy.

The `HibernateTemplate` handles most of the boilerplate operations required by Hibernate, delegating to your code for the important parts. When working with Hibernate (or any persistence framework), a fair amount of resource management is required to get everything working reliably. For instance, before performing a persistence-related operation, some setup is required. You need to open a database connection and get a Hibernate session. You also may set up transactional requirements or check if there is an existing transaction that you should take part in. Finally, after an operation completes, some cleanup is required, ensuring that the session is closed and transactions are properly committed or rolled back.

The `HibernateTemplate` takes care of these arduous steps. It also catches any exceptions that may occur and translates them into Spring's own data-access exceptions. This conversion allows you to work with a consistent exception hierarchy that is not tied to a specific persistence framework, so you can easily switch between disparate persistence technologies without needing to change the exception handling throughout your code.

■ **Note** Spring's exception hierarchy does not use checked exceptions, meaning you aren't required to catch any of these exceptions. When it comes to database operations, unchecked exceptions are far more pragmatic. If something goes awry when you are trying to write to the database, chances are there's nothing your application can do to recover. So what is the point of handling this exception if you can't do much about it anyway?

Building a DAO

We'll start with the `CategoryDAO` implementation for our gallery application. `ArtEntity` domain classes can be organized into one or more categories. This feature allows end-users to browse for photos and artwork by categories. We define the `CategoryDao` interface as follows:

```
public interface CategoryDao {

  public List<Category> getCategories() throws DataAccessException;

  public Category getCategory(Long catId) throws DataAccessException;

  public List<ArtEntity> getArtworkInCategory(Long catId)
      throws DataAccessException;

  public void saveCategory(Category category) throws DataAccessException;

}
```

■ **Note** Although we introduced our `GenericDao` approach earlier in this book, we are going to take a step back and examine rolling a DAO from scratch. Typically, we would extend from our `GenericDao` implementation and define those additional methods not provided by the `GenericDao` base class.

With these methods, we can load an individual category, find all the categories, and access artwork within a particular category. The CategoryDao enables us to save new instances of Category objects as well. Of course, our application might also define a few additional Category-related persistence methods, but this interface is sufficient for illustrative purposes.

Using Spring's Hibernate Support Classes

Spring excels at reducing the amount of code you need to write in order to get something to work. When it comes to building Hibernate DAO classes, you have several options. One of the more common solutions is to extend Spring's HibernateDaoSupport class. This abstract class requires that you pass in a Hibernate SessionFactory via the setSessionFactory(SessionFactory sessionFactory) setter method. You should, of course, configure your SessionFactory in Spring so that it can be easily injected via configuration. We will demonstrate this process shortly.

When a valid SessionFactory is injected into a class that extends HibernateDaoSupport, a HibernateTemplate instance is automatically created for you, using the SessionFactory reference that was passed in. The HibernateTemplate works in a similar fashion to the Spring Framework's other template abstractions, such as the JDBCTemplate and TransactionTemplate. Following the Template design pattern, this class handles all the heavy lifting required by Hibernate so that you can focus on the persistence logic. The result is cleaner code that usually reflects very little other than the Hibernate persistence operations you are implementing.

Extending the HibernateDaoSupport class is ideal for reducing code, since it automatically defines a setter for your Hibernate SessionFactory and handles the creation of a HibernateTemplate. However, if your DAO needs to extend from a different base class, you won't be able to extend HibernateDaoSupport as well. Of course, flexibility and decoupling are key Spring philosophies, and therefore you are rarely required to extend from framework classes (although this is sometimes preferred). Instead, you can simply create your HibernateTemplate directly:

```
@Repository("categoryDao")
public class CategoryDaoImpl implements CategoryDao {

    private SessionFactory sessionFactory;
    private HibernateTemplate hibernateTemplate;

    @Autowired
    public void setSessionFactory(SessionFactory sessionFactory) {
        this.sessionFactory = sessionFactory;
        this.hibernateTemplate = new HibernateTemplate(sessionFactory);
    }

}
```

This approach requires a little more plumbing, but you are now free from extending any framework-specific classes. Notice that we created our HibernateTemplate within our setSessionFactory(SessionFactory sf) setter method. This way, when Spring injects the Hibernate SessionFactory, the HibernateTemplate will be automatically created. We applied the @Repository annotation to help Spring find our DAO via component scanning, and used the @Autowired annotation to inject the SessionFactory.

In the above snippet, we are using the @Autowired annotation to automatically inject a bean of type DataSource. Provided we have only a single bean of type DataSource, this example will work fine. If your application requires multiple datasources, you will need to ensure that you remove any potential for ambiguity. As discussed in Chapter 2, you can use the `@Qualifier` annotation to provide Spring with the necessary hints so that it is able to distinguish among your datasources.

The choice over which configuration approach to use largely depends on your coding style. In the preceding example, we use the `@Repository` annotation, indicating that we are configuring a class with persistence-related functionality. This annotation is used by Spring's component-scanning facility, which we introduced in Chapter 3. With component scanning, Spring searches a specified package structure to find those classes annotated as components so that they can be managed by Spring and play a role in dependency injection.

Spring defines three core stereotype annotations, each representing a layer within a typical application:

- `@Repository` is used to delineate those classes that provide *data repository* functionality. In this case, it is our DAO implementation, as it serves the purpose of abstracting all data-access functionality that relates to the `Category` domain object.

- `@Controller` is used to delineate controller classes, which are used in the web layer to handle requests.

- `@Service` defines a service facade. Typically, the service layer wraps the DAO layer, providing a coherent, transactional service that often serves as the business logic for an application. The service layer is often called a *façade*, since it serves as an abstraction over the data-access code, hiding the lower-level implementation details and providing a business-specific API. We will discuss the service layer in more detail in Chapter 8.

These three annotations logically extend from the `@Component` annotation, which defines any bean intended to be managed by the Spring container. In fact, we could just as easily have used `@Component` instead of `@Repository` in our example, but we would lose the intention of our class as a DAO. In other words, we use the `@Repository` annotation to clue Spring in to the fact that our class is a DAO.

To ensure that our `CategoryDao` class will be configured into our Spring `ApplicationContext`, we will need to add a component-scanning bean like the following to our Spring XML configuration:

```
<context:component-scan base-package=
        "com.prospringhibernate.gallery.dao.hibernate">
    <context:include-filter type="annotation" expression=
        "org.springframework.stereotype.Repository"/>
</context:component-scan>
```

This XML snippet tells Spring to look for classes annotated with `@Repository` within the `com.prospringhibernate.gallery.dao.hibernate` package. Eventually, we will have multiple DAO implementations in this package, all configured in a similar fashion.

Enabling Query Caching with the HibernateTemplate

The `HibernateTemplate` includes two methods needed to facilitate query caching. Using a query cache with Hibernate can provide a significant performance boost by minimizing the number of trips to the database. However, you should verify the performance benefits of query caching carefully, as sometimes query caching can actually have a detrimental effect on application performance. We discuss this in more detail in Chapter 9.

There are several different strategies for enabling query caching. One approach is to configure a `HibernateTemplate` directly in your Spring configuration. This way, you can externalize and centralize query cache specifics:

```
<bean id="hibernateTemplate"
      class="org.springframework.orm.hibernate3.HibernateTemplate">
    <property name="sessionFactory" ref="sessionFactory"/>
    <property name="queryCacheRegion" value="querycache_artwork"/>
    <property name="cacheQueries" value="true"/>
</bean>
```

■ **Note** You must first enable query caching globally by adding the following hibernate property to the hibernateProperties map when creating your `SessionFactory`:

```
<prop key="hibernate.cache.use_query_cache">true</prop>
```

You can then inject this preconfigured `HibernateTemplate` directly into your DAO implementation. If your DAO extends from the **HibernateDaoSupport** class, it will use the **SessionFactory** applied to your Spring-configured `HibernateTemplate` automatically. Using this strategy, you can ensure that query caching is enabled for all operations that make use of the `HibernateTemplate`. The downside to this technique is that you are using a centrally configured `HibernateTemplate`, which makes it difficult to apply customizations for specific DAOs that rely upon it. An alternative approach is to configure query caching details in code through extending `HibernateTemplate` or setting the query cache specifics directly.

Going Template-less

When you use Spring's template abstractions, you don't need to worry about handling boilerplate processes and resource management. Most Hibernate operations can be managed through the `HibernateTemplate`.

When working with Hibernate directly, you normally are required to create a new Hibernate **Session** from a **SessionFactory**. For most operations, you also need to be concerned with transactional details, ensuring that transactions are started at the beginning of an operation, and then either committed or rolled back when the operation completes. The `HibernateTemplate` (along with other Spring Framework classes) will ensure that the Hibernate **Session** is opened and closed, and that transactional semantics are properly applied. However, using a `HibernateTemplate` is not the only valid approach, when using Spring and Hibernate together.

■ **Note** You are free to specify transactional requirements all in code. However, doing so can be verbose and error-prone. Instead, we recommend specifying transactional requirements entirely via configuration, separating transactional details from our persistence logic. This is one of the key purposes of the service facade layer.

The introduction of the `HibernateTemplate` came early in Hibernate's development. Prior to Hibernate 3, Hibernate suffered from "a few architectural flaws." Unlike today's version, earlier versions of Hibernate had a checked exception hierarchy, which required developers to write messy DAO code as a result of attempting to handle Hibernate's exceptions through a series of nested `try-catch-finally` blocks.

With the release of Hibernate 3.0.1, things became a bit simpler. Hibernate swapped its checked exception hierarchy for unchecked exceptions, removing the requirement for sloppy `try-catch` blocks. Additionally, Hibernate introduced the concept of a *contextual session*, which allows Hibernate to associate and synchronize a single session with the current transaction. This is a similar to what Spring provides in its Hibernate support, allowing sessions to automatically participate in transactions.

In its Hibernate 3 support, Spring's `LocalSessionFactoryBean` classes integrate with Hibernate's contextual session support, creating a proxied Hibernate `SessionFactory` by default. This proxied version of the `SessionFactory` enhances its `getCurrentSession` method, allowing it to be automatically synchronized with Spring's resource management, such as transactional features.

Going with the standard Hibernate APIs rather than utilizing Spring's `HibernateTemplate` might simplify some development, but you lose some benefits. Spring's template support provides a level of consistency across various persistence technologies; for example, Spring's `JDBCTemplate` works in a similar fashion to the `HibernateTemplate` or the `JPATemplate`.

Additionally, Spring's template support automatically translates a particular persistence framework's exceptions into the appropriate exception from Spring's `DataException` hierarchy, further decoupling your code from a particular technology. But there is a way to achieve this without using the `HibernateTemplate`. If you add a BeanFactory PostProcessor, Spring can detect any DAO classes annotated with the `@Repository` annotation and automatically translate Hibernate exceptions into the Spring generic `DataAccessException` hierarchy. To make this work, simply add the following bean to your Spring configuration:

```
<bean class="org.springframework.dao.annotation.↵
                    PersistenceExceptionTranslationPostProcessor"/>
```

Then ensure your DAO classes are properly annotated with `@Repository`, and you will be able to use the Hibernate API directly in your DAO implementation, rather than relying on `HibernateTemplate`. You can instead just define getters and setters for the `Hibernate SessionFactory`, allowing the `AnnotationSessionFactoryBean` to inject a proxied `SessionFactory` into your class. Then you can implement your DAO methods by accessing the Hibernate session via the following:

```
this.getSessionFactory().getCurrentSession()
```

A more complete implementation might look like this:

```
@Repository("categoryDao")
public class CategoryDaoHibernate implements CategoryDao {

    private SessionFactory sessionFactory;

    public SessionFactory getSessionFactory() {
        return this.sessionFactory;
    }
```

```
@Autowired
public void setSessionFactory(SessionFactory sessionFactory) {
    this.sessionFactory = sessionFactory;
}

@SuppressWarnings("unchecked")
public List<Category> getCategories() throws DataAccessException {
    return this.getSessionFactory().getCurrentSession().createQuery(
        "select categories from Category categories"
    ).list();
}

. . .

}
```

This example is a bit contrived, but it should provide you with a clearer sense of how you can leverage the Hibernate API directly while still taking advantage of Spring's powerful resource-management features. Which approach you take depends on your preferences and specific requirements. For example, if your organization uses other persistence technologies, such as JDBC or iBatis, then using HibernateTemplate may still be a good idea, since it provides greater consistency within the organization and perhaps the code base. Additionally, HibernateTemplate can also provide a few shortcuts that are not available with the direct Hibernate APIs, such as setting default behavior (for example, to activate cache settings) across an entire DAO.

Although we focus on the usage of Hibernate a bit more than JPA in this chapter, keep in mind that the two approaches are quite similar—especially when it comes to HQL and JPQL syntax. For this reason, we aren't going to examine every example from both a Hibernate and JPA perspective. However, to give you a clearer sense of how we might set up a JPA-based DAO, let's look at a short example:

```
@Repository("categoryDao")
public class CategoryDaoHibernate implements CategoryDao {

    private EntityManager entityManager;

    @PersistenceContext
    public void setEntityManager(EntityManager entityManager) {
        this.entityManager = entityManager;
    }

    @SuppressWarnings("unchecked")
    public List<Category> getCategories() throws DataAccessException {
        return this.entityManager.createQuery(
        "select categories from Category categories"
        ).getResultList();
    }

    . . .

}
```

Notice that the JPA version of our simple DAO example is quite similar, with a few syntax differences. The most significant variation is the use of @PersistenceContext to inject our JPA EntityManager. This annotation depends on the inclusion of a BeanPostProcessor in our Spring configuration, which will help to perform the standard JPA configuration, using the persistence.xml file. You can add this BeanPostProcessor by adding the following to your Spring configuration:

```
<bean class="org.springframework.orm.jpa.support.↵
                    PersistenceAnnotationBeanPostProcessor" />
```

Throughout this book, we will include examples that use the Hibernate APIs, Core JPA and HibernateTemplate or JPATemplate to demonstrate a broader range of implementations.

Querying in Hibernate

Now that we've examined some approaches for implementing our DAO and have taken care of all the wiring details, let's move on to the actual implementation. We will consider the following as the first version of our CategoryDao implementation:

```
@Repository("categoryDao")
public class CategoryDaoImpl extends HibernateDaoSupport ↵
                                    implements CategoryDao {

    public List<Category> getCategories() throws DataAccessException {
        return this.getHibernateTemplate().find(
            "select categories from Category categories"
        );
    }

    public Category getCategory(Long catId) throws DataAccessException {
        return (Category) this.getHibernateTemplate()
          .load(Category.class, catId);
    }

    public List<ArtEntity> getArtworkInCategory(Long catId)
                                        throws DataAccessException {
        return this.getHibernateTemplate().findByNamedParam(
            "select art from Category cat " +
            "join cat.artEntities art "+
            "where cat.id = :catId ",
            "catId", catId
        );
    }

    public void saveCategory(Category category) throws DataAccessException {
        this.getHibernateTemplate().saveOrUpdate(category);
    }

}
```

If you're not attempting to access a single entity, you will likely need to execute a query using either HQL or the Hibernate Criteria API. Here, we will look at how to use HQL to meet our persistence requirements for the CategoryDAO. We will start with the fundamentals and gradually work our way up to the more complex querying approaches.

Loading an Entity

One of the most basic operations you can perform in Hibernate is loading an entity by its identifier. Hibernate provides two primary means of accessing an entity from the database: load and get. Although these two methods do the same thing, there are slight differences in how they behave.

For example, to load a Category instance from the database, we could use the getCategory method defined in our sample implementation. Alternatively, we could also use the Hibernate Core APIs directly:

```
public Category getCategory(Long catId) throws DataAccessException {
    return (Category) this.getSessionFactory().getCurrentSession()↵
                                      .load(Category.class, catId);
}
```

As you can see in this example, the load method takes the entity class, followed by the entity identifier.

We could instead implement the getCategory method using Session.get:

```
public Category getCategory(Long catId) throws DataAccessException {
    return (Category) this.getSessionFactory().getCurrentSession()↵
                                      .get(Category.class, catId);
}
```

The two methods seem nearly identical, but have subtle differences. Session.load will throw an exception if there is no row in the database that matches the specified identifier. However, when using Spring's persistence support, Hibernate exceptions should be automatically converted to Spring's consistent DataAccessException hierarchy. Session.get will return null if the entity doesn't exist. However, load provides performance benefits that get does not provide. For instance, load can return a proxy rather than immediately hitting the database, which can allow multiple load operations to be batched.

Querying for a Particular Type

A common HQL operation is to find a set of entities of a given type that match a specific condition. HQL is fairly close to SQL semantically, except that it offers an object-oriented perspective, compared with SQL's more table-based approach. Here's a very basic query:

```
select categories from Category categories
```

In this example, we are using the select keyword to indicate which items to return. We could instead return a list of strings representing the category names of all the Category entities, as follows:

```
select categories.name from Category categories
```

In these examples, we use the `from` keyword to indicate which entity types to query against. We then alias `Category` to `categories`, allowing us to use this alias within the `select` clause to further reference the `Category` entity in the query.

These two queries will attempt to work with all the rows in the `Category` table. To filter our results, we need to add a condition to our query. Let's look at conditional queries next.

Using Named Parameters

Let's jump ahead to the finder method that gets all `ArtEntity` instances within a particular `Category`:

```
public List<ArtEntity> getArtworkInCategory(Long catId)
                                            throws DataAccessException {
    return this.getHibernateTemplate().findByNamedParam(
        "select art from Category cat " +
        "join cat.artEntities art " +
        "where cat.id = :catId ",
        "catId", catId
    );
}
```

This method uses a more complex HQL query that joins `Category` with `ArtEntity`, specifying a `where` condition with a parameterized `CategoryId`. Joins in HQL allow you to query across multiple entities. In this example, we are referencing the `ArtEntity` domain class through the `artEntities` property of the `Category` entity.

In Hibernate, it is possible to join two entity types explicitly or implicitly. Implicit uses of join don't actually use the `join` keyword, but instead navigate across object properties and associations as part of a query. For example, we could implicitly join `Category` and `ArtEntity` domain objects using the following query:

```
from ArtEntity artEntities where artEntities.category.id = :catId
```

Here, we navigate across associations within the `where` condition. This returns the same result but through a different approach.

For this method, we are using `HibernateTemplate`'s `findByNamedParam` method. This method takes three parameters: the HQL query, the HQL parameter name, and the parameter itself. We recommend using named parameters instead of positional parameters to make your code significantly clearer and less brittle. Positional parameters rely on the order in which the parameters are passed in, which is ambiguous and more prone to errors.

Notice that our HQL query specifies the condition `where cat.id = :catId`. The `:catId` is Hibernate's way of defining a named parameter in a query. This name can then be referenced as the parameter name to the `HibernateTemplate`'s `findByNamedParam` method.

In the preceding example, we have only a single parameter, but this is not typically the case. When you require more than a single HQL parameter, you can use the overloaded version of `findByNamedParam` that takes a `String` array (as the second parameter) to define the parameter names you are passing into your finder method, and an `Object` array for the actual parameter values. This more flexible version works about the same as the preceding example, except the second and third parameters both take arrays instead of a `String` and an `Object`, respectively. For instance, let's take a look at our `authenticatePerson` method in the `PersonDaoImpl` class:

```
public Person authenticatePerson(String username, String password)
                throws DataAccessException, AuthenticationException {

    List<Person> validUsers = this.getHibernateTemplate().findByNamedParam(
        "select people from Person people where" +
        "people.username = :username " +
        "and people.password = :password",
         new String[] {"username", "password"},
         new String[] {username, password }
    );

    if (validUsers == null || validUsers.size() <= 0) {
        throw new AuthenticationException("No users found");
    } else {
        return validUsers.get(0);
    }

}
```

In this example, we are passing two conditions to our HQL query: `username` and `password`. The second argument contains a `String` array of HQL parameter names, and the third method argument takes a `String` array of values. The `HibernateTemplate` also offers overloaded alternatives in which you can specify an `Object` or `Object` array for parameter values, allowing you to use any Java type as a parameter value in an HQL query.

Querying Using Core Hibernate

In the previous section, we discussed how to execute HQL queries using the `HibernateTemplate`. Although this approach works reasonably well, you probably noticed that things can get somewhat confusing when specifying multiple named parameters. As we discussed earlier, `HibernateTemplate` isn't always the most ideal way to implement your DAOs. Let's now look at how the `authenticatePerson` method is implemented using the Hibernate Core APIs:

```
public Person authenticatePerson(String username, String password)
                throws DataAccessException, AuthenticationException {

    Person validUser =
        (Person) this.getSessionFactory().getCurrentSession().createQuery(
            "select people from Person people where" +
            "people.username = :username " +
            "and people.password = :password")
            .setString("username", username)
            .setString("password", password)
            .uniqueResult()
        );

    if (validUser == null) {
            throw new AuthenticationException("No users found");
```

```
    } else {
        return validUser;
    }

}
```

As you can see, this form is a bit clearer and more concise than the `HibernateTemplate` version. The Hibernate Core APIs provide an easy way to set named parameters, one at a time, using a chained syntax (meaning that each `Query` method returns the `Query` instance, allowing you to invoke multiple methods in a row). You can also return a list or call `uniqueResult()`, which assumes that the query will return only a single item, allowing you to return this item directly. If you want your query to return a list, you can invoke `.list()` instead of `.uniqueResult()`.

Hibernate also provides an `.iterate()` method on the `Query` class, which can be useful if there is a decent chance that most of the entities returned by the query are stored in cache. The `.iterate()` method will return only the identifiers of each entity, rather than the entire entity itself. Assuming the IDs are cached, this will result in a more performant operation.

Using Named Queries

Even though the Hibernate Core APIs help to simplify our implementation, the method still seems a bit complex, due primarily to the length of the query itself, which we break into chunks for readability. We also rely on `String` concatenation, which incurs a slight performance hit.

One approach to making HQL-based methods clearer is to use a *named query*. Named queries allow you to externalize queries from the code itself. This can improve code clarity, while centralizing queries either outside the code entirely or grouped within a particular part of the file.

If you use Hibernate XML mapping files, you can define named queries directly within those files. This makes it possible to alter queries without needing to recompile your Java code. Alternatively, you can define named queries within your code by using the `@NamedQuery` annotation.

Once you have specified your named queries, you can easily access them using the following syntax (assuming the query is named `my.named.query.name`):

```
Query query = this.getSessionFactory().getSession().getNamedQuery("my.named.query.name");
```

Once you have a `Query` reference, you can work with it in exactly the same way as if you had created the query directly in code.

We recommend that you avoid placing HQL queries directly within the DAO code. Instead, use Hibernate's named query feature. This allows you to centralize your HQL queries within Hibernate mapping files or within domain class files using the `@NamedQuery` annotation. As we mentioned earlier, keeping named queries within XML mapping files also lets you tweak your queries without needing to recompile classes, which can come in handy when debugging a crisis in a development or Staging environment.

Working with Polymorphic Queries

In Chapter 5, you learned about the different strategies for mapping a Java class hierarchy. You can see some of the benefits of Hibernate's support for polymorphism when you consider the querying features.

For instance, in Chapter 5, we defined a class hierarchy intended to encapsulate the different image resolutions persisted within the gallery application: `ArtData`, `ArtData_Gallery`, `ArtData_Thumbnail`, and `ArtData_Storage`. In this hierarchy, the latter three classes extend from the `ArtData` base class. Now suppose that we want to find all instances that extend from `ArtData`. We can accomplish this with the following query:

```
Select artData from ArtData artData
```

This will return all instances of `ArtData`, including entities such as `ArtData_Gallery` and `ArtData_Thumbnail`, which extend from the `ArtData` parent class. Hibernate's support for polymorphism is extremely powerful, as it allows us to restrict or broaden a query across a class hierarchy. In fact, we could query for all instances of every domain object in our application by running the query:

```
From Object
```

The above query would load our entire database, since every domain object implicitly inherits from `Object`. Obviously, we strongly discourage you from trying this in a production application!

Persisting Data with Hibernate

Now that we've discussed a few options for defining finder methods using `HibernateTemplate` and the Hibernate Core APIs, how do we actually persist data?

Saving and Updating Data

Our `CategoryDaoImpl` class defines a save method for the `Category` instance as follows:

```
public void saveCategory(Category category) throws DataAccessException {
    this.getHibernateTemplate().saveOrUpdate(category);
}
```

Using `HibernateTemplate`'s `saveOrUpdate` is similar to calling `Session.saveOrUpdate(Object)` using the Hibernate Core APIs. Other saving options are available in the `HibernateTemplate`, such as merge, save, and update, if you want more specific kinds of persisting behavior.

It is even possible to perform batch operations using Hibernate, updating multiple objects using a `where` condition to determine which entities should be updated. You can also update a collection of domain objects by iterating through the entities and calling `saveOrUpdate` on each entity. We will discuss performance optimization strategies for saving objects in Chapter 9.

Handling Binary Data

Our `CategoryDao` is fairly straightforward, as it needs to manipulate only simple `String` fields. However, since we are building a gallery application, we will need to handle large data types in order to manage the data used to represent imagery. We could choose to store image data on the file system, storing only path references to the location where images are stored. However, we've found that it is often more flexible to persist everything in the database, ensuring your application data is completely centralized. This also helps to reduce coupling to the file system, and can make it easier to back up and migrate data.

In the database world, large objects (LOBs) are used to represent large binary fields. Typically, LOBs or BLOBs represent binary data while CLOBs are used to represent exceedingly large (typically more than 4,000 characters) character data. The process for working with these field types in Spring is similar.

First, we need to create a `DefaultLobHandler` reference to be used within our inserts and queries. This Spring abstraction is intended to simplify the manipulation of LOB fields. We can create our `DefaultLobHandler` by adding the following snippet to our Spring configuration:

```
<bean id="defaultLobHandler"
      class="org.springframework.jdbc.support.lob.DefaultLobHandler" />
```

Next, we need to inject our `defaultLobHandler` reference into our DAO layer. We don't need LOB support in our `CategoryDao` implementation, and we haven't defined our `ArtEntityDao` just yet. To conserve space, we won't get into the details of our `ArtEntityDao` here. Just keep in mind that this interface will handle persistence operations for the `ArtEntity` domain object (which represents a particular image within our gallery application). Additionally, remember that LOB fields within the domain model should be annotated with @Lob, to indicate that the property should be mapped to a database Lob type.

Let's begin stubbing out our `HibernateArtEntityDao` implementation:

```
public class HibernateArtEntityDao implements ArtEntityDao {
    private HibernateTemplate template;
    private LobHandler defaultLobHandler;
    // getters and setters omitted
}
```

We will need to ensure our `LobHandler` reference is injected into our `HibernateArtEntityDao` class.

Next, let's define a `saveArtEntity` method that takes an `ArtEntity` parameter, which encapsuates information about our image as well as the image data itself. (Again, keep in mind that this is a simplification of our actual `ArtEntityDao` interface and domain entity.) Our `saveArtEntity` method might look like the following:

```
public void saveArtEntity(ArtEntity artEntity) throws DataAccessException {
    this.getHibernateTemplate().saveOrUpdate(artEntity);
}
```

Understanding the Benefits of the Criteria API

Although HQL and JPQL are effective and concise strategies for expressing a query, they both suffer from a few limitations. First, because these query languages are articulated as plain text, they are prone to errors which are unable to be caught or verified by the compiler. Methods containing significant errors in the HQL or JPQL queries will compile perfectly, only to throw exceptions at runtime — or perform in unexpected ways.

HQL and JPQL are also not conducive to expressing dynamic queries, in which the attributes of the query are not fully known until runtime. For instance, if we would like our users to be able to search for images by specifying any number of tags, it would be difficult to represent this sort of query using HQL or JPQL. To accomplish this, we might try dynamically generating a JPQL query string by concatenating the conditions of each tag parameter. Clearly, this is a fragile and awkward solution to this problem.

To address these limitations, Hibernate offers the Criteria API. Until recently, JPA did not include a Criteria API, forcing developers that needed this type of functionality to go outside of the JPA standard. However, with the release of JPA 2.0, a standards-based Criteria API is now available.

Using the JPA 2.0 Criteria API

We've focused more on Hibernate-specific querying, so let's examine the new JPA 2.0 Criteria API. To illustrate the Criteria API, we will define a new DAO method for our **CategoryDao** interface:

```
public List<ArtEntity> getArtEntitiesByTitle(String title);
```

This method will return all those **ArtEntity** instances that match the specified title. Obviously, we could express this query using JPQL, however the Criteria API offers some advantages. One of the primary benefits is that we can leverage compile-time checking to ensure that our query is valid and fits within the constraints of our domain model. Later in this section, we will also examine some other advantages of the Criteria API, such as applying dynamic constraints on our query, including pagination, filtering, and ordering details.

First, let's take a look at our query:

```
public List<ArtEntity> getArtEntitiesByTitle(String title) {
    CriteriaBuilder criteriaBuilder = entityManager.getCriteriaBuilder();
    CriteriaQuery<ArtEntity> criteriaQuery =
        criteriaBuilder.createQuery(ArtEntity.class);
    Root<ArtEntity> root = criteriaQuery.from(ArtEntity.class);
    Path<String> path = root.<String>get("title");
    criteriaQuery.where(criteriaBuilder.equal(path, title));
    return entityManager.createQuery(criteriaQuery).getResultList();
}
```

If you consider the structure of a JPQL query, then you should be able to infer what the above method is doing. The first line gets a reference to a **CriteriaBuilder**. The **CriteriaBuilder** class is necessary for generating important aspects of our Criteria query, as we will see shortly. The next line then uses our **CriteriaBuilder** reference to create a **CriteriaQuery** instance. Notice that we pass **ArtEntity.class** as the single parameter to the **createQuery** method. We are essentially requesting that we would like a generically typed **CriteriaQuery** instance, using our **ArtEntity** type. Our intention in doing this is to specify that we want our query to return results of type **ArtEntity**. This doesn't necessarily imply that we are querying against an **ArtEntity** instance. In fact, we could specify a type of **Long.class** to the **createQuery** method, to indicate that our query should return a **Long**, which is typical when performing projection or aggregate queries.

Now that we have our **CriteriaQuery** instance, we need to declare what type we intend to query against. We call the **from** method on our **CriteriaQuery** instance, specifying a parameter of **ArtEntity**. This line of code in our example is similar to a JPQL clause that reads: "**from ArtEntity**". In other words, we are expressing our intention to query against the **ArtEntity** type. We are returned a **Root** instance as a result of this method call, which is generically typed to our **ArtEntity** instance. The **Root** instance can now be used as a means for referencing properties on the **ArtEntity** class that we wish to use as conditions in our query.

The next line in our method uses our **Root** instance to access the title field on our **ArtEntity** domain class, by calling the **get** method on the **Root** instance and specifying the string "**title**" (which is the appropriate property name on the **ArtEntity** class). This returns a **Path** instance, which we can use to represent the title property, in order to express a condition in our query. To express this condition, we call the **where** method on our **CriteriaQuery** instance. Notice that as a parameter to the **where** method, we have used a nested method call of **criteriaBuilder.equal(path, title)**. We use the **criteriaBuilder** as a factory to construct the **equal** condition, which returns a **Predicate** instance. Predicates represent encapsulated logic that will return either true or false, and are used as building blocks in the Criteria API to form complex queries. In our case, we have created a `Predicate` to represent the comparison logic between the `Path` instance (which represents our `ArtEntity.title` field) and the `String` title parameter, that was passed in to this method.

Now that we've articulated the requirements and conditions for our `CriteriaQuery`, we need to actually execute our query so that we can access the results. This part of the method works in a similar fashion to executing a JPQL query. We invoke `createQuery` on our `EntityManager` reference, passing in our `CriteriaQuery` instance. The `createQuery` method will actually return a `TypedQuery` instance that is generically typed to our `ArtEntity` domain class. However, to keep our method streamlined, we call `getResultList()` on the method chain to directly return a `List` of `ArtEntity` instances that match our query's conditions.

You're probably thinking that the above example required quite a bit of work to define a query that might be defined in JPQL as:

```
public List<ArtEntity> getArtEntitiesByTitle(String title) {
    Query query = this.entityManager.createQuery(
        "select art from ArtEntity where art.title = :title "
    );
    query.setParameter("title", title);
    return query.getResultList();
}
```

It's true that the JPQL version is a bit more concise. However, what about our earlier concerns about a lack of compile-time checking on the validity of our query? With the Criteria API approach, we benefit from some assurance that the syntax of our query is verifiable, whereas in JPQL we won't be aware of issues until runtime. However, in our Criteria API example, we are actually short-changing ourselves a bit. Remember that in order to represent the `ArtEntity.title` field as a `Path` reference, we used the following code:

```
Path<String> path = root.<String>get("title");
```

This line is intuitive, but we are still opening ourselves up to the potential for error since we could misspell our title field, or specify a domain class property that simply doesn't exist. Additionally, when we get into more complex queries, such as those involving associations, we could lose track of the correct field type or plurality.

To address this problem, the JPA 2.0 Criteria API provides a `MetaModel`, which can be used to describe the metadata related to your domain model. While it is possible to manually define your own `MetaModel`, in order to mirror the structure of each of your domain classes, the easier bet is to use the annotation processing feature of Java 1.6. Hibernate offers the hibernate-jpamodelgen jar, which can be used to analyze your domain model classes and then automatically generate the sourcecode for the `MetaModel`. The first step in getting this to work is to add the hibernate-jpamodelgen to your Maven pom.xml file as a dependency:

```
<dependency>
    <groupId>org.hibernate</groupId>
    <artifactId>hibernate-jpamodelgen</artifactId>
    <version>1.0.0.Final</version>
</dependency>
```

Once you've added this dependency, you will be able to have your `MetaModel` automatically generated and updated whenever your code is compiled. While it is possible to make this process more implicit, we recommend installing a Maven plugin to provide some level of control and configuration. For example, you will probably want to specify where the `MetaModel` classes should be located. Copy the following plugin configuration into the <plugins> block of your pom.xml:

```
<plugin>
  <artifactId>maven-compiler-plugin</artifactId>
  <configuration>
    <source>1.6</source>
    <target>1.6</target>
    <compilerArguments>
      <processor>
        org.hibernate.jpamodelgen.JPAMetaModelEntityProcessor
      </processor>
    </compilerArguments>
  </configuration>
</plugin>

<plugin>
  <groupId>org.bsc.maven</groupId>
  <artifactId>maven-processor-plugin</artifactId>
  <executions>
    <execution>
      <id>process</id>
      <goals>
        <goal>process</goal>
      </goals>
      <phase>generate-sources</phase>
      <configuration>
        <!-- source output directory -->
        <outputDirectory>src/main/generated-java</outputDirectory>
      </configuration>
    </execution>
  </executions>
</plugin>

<plugin>
  <groupId>org.codehaus.mojo</groupId>
  <artifactId>build-helper-maven-plugin</artifactId>
  <version>1.3</version>
  <executions>
    <execution>
      <id>add-source</id>
      <phase>generate-sources</phase>
      <goals>
        <goal>add-source</goal>
      </goals>
      <configuration>
        <sources>
          <source>src/main/generated-java</source>
```

```
        </sources>
      </configuration>
    </execution>
  </executions>
</plugin>
```

It may also be necessary to add a `<pluginrepositories>` block to your pom.xml, if you have trouble automatically installing the above plugins. You can add the following block, to ensure that the necessary plugins can be downloaded:

```
<pluginRepositories>
  <pluginRepository>
    <id>maven-annotation</id>
    <url>
      http://maven-annotation-plugin.googlecode.com/svn/trunk/mavenrepo/
    </url>
  </pluginRepository>
</pluginRepositories>
```

Once you've updated your Maven configuration, you should be able to run mvn compile in order to trigger the annotation processing to have your MetaModel generated. The above Maven configuration will generate the `MetaModel` source to src/main/generated-java, but feel free to update the location to suit your own needs.

Once you have generated your `MetaModel`, you should be able to find these classes in the appropriate location. The `MetaModel` classes mirror your own domain model classes, except that an underscore is suffixed to the class name. For instance, our `ArtEntity` domain class would have a corresponding MetaModel class in the same package structure but with the name `ArtEntity_`. Let's take a look at what our `ArtEntity` `MetaModel` class looks like:

```
@StaticMetamodel(ArtEntity.class)
public abstract class ArtEntity_ {

    public static volatile SingularAttribute<ArtEntity, String> displayDate;
    public static volatile SingularAttribute<ArtEntity, Integer> width;
    public static volatile SingularAttribute<ArtEntity, Integer> hashCode;
    public static volatile SingularAttribute<ArtEntity, String> caption;
    public static volatile SingularAttribute<ArtEntity, Boolean> ↵
                                                    privilegeViewable;
    public static volatile SingularAttribute<ArtEntity, Boolean> ↵
                                                    generalViewable;
    public static volatile SingularAttribute<ArtEntity, Integer> version;
    public static volatile SingularAttribute<ArtEntity, Long> id;
    public static volatile SingularAttribute<ArtEntity, String> subTitle;
    public static volatile SingularAttribute<ArtEntity, String> title;
    public static volatile SingularAttribute<ArtEntity, Integer> height;
    public static volatile SingularAttribute<ArtEntity, String> description;
    public static volatile SingularAttribute<ArtEntity, ArtData_Gallery> ↵
                                                    galleryPicture;
```

```
        public static volatile SetAttribute<ArtEntity, Category> categories;
        public static volatile SingularAttribute<ArtEntity, ArtData_Thumbnail> ↵
                                                         thumbnailPicture;
        public static volatile SingularAttribute<ArtEntity, String> media;
        public static volatile SetAttribute<ArtEntity, Comment> comments;
        public static volatile SingularAttribute<ArtEntity, ArtData_Storage> ↵
                                                         storagePicture;
        public static volatile SingularAttribute<ArtEntity, Date> uploadedDate;
}
```

Notice that the class is quite simple, containing only static volatile properties that correspond to each of our `ArtEntity`'s domain class properties. Since most of the fields in our `ArtEntity` domain class are scalar properties, they are represented by the `SingularAttribute` type. However, notice that each `MetaModel` property is generically typed to indicate both the domain class type (in this case, `ArtEntity`), as well as the type of the field. This metadata will prove valuable for leveraging compile time checking for all aspects of our Criteria API query — even conditions that reference particular fields.

We should also point out that the `comments` and `categories` properties are represented by the `SetAttribute` type, rather than the `SingularAttribute` type. Unlike the other fields in the `ArtEntity` class, the categories and comments properties are collection associations, represented by a `java.util.Set`.

Now that we have a clearer understanding of the `MetaModel` and how we can generate it, let's get back to the Criteria API to see how we can use this feature. To better illustrate some other features of the Criteria API, we will examine a different query that will return the count of all `ArtEntity` instances that fall within a minimum and maximum width and height. Let's take a look at the method:

```
public Long getCountOfArtEntitiesBySize(MaxMin widthRange,
                                        MaxMin heightRange,
                                        QueryOpts queryOpts) {
    CriteriaBuilder criteriaBuilder = entityManager.getCriteriaBuilder();
    CriteriaQuery<Long> criteriaQuery =
        criteriaBuilder.createQuery(Long.class);
    Root<ArtEntity> root = criteriaQuery.from(ArtEntity.class);
    Path<Integer> widthPath = root.get(ArtEntity_.width);
    Path<Integer> heightPath = root.get(ArtEntity_.height);
    criteriaQuery.where(criteriaBuilder.and(
        criteriaBuilder.between(widthPath,
                                widthRange.getMin(),
                                widthRange.getMax()),
                                criteriaBuilder.↵
                                    between(heightPath,
                                            heightRange.getMin(),
                                            heightRange.getMax())));

    criteriaQuery.select(criteriaBuilder.count(root));
    Long count = entityManager.createQuery(criteriaQuery).getSingleResult();
    return count;
}
```

Unlike our previous example, this method returns a `Long`, since we don't want a list of the `ArtEntity` instances themselves, but rather a count of how many instances match the specified condition. Notice that we have encapsulated the minimum and maximum values for both the height and width respectively through a custom `MaxMin` class. For clarity, here is the `MaxMin` class (which is an inner class of our `Dao`):

```
public static class MaxMin {

    private final int max;
    private final int min;

    public MaxMin(int max, int min) {
        this.max = max;
        this.min = min;
    }

    public int getMax() {
        return max;
    }

    public int getMin() {
        return min;
    }

}
```

Since our query will return a `Long` value, we invoke `criteriaBuilder.createQuery(Long.class)` to indicate that the intended return value for our query. We use the `criteriaQuery.from()` method to indicate that we wish to query against the `ArtEntity` class, which returns a `Root<ArtEntity>` instance — just as in the previous example. However, notice that on the next line we call `root.get(ArtEntity_.width)` to return a `Path<Integer>` reference, used to indicate the `ArtEntity.width` field. Unlike in our previous example, we are using our `ArtEntity_ MetaModel` class to reference attributes of the `ArtEntity` domain class in a consistent and type-safe way. Notice that we are returned a `Path<Integer>` instance that reflects the correct generic type. If we simply specified a string value of "width" instead of using the `MetaModel`, we would not have assurance that our query was accurately reflecting the correct field types.

Next, we use a `where` condition in which we nest an **and** expression, into which we further nest two `Predicate` clauses that articulate the **between** conditions for our query. We use our `CriteriaBuilder` as a factory to generate an **and** `Predicate`, which takes a variable number of `Predicate` arguments — all of which must evaluate to true in order for the query condition to be met.

Finally, we invoke `criteriaQuery.select()`, passing in a nested call of `criteriaBuilder.count(root)`. The inner expression defines an aggregate query of `count`, specifying our `Root` instance. This essentially boils down to counting all the `ArtEntity` instances that match the `where` condition defined above. The `criteriaQuery.select()` invocation is used to indicate what is to be selected in the query, which is effectively similar to the select keyword in a JPQL query. The last step is to use the `entityManager` reference to call `createQuery`, using our configured `CriteriaQuery` as a parameter, and then chaining a call to `getSingleResult()`. Since this query is intended to return the result of an aggregate query, we want to call `getSingleResult()`, rather than `getResultList()`.

So far, we have seen the benefits of using the Criteria API through the assurances gained by compile-time checking and verification of both the query structure and syntax, as well as the structure of our domain model. Let's look at one more example that touches on some of the benefits of the

CriteriaAPI in being able to express queries in which the structure, conditions, and complexity are dynamic in nature. In this example, we define a method that allows us to specify a `QueryOpts` instance as a parameter, which encapsulates ordering and pagination information, The key differentiator in this (somewhat simplified) example, is that we are able to define a variable-length list of fields we wish to order the results by. However, we could extend this example further, allowing us to also specify dynamic filter criteria as well.

First, let's examine the `QueryOpts` class, which is simply a wrapper for our pagination and ordering requirements:

```
public class QueryOpts {
    private int pageNum;
    private int pageSize;
    private List<FieldOrder> orderList;

    public QueryOpts() {

    }

    public QueryOpts(int pageNum, int pageSize, List<FieldOrder> orderList) {
        this.pageNum = pageNum;
        this.pageSize = pageSize;
        this.orderList = orderList;
    }

    public int getPageNum() {
        return pageNum;
    }

    public void setPageNum(int pageNum) {
        this.pageNum = pageNum;
    }

    public int getPageSize() {
        return pageSize;
    }

    public void setPageSize(int pageSize) {
        this.pageSize = pageSize;
    }

    public List<FieldOrder> getOrderList() {
        return orderList;
    }

    public void setOrderList(List<FieldOrder> orderList) {
        this.orderList = orderList;
    }


    public static class FieldOrder {
        private String field;
```

```
        boolean ascending;

        public FieldOrder() {

        }

        public FieldOrder(String field, boolean ascending) {
            this.field = field;
            this.ascending = ascending;
        }

        public String getField() {
            return field;
        }

        public void setField(String field) {
            this.field = field;
        }

        public boolean isAscending() {
            return ascending;
        }

        public void setAscending(boolean ascending) {
            this.ascending = ascending;
        }
    }

}
```

Notice that the QueryOpts also contains the static inner-class FieldOrder, which is used to represent a field name and its order direction (i.e. whether it is ascending or descending).

Now that we have a better handle on the QueryOpts class, let's take a look at the method which defines our dynamic query:

```
public List<ArtEntity> getArtEntitiesByTitle(String title,
                                             QueryOpts queryOpts) {

    CriteriaBuilder criteriaBuilder = entityManager.getCriteriaBuilder();
    CriteriaQuery<ArtEntity> criteriaQuery =
        criteriaBuilder.createQuery(ArtEntity.class);
    Root<ArtEntity> root = criteriaQuery.from(ArtEntity.class);
    Path<String> path = root.get(ArtEntity_.title);
    criteriaQuery.where(criteriaBuilder.equal(path, title));
    List<Order> orderList = criteriaQuery.getOrderList();
    List<Order> newOrderList = new ArrayList<Order>(orderList);

    for (QueryOpts.FieldOrder fieldOrder : queryOpts.getOrderList()) {
        Order order = null;
        if (fieldOrder.isAscending()) {
            order = criteriaBuilder.asc(root.get(fieldOrder.getField()));
```

```
    } else {
        order = criteriaBuilder.desc(root.get(fieldOrder.getField()));
    }
    newOrderList.add(order);
}

criteriaQuery.orderBy(newOrderList);
TypedQuery<ArtEntity> query =
    entityManager.createQuery(criteriaQuery);
query.setFirstResult(queryOpts.getPageNum() * ↵
    queryOpts.getPageSize());
query.setMaxResults(queryOpts.getPageSize());

return query.getResultList();
}
```

Once again, we are querying for ArtEntities that match a specified title. However, this method also takes a second parameter of type QueryOpts. Most of this method is similar to our first Criteria API example. However, notice how we specify the "order by" criteria for our query. We call criteriaQuery.getOrderList() in order to gain access to a List of Order classes. It is important to note that we can't directly change this list, but instead must create a new ArrayList, copying any Order items from the original list into the new list. Next, we use a for loop to iterate through our "order criteria" embedded within the QueryOpts parameter. We perform a few checks to determine whether a particular QueryOpts.FieldOrder item is ascending or descending, and then instantiate the appropriate javax.persistence.criteria.Order instance, using either criteriaBuilder.asc or criteriaBuilder.desc. In either case, notice that we extract a Path instance using root.get(), passing in the field name we wish to order by. Each newly created javax.persistence.criteria.Order instance is added to our newOrderList.

After we have finished looping through our order requirements, we call criteriaQuery.orderBy(), passing in our newOrderList as a parameter. This method call effectively sets our order by criteria, overwriting any previously specified order requirements for this query.

Finally, we use our entityManager reference to create a TypedQuery<ArtEntity> reference, and then use the pagination details embedded in our QueryOpts parameter to set the firstResult and maxResults properties, effectively controlling the range and page-size for our query.

As you can see, the Criteria API is a powerful tool for dynamically expressing queries in an object-oriented way. The Criteria API also supports more advanced features, such as joins and compound predicate expressions, as well as unique capabilities, such as "query by example." For some queries, whether to use JPQL or the Criteria API may be a matter of style. However, we believe it is important to have a thorough understanding of the Criteria API so that you can effectively leverage this feature — especially in those circumstances in which JPQL doesn't offer an elegant or viable solution.

Summary

In this chapter, we introduced some core ORM concepts, and you learned more about how Spring and Hibernate can be used together. We also reviewed some key design patterns that are instrumental to the way in which Spring integrates with many persistence frameworks. Through our gallery application examples, we demonstrated how to implement an effective DAO layer. We examined several options for integrating Hibernate—using the HibernateTemplate as well as using the Hibernate Core APIs.

The DAO pattern is considered a best practice for abstracting persistence-related functionality. Using Hibernate, we demonstrated how to load entities via their identifier, save or update individual entities, and query for domain objects using HQL. We discussed some querying techniques and examined various approaches for performing joins, using both implicit and explicit forms. We also contrasted implementation strategies using Spring's `HibernateTemplate` and Hibernate Core APIs. Although `HibernateTemplate` has played a significant role in both Spring and Hibernate's history, its use is becoming less important due to improvements to the Hibernate architecture after version 3.0.1.

This chapter discussed several implementation options for building our gallery application's DAO layer. We built on some of the concepts introduced in the previous chapter, which illustrated mapping strategies for our application's domain model. In the next chapter, we will build on the DAO layer introduced in this chapter, demonstrating how the service layer can be used to define an application's transactional business logic.

CHAPTER 7

■■■

Transaction Management

Database transactions help you group a set of operations into a single unit of work. All operations either succeed or fail as a group.

Spring's powerful and flexible transaction support is another factor responsible for the framework's success and popularity. Before Spring, complex or declarative transactional features typically required that an organization use EJB, along with a heavyweight JEE container. Using aspect-oriented programming (AOP) techniques, Spring helped democratize enterprise-level transactional support, allowing developers to cleanly apply transactional rules to their code whether they were using a full-fledged JEE application server, a lighter-weight web container, or even a stand-alone unit test.

Not only did Spring help to obviate the need for a heavyweight container, but it also provided a generalized abstraction for transaction management. It no longer mattered whether you were using Hibernate transactions, local database transactions, or even the Java Transaction API (JTA), which allows for distributed transactions across multiple datasources. In much the same way that Spring provides a generic `DataAccessException` hierarchy, Spring's abstraction for transaction management and demarcation helps to simplify and decouple transactional specifics from application code and business logic.

Much of the popularity of EJB stemmed from its transactional support. EJB provided a way to specify transactional rules via configuration, preventing these details from adding too much complexity to data access code. By leveraging its AOP features, Spring is able to offer similar flexibility, but without the overhead of a heavy EJB container or the addition of complexity or features that an organization doesn't require.

Using Spring, transactional rules can be consolidated into configuration so that code need not be muddied with these types of concerns. Switching between a JEE application server using a JTA datasource and a simple unit test using a local datasource is just a matter of modifying the Spring configuration— no code needs to be altered. Spring can leverage some of the advanced features offered by JTA when employing a JTA transaction manager. The key benefit, however, is that Spring provides a transactional programming model that is consistent—whether you need to have transactions span across multiple datasources (a feature offered by JTA) or across a single datasource, the way you define these transactional concerns will always be the same.

In rare cases where you actually want to define transactional rules for your application programmatically, Spring offers a means for accomplishing this as well. You could just rely on Hibernate's transactional programming model, but by leveraging Spring's abstractions, you reduce your coupling to Hibernate by basing your persistence code on generalized APIs. This might come in handy if you decide to move away from Hibernate in the future, or (more likely) if your persistence layer utilizes both Hibernate and JDBC.

Spring allows you to control how transactions are performed at a per-method level. Transaction management can be applied via XML configuration or using annotations. In this chapter, we will demonstrate both approaches. However, we recommend using annotations, as this strategy is the most intuitive, and allows transactional metadata to be embedded directly within a service layer class or interface.

The Joy of ACID

Before we begin adding transactions to our application using Spring, let's discuss some of the fundamental and theoretical concepts. There's quite a bit to know about transactions, but the most important details to understand are encapsulated in the acronym ACID, which defines the four core requirements of a transaction:

Atomicity specifies that all operations within a single transaction must complete together or not at all. In other words, a transaction allows multiple database operations to be applied together. In the event of an error, the entire set of operations is rolled back.

Consistency refers to the requirement that transactions must transition a database from one consistent state to another consistent state. A successful transaction cannot leave the database in a state that violates the integrity constraints of the database or the schema. In other words, transactions must comply with database constraints and referential integrity rules during every insert, update or delete before a transaction may be committed.

Isolation defines the rules about how one running transaction affects or interacts with other concurrently running transactions. The isolation strategy used on a transaction is very important. If the chosen isolation level is too loose, hard-to-find bugs can be introduced, which may adversely impact the integrity of your data. If your isolation level is too high, however, you run the risk of slowing down your application or deadlocking your database. This setting is both application server and database server dependent. While there are technically eight isolation levels, generally you will only need to concern yourself with the four that are defined by the ANSI/ISO SQL standard. You should also note that the default isolation level varies quite a bit amongst DBMS vendors.

Durability ensures that once a transaction is committed, the changes will not be lost and should survive database failures.

In this chapter, we will cover the fundamentals of ACID transactions, as well as how to declaratively apply transactions using Spring. These concepts will undoubtedly prove useful for any type of application development, and might also come in handy during your next job interview! (Although we recommend waiting for these topics to come up themselves in the context of a job interview—we do not recommend starting out by confessing your love for ACID.)

ACID can be perceived as a bit trippy, but it has a way of keeping your data safe and will definitely maintain your sanity when dealing with persistence.

So why should you care about ACID? It's important to understand the available rules and options of database behavior so that you can effectively leverage these features in the context of your application.

These details are critical for controlling how a group of operations are applied to a database or how concurrent database modifications can affect each other. Improper transaction management can also adversely affect performance in an enterprise application.

Understanding Isolation Levels

The four isolation levels that you'll encounter in practice, listed from least isolated to most isolated, are **Read Uncommitted**, **Read Committed**, **Repeatable Read**, and **Serializable**. These isolation levels also have an impact on concurrency. The least stringent isolation level allows for the highest number of concurrent database operations, while the most stringent are all but guaranteed to slow down your systems. Figure 7-1 highlights the ramifications of each isolation level including a demonstration of the correlation between isolation level and concurrency.

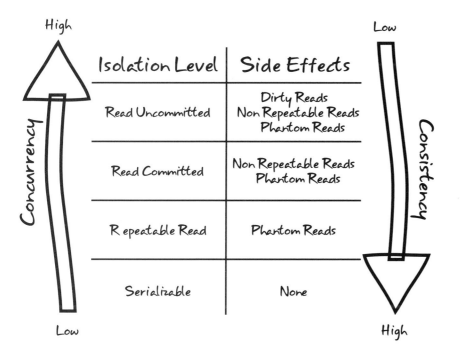

Figure 7-1. Isolation levels mandate tradeoffs between consistency and concurrency

In order to explain the side effects outlined in Figure 7-1, consider the following scenario in our art gallery application:

1. Paul opens a database transaction, T1, and SELECTs everything from the ArtEntity table.

2. Brian initiates a separate transaction, T2, to DELETE a piece of art from the ArtEntity table.

3. Brian, still in his same T2 transaction, UPDATEs a record in the ArtEntity table, correcting a typo.

4. Paul, still in his same T1 transaction, SELECTs all pieces of art in the ArtEntity table a second time.

5. Brian's transaction, T2, COMMITs.

6. Mary initiates a new transaction, T3, and INSERTs a new piece of art to the ArtEntity table.

7. Paul, still in his same T1 transaction, SELECTs all pieces of art in the ArtEntity table a third time.

8. Mary's T3 transaction COMMITs.

9. Paul, still in his same T1 transaction, SELECTs all pieces of art in the ArtEntity table a fourth time.

10. Paul's transaction, T1, finally COMMITs.

What should Paul see in step four? What about steps seven and nine? Your database vendor will have default behaviors defined, but it's important to know that you have absolute control over the outcome by choosing the isolation level you prefer for your transactions. Let's take a look at how the four isolation levels impact this scenario.

Serializable

The easiest isolation level to understand is serializable, which mandates complete isolation. If we choose serializable as our isolation level, Paul will never see any of Brian's or Mary's changes until Paul begins a new transaction. From Paul's perspective, the database remains completely consistent and there are no side effects; Paul will see the same results for his query all four times because they all take place within a single transaction that is insulated from any other modifications. That sounds pretty ideal, right? So what more is there to talk about? Unfortunately, there is a lot of overhead associated with this setting. Using serializable vastly reduces the number of concurrent operations that may occur and can result in nasty performance problems involving database locks. As such, the serializable isolation level should be used sparingly, when the use case really requires absolute consistency and it's acceptable to risk the chance that concurrent transactions may be forced to abort with an error.

Repeatable Read

Relaxing isolation a bit by employing the repeatable read isolation level in our scenario would allow Paul to see any inserts that are committed, but not updates or deletes. In order to guarantee that rereads of the same row stay consistent, the underlying database will ordinarily implement either row-level, shared read locks or multiversioning. Under this isolation level setting, Paul would not see Brian's update or delete at any point in the scenario. However, Paul will see Mary's insert at step nine after she has committed her transaction. This side effect—where newly inserted and committed rows are visible to Paul's query (step nine) that weren't visible earlier (steps four and seven) within a single transaction (T1)—is known as a **phantom read**.

Read Committed

Read committed is the default isolation level used by most RDBMS vendors, including Oracle and PostgreSQL. This isolation level states that a transaction may read only data that has been committed in the database. When choosing read committed, Paul will see any changes made by Brian or Mary after their respective transactions have completed and been committed. This provides some data consistency while still delivering high concurrency. As with the repeatable read isolation level, Paul is still susceptible to **phantom reads**. As was the case with the repeatable read isolation level, Paul's query at step nine will return a new record that wasn't visible earlier in his transaction. When choosing read committed, Paul is also exposed to a second type of side effect; a **nonrepeatable read**. A nonrepeatable read occurs when rereads of the same row return different data within the same transaction. This becomes possible after Brian's update and delete are committed in step five. Unlike what happened under the serializable or repeatable read isolation levels, these row level modifications become visible to Paul in step seven, even though Paul read these two rows earlier and he's still in the context of his first and only transaction, T1. When in doubt, choose the read committed.

Read Uncommitted

On the polar opposite end of the spectrum from serializable is the read uncommitted isolation level. If we employ read uncommitted for our scenario, there will be no transactional isolation whatsoever. Consequently, Paul's first three identical queries will all return different results. If Mary's commit in step eight succeeds, Paul's fourth query will return the same results as his third query.

At step four, Paul sees Brian's typo correction (SQL **UPDATE**) as well as the removal he performed (SQL **DELETE**) before Brian's transaction commits. This third side effect is commonly referred to as a **dirty read** because Paul is reading in **tentative data**. If Brian's commit fails at step five, forcing his transaction to roll back, the data Paul is looking at will be rendered completely inaccurate. Reading in Mary's insert at step seven, prior to her commit, is also representative of a dirty read because that too represents tentative data.

Choosing the read uncommitted isolation level exposes you to all three of the possible side effects. Intuitively, this represents a strategy that is not ideal. However, there is a silver lining with the read uncommitted isolation level. Because this isolation level offers the highest degree of concurrency, one can expect each of Paul, Brian, and Mary's SQL operations to be incredibly fast. You might adopt this isolation level when you need to emphasize speed and you're confident that your application can cope with the side effects. As with serializable, read uncommitted should only be considered for fringe use cases.

Controlling ACID Reflux

Transactions define how and when data is committed to a database. They are indispensable in grouping persistence logic together, ensuring that all methods complete successfully or that the database is rolled back to its previous state. For most operations, you also need to be concerned with transactional details, ensuring that transactions are started at the beginning of an operation and are either committed or rolled back when the operation completes. Spring enables these features through three core concepts:

- *Platform transaction management* refers to Spring's abstraction for handling commits and rollbacks. Frameworks like Hibernate and iBatis have their own transaction implementations. Furthermore, transactions typically operate differently in a testing environment than within an EJB server. Spring's platform transaction management abstraction hides these details, allowing developers to specify transactional rules in a consistent manner.

- *Declarative transaction management* allows developers to specify the transactional requirements for a particular method through metadata or configuration. Obviously, the code to set up, commit, and roll back a given transaction is still being executed. However, these details may be separated from the code itself and externalized into configuration files or annotations.

- *Programmatic transaction management* explicitly controls the transaction through code. Spring provides a `TransactionTemplate` class that can greatly simplify the code required to apply transactional semantics to a given method. However, this approach requires that transactional details be blended with business logic and requires your code to directly interact with the Spring APIs.

We'll look at each of these types of transaction in the following sections.

Platform Transaction Management

Spring offers several `TransactionManager` implementations, each of which fills the role of (drum roll please) managing transactions. `TransactionManager` instances typically extend the `AbstractPlatformTransactionManager` class, which in turn implements the `PlatformTransactionManager` interface. These classes form the foundation of Spring's transactional support, and provide the know-how to access, initiate, rollback, and commit transactions. The interface looks like this:

```
public interface PlatformTransactionManager {
    TransactionStatus getTransaction(TransactionDefinition definition)
        throws TransactionException;

    void commit(TransactionStatus status) throws TransactionException;

    void rollback(TransactionStatus status) throws TransactionException;
}
```

There are quite a few `TransactionManager` implementations. For example, the `DataSourceTransactionManager` is used for JDBC and iBATIS implementations. For our purposes, we are predominantly interested in Spring's ORM-based `TransactionManager` implementations: `HibernateTransactionManager` and `JpaTransactionManager`.

You'll even find `TransactionManager` implementations for JTA used by EJB. JTA is typically used to enable transactions to span across multiple databases and even disparate technologies, such as Java Message Service (JMS). These include the generic `JtaTransactionManager` and implementations for specific EJB servers like `OC4JJtaTransactionManager` for Oracle's server, `WebLogicJtaTransactionManager` for BEA's server, and `WebSphereUowTransactionManager` for IBM's server.

By adding the `<tx:jta-transaction-manager/>` XML tag to your Spring configuration, you can empower Spring to determine which JTA transaction manager to use, based on runtime information, so that you don't need to explicitly reference the platform-specific details in your configuration.

You might have noticed the `TransactionStatus` and `TransactionDefinition` interfaces that are part of the `PlatformTransactionManager` interface. You rarely need to use these interfaces yourself. They are set up by Spring's declarative transaction management (discussed in the next section), but they are still worth knowing about, as these details help to explain how Spring's transactional features work under the hood.

> `TransactionStatus`: Encapsulates key information related to an actively running transaction, such as whether a new transaction has been created and whether the transaction should be rolled back or committed. It also allows the transaction to be marked as `Rollback-Only`. Setting a running transaction to be `Rollback-Only` tells the transaction system that the transaction should be rolled back. For example, in the event of an error condition, you might write code to call `setRollbackOnly()` on a `TransactionStatus` instance, which will ensure that the actively running transaction is rolled back.

> `TransactionDefinition`: Defines the ACID properties we talked about earlier, including details such as the isolation rules for the transaction, whether your transaction will perform any writes (or is read-only), how long the transaction is allowed to run before timing out, and how to handle transaction propagation.

We will learn more about how these classes are used later in this chapter when we discuss programmatic transaction management.

Declarative Transaction Management

Declarative programming employs metadata to define the requirements for a particular set of application logic, rather than coding the steps that define this behavior directly. Typically, you use declarative programming within the context of a framework, which is designed to analyze the metadata in order to tailor its behavior accordingly. Using declarative transaction management, therefore, implies that you define the rules or attributes that compose your transactions' behavior, rather than interspersing this logic directly in your code. As you can probably guess, Spring applies these cross-cutting concerns to your code by levering its excellent AOP support. However, because transactions are such a prevalent and critical feature, the AOP details are a bit abstracted to provide a clearer and more transaction-specific approach.

Spring has a fantastic annotation-driven approach for transaction management. An alternative is to use an XML-driven strategy based on Spring configuration. We will discuss both of these approaches, beginning with annotation-based transaction management, since you have seen examples of this in earlier chapters.

Transactional Annotations

Using the `@Transactional` annotation, you can set some transactional behavior and attributes.

`Propagation` defines the transactional behavior for the specified method. This setting determines whether a new transaction should always be created, whether a nested transaction should be created, or even if no transaction should be created at all. Here are the `Propagation` values you can use in Spring:

- `REQUIRED`: If there's a transaction, support it; otherwise, create a new one.

- `SUPPORTS`: If there's a transaction, it will be supported, but this is not a requirement.

- MANDATORY: There must be a transaction; otherwise, throw an exception.

- REQUIRES_NEW: Create a new transaction and suspend the current one if it exists.

- NOT_SUPPORTED: Execute the code within the "transactionalized" method non-transactionally and suspend the current transaction.

- NEVER: Throw an exception if a transaction exists.

- NESTED: Perform a nested transaction if a transaction exists; otherwise, create a new transaction. Nested transactions offer a way to provide more granular transactional behavior, allowing a group of inner transactions to be executed. This can be useful, for example, for cases in which some nested transactions may get rolled back, but without aborting the entire operation.

Isolation is the "I" in ACID, and defines how a running transaction affects (and is affected by) other database processes occurring within the application. The settings to control isolation behavior for a given transaction are:

- DEFAULT: Let the datastore define the isolation level.

- READ_UNCOMMITTED: This isolation level allows changes made by other running transactions to be read by the actively running transaction, even when the other transactions have not committed. In other words, this setting enables dirty reads.

- READ_COMMITTED: Dirty and nonrepeatable reads are not allowed, but phantom reads are. Only changes applied by successfully committed transactions are visible.

- REPEATABLE_READ: Indicates that dirty reads and nonrepeatable reads are prevented but phantom reads may occur.

- SERIALIZABLE: Indicates that dirty reads, nonrepeatable reads and phantom reads are prevented.

Spring also provides a way to specify some of the fundamental attributes of a transaction. For instance, you can use the readOnly attribute to indicate whether a transaction is read-only (as opposed to a transaction in which inserts or updates are performed). A readOnly value of true ensures that the method performs only read operations.

The timeout attribute defines how long a transaction can live without committing or rolling back. If the timeout for a running transaction elapses without the transaction completing, Spring will automatically roll back the transaction.

Spring's transactional support provides a means to specify how a transaction should behave if an exception is thrown. For example, we could specify that whenever an InvalidImageException is thrown from a method within our ArtEntityService, the currently running transaction should be rolled back. Spring provides the attributes rollbackFor and rollbackForClassName to enable this behavior. This setting allows you to specify an array of either classes or class names (depending on the setting used) of exceptions that, when thrown, will trigger the currently executing transaction to be automatically rolled back.

Similarly, you may specify the inverse of this behavior (which exceptions should not trigger a rollback) through the use of the noRollbackForClass and noRollbackForClassName attributes. These options work the same way as rollbackFor and rollbackForClassName, but prevent a transaction from being rolled back if one of the specified exception classes is thrown while this transaction is being executed.

Armed with a clearer understanding of some of the configuration options for Spring transactions, let's take a look at how we can specify the transactional semantics for our service class. To keep things simple, we will examine a scaled-back version of our `ArtEntityService` class.

```
class ArtEntityServiceImpl implements ArtEntityService {

    @Transactional(rollbackFor=InvalidImageExeption.class,
                    readOnly=false,
                    timeout=30,
                    propagation=Propagation.SUPPORTS,
                    isolation=Isolation.DEFAULT)
    public void saveArtEntity(ArtEntity artEntity) throws InvalidImageException {
        this.getArtEntityDao().saveArtEntity(artEntity);
    }

}
```

Here, we define a transactional service method that specifies a timeout of 30 seconds, and will automatically roll back if an `InvalidImageException` is thrown. Notice that we have also configured the transaction to be writable (`readOnly` is set to `false`).

Now that we've configured the details of our transaction, we need to set up our transaction manager. As noted earlier, Spring provides a `PlatformTransactionManager` interface, along with a set of implementations for use with different persistence strategies. For global transactions that span multiple datasources, we would need to use Spring's JTA support. For our example, we will use Spring's `JpaTransactionManager`. Our `spring-jpa.xml` should be updated to reflect the following (the important bits for transaction support have been bolded):

```
<?xml version="1.0" encoding="UTF-8" standalone="no"?>
<beans xmlns="http://www.springframework.org/schema/beans"
      xmlns:p="http://www.springframework.org/schema/p"
      xmlns:tx="http://www.springframework.org/schema/tx"
      xmlns:aop="http://www.springframework.org/schema/aop"
      xmlns:context="http://www.springframework.org/schema/context"
      xmlns:xsi="http://www.w3.org/2001/XMLSchema-instance"
      xsi:schemaLocation="http://www.springframework.org/schema/beans
          http://www.springframework.org/schema/beans/spring-beans-3.0.xsd
          http://www.springframework.org/schema/context
          http://www.springframework.org/schema/context/spring-context-3.0.xsd
          http://www.springframework.org/schema/tx
          http://www.springframework.org/schema/tx/spring-tx-3.0.xsd">

    <!-- JPA Entity Manager Factory -->
    <bean id="entityManagerFactory"
        class="org.springframework.orm.jpa.LocalContainerEntityManagerFactoryBean"
        p:dataSource-ref="galleryDataSource"/>

    <bean
        class="org.springframework.orm.jpa.support.PersistenceAnnotationBeanPostProcessor" />
```

```
<!-- Database LOB Handling -->
    <bean id="defaultLobHandler"
          class="org.springframework.jdbc.support.lob.DefaultLobHandler" />

    <!-- Read in DAOs from the JPA package -->
    <context:component-scan base-package="com.prospringhibernate.gallery.dao.jpa" />

<!-- Transaction Config -->
<bean id="transactionManager"
            class="org.springframework.orm.jpa.JpaTransactionManager"
            p:entityManagerFactory-ref="entityManagerFactory"/>

<tx:annotation-driven mode="aspectj" transaction-manager="transactionManager"/>

</beans>
```

The XML configuration in this example specifies our `artEntityService` bean, along with our `PlatformTransactionManager`. We are using Spring's `JpaTransactionManager`, but the way in which we are able to declaratively configure transactions would not be different if we decide to create a JDBC implementation, or even if we required global transactions via JTA. Spring allows us to use a consistent strategy for specifying transactions, regardless of the underlying implementation details.

Also notice the `tx:annotation-driven` bean that Spring includes in its `tx` namespace. This XML snippet is necessary to enable the usage of our `@Transactional` annotations. Without it, Spring would not enable transactions for our `ArtEntityService`. The `tx:annotation-driven` annotation supports the following features:

- **transaction-manager**: This supplies the name of the bean used for the transaction manager. Theoretically, you can have more than one transaction manager in your Spring application context and use only one. The default value is `transactionManager`.

- **mode**: This specifies the type of proxying mechanism you want. You have a choice of **proxy** to use Spring proxying or **aspectj** to use AspectJ, an industrial-strength AOP framework. The default is **proxy**.

- **proxy-target-class**: By default, Spring creates a Java proxy object, and attaches only the interfaces that the object implements. For example, if you have a `PersonDaoJPA` class that implements a `PersonDao` interface, the proxying process will create an object that implements `PersonDao`, adds on the implementation of your transactional semantics, and passes the request on to your implementation. If the class doesn't implement any interfaces or you need the proxy to extend the class and not just its interfaces, Spring will then use the Code Generation Library (CGLIB) open source bytecode manipulation framework to perform the proxying. The CGLIB approach does have a limitation: you need to put the transactional annotations on the class itself, not on the interface.

- **order**: There are plenty of other frameworks that take advantage of proxying, but to use them, you may need to explicitly order the transactional and other proxying mechanisms. Lower order numbers are processed first.

Declarative Transactions via XML

Rather than using the @Transactional annotation for applying transactional semantics, you can take a pure XML-driven approach. This approach is useful in cases where you prefer not to apply annotations, or you can't use annotations because you need to use JDK1.4 or you want to apply transactional semantics to a library that you can't change.

Coupling the tx:advice XML configuration with an XML-based AOP configuration makes for a synergistic combination. For example, you can use method names to automatically figure out what kind of transactionality you want to apply.

Here's an example that specifies that methods starting with save, update, and delete require a transaction, and everything else supports (but does not require) a read-only transaction:

```
<tx:advice id="txAdvice" >
    <tx:attributes>
        <tx:method name="save*" propagation="REQUIRED"/>
        <tx:method name="update*" propagation="REQUIRED"/>
        <tx:method name="delete*" propagation="REQUIRED"/>
        <tx:method name="*" propagation="SUPPORTS" read-only="true"/>
    </tx:attributes>
</tx:advice>
```

tx:advice does support a transaction-manager XML attribute, but by default, it uses the name transactionManager, just like tx:annotation-driven.

In addition to the flexible method name matching, the tx:method element has the same types of parameters as the @Transactional annotation. You can set values for propagation, isolation, timeout, read-only, rollback-for, and no-rollback-for. These tx:method XML attributes have the same values as their @Transactional counterparts.

One more detail needs to be added to this example in order to make it complete. You need to use Spring's AOP framework to define which beans require the advice. You can accomplish this by using the aop namespace in your Spring XML file. For example, if we wanted to apply the transactional advice to all of the classes that are in the com.prospringhibernate.gallery.service package, we can add the following to our Spring XML file:

```
<aop:config>
    <aop:pointcut id="allServices"
                  expression="execution(*com.prospringhibernate.gallery.service.*.*(..))"/>
    <aop:advisor advice-ref="txAdvice" pointcut-ref="allServices"/>
</aop:config>
```

Spring AOP is pretty flexible, and even lets you use annotations to define the pointcut. If you want to apply txAdvice to any class that is annotated with @Transactional, you can change the allServices pointcut to this:

```
<aop:pointcut id="allServices"
              expression="@target(org.springframework.transaction.annotation.Transactional)"/>
```

You can even combine the two pointcut approaches, like so:

```
<aop:pointcut
    id="allServices"
    expression="execution(*com.prospringhibernate.gallery.service.*.*(..)) &&
        @target(org.springframework.transaction.annotation.Transactional)"/>
```

Let's take a look at one more Spring AOP trick: using the bean name to define a pointcut. Here's how to apply a transaction to a bean named **personService**:

```
<aop:pointcut id="allServices" expression ="bean(personService)"/>
```

You can also use the asterisk (*) wildcard character to match against all beans that end with **Service** or **Dao**, as follows:

```
<aop:pointcut id="allServices" expression ="bean(*Service) || bean(*Dao)"/>
```

If applying complex AOP pointcuts to ACID transactions is still a bit too mind-altering for you, you'll find plenty of documentation out there.[1] However, the information you've gleaned here should give you a running start in understanding how to get your ACID transactions in order.

Programmatic Transaction Management

We can't think of many real-world use cases for working with programmatic transactions rather than leveraging Spring's simpler declarative transaction support. However, understanding programmatic transactions can prove helpful in comprehending the way in which Spring transactions work under the hood.

To demonstrate how programmatic transactions work, we will rework the **ArtEntityService** example to use programmatic transactions, as follows;

```
public class ArtEntityServiceImpl implements ArtEntityService {

    private TransactionTemplate transactionTemplate;

    public ArtEntityServiceImpl(PlatformTransactionManager transactionManager) {
        this.transactionTemplate = new TransactionTemplate(transactionManager);
    }

    public Object saveArtEntity(ArtEntity artEntity) {
        return transactionTemplate.execute(
            new TransactionCallback() {
                public Object doInTransactionWithoutResult(TransactionStatus status) {
                    try {
                        this.getArtEntityDao().saveArtEntity(artEntity);
```

---

[1] If you would like to learn more about the huge and important field of transaction processing, consider reading *Transaction Processing: Concepts and Techniques* by Jim Gray and Andreas Reuter (Morgan Kaufmann, 1992); *Principles of Transaction Processing*, Second Edition, by Philip A. Bernstein and Eric Newcomer (Morgan Kaufmann, 2009); and *Pro JPA 2: Mastering the Java Persistence API* by Mike Keith and Merrick Schincariol (Apress, 2009).

```
                        } catch (ImageErrorException e) {
                            status.setRollbackOnly();
                        }
                        return;
                    }
                }
            );
        }

    }
```

In this snippet, we rely on constructor injection to provide a reference to our `JpaTransactionManager` (which is an implementation of the `PlatformTransactionManager` interface). Using `transactionManager`, we create an instance of `TransactionTemplate`, which we use to wrap our persistence behavior within the scope of a transaction.

The usage of the `TransactionTemplate` should look very familiar to you. This is a common Spring idiom, and works in a similar fashion to the `HibernateTemplate` we use within our DAO classes. The key difference here is that we are using the `TransactionTemplate` to handle the boilerplate process of transactions, rather than database connection setup and closing.

To wrap our persistence code within a transaction, we call the `execute` method on our `transactionTemplate` property, passing in an anonymous implementation of `TransactionCallback` as a parameter. In the example, our service method does not return a value, so we implement the method `doInTransactionWithoutResult`. However, if we needed to return a value from our transaction, we would instead use `doInTransaction`.

Within the scope of the `TransactionCallback`, we are calling the same persistence code that we used in our annotation-based example. We delegate to our `artEntityDao` to do the heavy lifting. Notice, however, that we catch the `ImageErrorException`, and should the exception get thrown, we use the `TransactionStatus` parameter to rollback the transaction.

Clearly, this approach is not as clear or as elegant as using declarative transactions in Spring. Nevertheless, it is helpful to see how the various components fit together without relying on AOP to inject this behavior implicitly.

Transactional Examples

Now that we've covered the main transactional concepts, let's go through a couple of real-world scenarios. We'll look at a batch application and transactions involving two datasources.

Creating a Batch Application

Batch applications can be a bit of a drag, especially with ORM frameworks. Both the database and the ORM framework need to reserve valuable resources for each operation performed in a transaction. The database needs to keep locks on the tables that you've changed. The ORM, for a variety of reasons, needs to cache the objects that you've persisted and read from the database. The more operations a transaction executes, the more resources the ORM and database need to dedicate to it.

Let's start out with the following example, which updates a whole bunch of records:

```
@Transactional(readOnly = false, propagation = Propagation.SUPPORTS)
public void batchProcessAll() {
    int count = dao.getCount();
    // do your ACID business in a big for loop
}
```

Here, we're attempting to update all of the data in a single transaction. Depending on the amount of data and system resources, this may not be possible, or it may lead to degraded performance for our application. Instead, we may be able to find a way to define smaller units that can be committed, which will free up some of the resources utilized by the database and ORM framework. However, the process of committing the transaction consumes resources as well. If we commit too often, we'll probably decrease performance. There's a balance between committing too often and too little—for example, committing after a certain number of items have been processed.

We can create a method that processes *x* number of units and commits after it completes. It's actually quite simple to set this up. We'll choose 100 as an arbitrary number of *units of work*.

```
// no transaction on this method anymore
public void batchProcessAll() {
    int count = dao.getCount();
    for(int i=0; i<count; i+= 100) {
        doMyUnit(i, i+100);
    }
}

@Transactional(readOnly = false, propagation = Propagation.REQUIRES_NEW)
public void doMyUnit(int start, int finish) {
    // do your ACID business from the unit's
    // start to finish
    dao.flush();
}
```

Note the use of `Propagation.REQUIRES_NEW`. It tells Spring that a new transaction begins when the method gets invoked and commits when the method completes. It's just that simple to create and commit a transaction. There are many variables, ranging from server capacity to application load, to be able to prescribe an ideal batch size, so determining the best size for your application will likely require some trial and error.

Using Two Datasources

Assume you have two databases, and you want to apply the right transactions to the right beans. You need to create two different `transactionManagers` that must be applied to the appropriate subsets of Spring beans. You can do that with some fancy AOP work.

Assume that you have already configured `transactionManager1` and `transactionManager2` beans. You'll need to start with the following XML:

```
<tx:advice id="txAdvice1" transaction-manager="transaction-manager1" >
    <tx:attributes>
        <tx:method name="save*" propagation="REQUIRED"/>
        <tx:method name="update*" propagation="REQUIRED"/>
        <tx:method name="delete*" propagation="REQUIRED"/>
```

```
            <tx:method name="*" propagation="SUPPORTS" read-only="true"/>
        </tx:attributes>
    </tx:advice>

    <tx:advice id="txAdvice2" transaction-manager="transaction-manager2" >
        <tx:attributes>
            <tx:method name="save*" propagation="REQUIRED"/>
            <tx:method name="update*" propagation="REQUIRED"/>
            <tx:method name="delete*" propagation="REQUIRED"/>
            <tx:method name="*" propagation="SUPPORTS" read-only="true"/>
        </tx:attributes>
    </tx:advice>

    <aop:config>
        <aop:advisor advice-ref="txAdvice1" pointcut-ref="allDatabaseOneBeans"/>
        <aop:advisor advice-ref="txAdvice2" pointcut-ref="allDatabaseTwoBeans"/>
        <!-- Add pointcuts here -->
    </aop:config>
```

The `tx:advice` element tells Spring what needs to be done, and the `aop:config` element tells Spring where it needs to be done.

The question now is what beans should have which advice? Some beans need **txAdvice1**; others need **txAdvice2**; and others may need both. Thankfully, Spring AOP provides several mapping options. You might chose to organize your classes into packages that differentiate between the two datasources to which they relate and apply an expression pointcut, or you can devise logical bean names that clearly infer which advice to apply. You can also create our own annotations, `@Transaction1` and `@Transaction2` for example, and use the `expression="@target(...)"` approach.

Let's go through a quick bean name example. Imagine we have two datasources: `datasource1` and `datasource2`. Let's say that all of the `datasource1` beans have `ds1` as part of their bean name. For example, if `PersonDao` is intended to interface with `datasource1`, it would be called `ds1.personDao`. If `PersonService` depends on `personDao` as well as a DAO from `datasource2`, it should be called `ds1.ds2.personService`. Our pointcuts will look like the following:

```
<aop:pointcut id="allDatabaseOneBeans" expression ="bean(*ds1*)"/>
<aop:pointcut id="allDatabaseTwoBeans" expression ="bean(*ds2*)"/>
```

We've defined two pointcut expressions that utilize a bean-naming convention to properly infer which datasource and `transactionManager` to utilize for a given transaction.

Summary

In this chapter, you've learned both the fundamentals and low-level details for managing database transactions with Spring. We've explored two different avenues for applying transactions declaratively with Spring: via annotation and through XML-based Spring configuration. It's also possible to utilize Spring's transaction management programmatically, through the use of the `TransactionTemplate`. However this approach couples transactional behavior with the application's business logic.

Understanding how transactions work, along with the available configuration options, is critical for developing and debugging multiuser applications. We've discussed both simple and complex scenarios in this chapter, and we hope they give you a taste of what's possible when using Spring for transaction management.

Most important, Spring provides a consistent approach for applying transactional semantics to an application, no matter what the architecture or environment. This means that you can configure and code your application the same way, regardless of whether you're deploying to a JEE app server using a JTA datasource or to a lightweight container with a local datasource. The difference is just a matter of configuration.

CHAPTER 8

■ ■ ■

Effective Testing

Automated testing, and unit testing in particular, is now universally regarded as a best practice for software development. A number of testing frameworks are available, and there remains plenty of room to debate the merits of unit testing versus integration testing, whether to mock objects with interesting behavior with frameworks like jMock or EasyMock or take a more classic approach with basic stubs, when to apply test-driven development (TDD), whether behavior-driven development (BDD) will become commonplace, and so on.

Throughout this book, we've highlighted several best practices, including layering your application and coding to interfaces. In this chapter, we'll demonstrate how these principles lend themselves to building solid test coverage with proper emphasis on exercising aspects of an application in isolation.

A code base that is broken down into layers so that each layer has a unique responsibility is much more testable than code that attempts to combine multiple aspects of functionality into a single class. Testable code is code that is decoupled and divided into logical layers, and well-layered code is testable because it produces small, defined parts of an application's overall vision. By coding to interfaces and leveraging Spring's dependency-injection capabilities, you gain the ability to mock or stub one layer (such as the DAO layer) when you're testing the layer above it (in this case, the service layer that uses DAOs).

Dependency-injection frameworks like Spring are tremendously useful for testing because they make it relatively easy to instantiate classes directly, providing collaborators through code. With Spring in particular, you can automatically inject dependencies within your test classes simply by specifying the appropriate annotations. This allows you to construct an application context for your tests that uses configuration options that may differ quite a bit from your production setup. This flexibility enables you to test your code against a large number of potential inputs.

When it comes to verifying assertions of a persistence tier, it is important to verify the behavior of your DAO and service classes, the configuration details and behavior of your domain classes, and even the collaboration and wiring of dependencies.

We will skim the surface of these strategies in this chapter, but it is important to keep in mind that an effective testing strategy should incorporate both unit and integration tests. Luckily, Spring helps to simplify the creation of both of these kinds of tests, as well as other forms of automated testing, such as functional testing with tools like Selenium.

Unit, Integration, and Functional Testing

Spring makes it easy to test specific parts of your code without relying on an application server or other infrastructural details. You can switch between different database implementations and datasources, or test your DAO classes in isolation by mocking these details.

Unit testing is an effective strategy for verifying that a particular class works properly in isolation. Assessing classes in isolation is very valuable, and there is no commensurate replacement for a good unit test. Writing an effective unit test involves the definition of assertions regarding the behavior of specific areas of a class in isolation. Good test coverage is related to which lines of code have their expected behavior verified.

Unlike unit testing, *integration testing* typically verifies multiple components simultaneously, often by running the same implementation layers used within the production version of an application. For instance, a common practice for integration testing is to instantiate the Spring `ApplicationContext` and test a DAO implementation using a real database along with the Spring Hibernate abstractions. The advantage of this approach is that you are touching multiple components, ensuring that all the pieces are working together properly. The disadvantage is that it doesn't provide much granularity to ascertain whether a particular component works properly on its own. For a comprehensive testing strategy, we recommend including both integration and unit tests.

A *test suite* is a set of individual test classes that are designed to run together and that typically make assertions related to a particular layer or component. For example, you can create a DAO test suite composed of all of your DAO tests. The following example shows all you need to do to create a suite of tests:

```
public void static testSuite() {
    return new TestSuite(ArtworkDao.class,
                         CategoryDao.class,
                         ExhibitionDao.class,
                         PersonDao.class);
}
```

Modern IDEs (Eclipse, IntelliJ IDEA, NetBeans, and many more) and other runtime environments (such as Ant and Maven) know how to run both individual unit tests and test suites, which can include both unit and integration tests. It's common to use the notion of suites to strategically bundle tests together. For example, you might want a test suite of fast unit tests that are run on every commit and a different test suite composed of longer-running integration tests, which are done on some scheduled interval.

Functional tests are another strategy for verifying your application is behaving properly. Functional tests provide the most high-level assessment of a code base, and typically require that an application run within a production environment container—for instance, using a servlet container.

Functional tests in a web application context usually involve a series of HTTP requests and then assertions as to the responses that should be returned. For example, a REST web service might include a battery of functional tests that verify the data that is returned when a chunk of XML is `POST`ed to a particular URL. Another type of functional test might verify certain HTML elements within a returned HTTP response, given a particular URL.

The downside of functional tests, especially as they relate to verifying HTML markup, is that they tend to be very brittle—meaning they are likely to break as a result of minor changes to the application. However, functional tests do have their place, and they are often an effective tool to verify basic assumptions regarding an application's behavior.

Using JUnit for Effective Testing

The two biggest unit testing frameworks in the Java community at present are JUnit and TestNG. For our examples, we will use JUnit. JUnit 4's approach is highly annotation-based. The @Test annotation is all you need to add to define a test:

```
package com.prospringhibernate.gallery.test;

import org.junit.Test;
import org.junit.Assert;

public class TrivialJUnitTest {

    @Test
    public void testSimpleStuff() {
        String name = "ProSpringHibernate";
        Assert.assertEquals("ProSpringHibernate", name);
    }

}
```

A couple of additional basic JUnit annotations can help define the life cycle of the test. You can run some code immediately before and after each test method using the @Before and @After annotations. Guess which one comes before a test? You can also run code before and after all tests in a particular class using @BeforeClass and @AfterClass. (Note that the @BeforeClass method must be static.) There's also an @Ignore annotation, which allows you to use a @Test annotation and not run a particular method.

Of course, the main point of a test is to set up a scenario, and then verify a group of assertions. JUnit provides several built-in assertions, such as verifying that two values should be equal, a returned value is not null, and so on. You'll notice many of these annotations in the following example.

```
package com.prospringhibernate.gallery.test;

import org.junit.Test;
import org.junit.Ignore;
import org.junit.Assert;
import org.junit.Before;
import org.junit.BeforeClass;

public class SimpleJUnitTest {

    public static String staticName = null;
    public String memberName = null;

    @BeforeClass
    public static void initializeClass() {
        staticName = "Rod Johnson";
    }
```

```
@Before
    public void initializeTest() {
        memberName = "Gavin King";
    }

    @Test
    public void simpleEqualsAssertion() {
        Assert.assertEquals("Rod Johnson", staticName);
    }

    @Test
    public void simpleBooleanAssertion() {
        Assert.assertFalse(staticName.equals(memberName));
    }

    @Test
    @Ignore
    public void dontTestThis() {
        // notice that this would fail without @Ignore
        Assert.assertEquals("Rod", memberName);
    }

}
```

Now let's move beyond the basics and apply some tests to our art gallery application.

Unit Testing with Mocks

The tests in the previous examples are fairly simple, in that they don't have any dependencies on either the Spring container or implementations of other classes or components. Because our tests are isolated to a specific class, they qualify as unit tests. Most of the time, you'll need to go beyond such basic testing to simulate the effects of two or more classes interacting with each other. Integration tests are one way to achieve this, but that generally entails a fair amount of code and tight coupling of tests. An alternate strategy is to use stubs or mocks.

Stubbing and mocking both attempt to simulate the behavior of a particular component or layer within an application, without relying on an actual, full-featured implementation. This approach helps to focus your testing concerns on the code actually being tested, rather than the details of other layers.

Stubbing usually implies that a particular component is faked, with "canned responses" being returned so that the layer being tested is fooled into believing that it is talking to the actual live implementation. Mocking also attempts to simulate a particular layer, but it does more than just return canned responses. A mocked object can also be used to validate expected behavior relating to the layer it is intended to represent. For example, it is possible to specify that a certain method is called on the mock as well as other details that help to provide valuable assertions about how the code you are testing integrates with the mocked layer.

Spring provides several useful mock layers, which can be used as drop-in replacements for various layers within your application. For example, JNDI, Servlet-API, and Portlet mock layers that simulate behavior and associated expectations for their respective layers. For mocking other components, it is possible to use frameworks like jMock, EasyMock or MockObjects. These frameworks provide an extensible means for defining your own mocks dynamically.

For our examples, we will use the very powerful jMock framework. JMock allows you to define the behavior for a particular class, as well as expectations for how particular methods on the class will be called and what they will return within the context of a unit test. jMock employs a simple DSL that allows you to specify a fairly flexible range of behavior. We'll point out a few of the basic jMock concepts when we look at a unit test with mocks later in this chapter.

Let's look at a unit test that attempts to verify the behavior of our **ArtworkService** implementation:

```
package com.prospringhibernate.gallery.test;

import com.prospringhibernate.gallery.domain.Person;
import com.prospringhibernate.gallery.exception.AuthenticationException;
import com.prospringhibernate.gallery.service.ArtworkFacade;

import org.junit.Test;
import org.junit.Before;
import org.junit.runner.RunWith;

import org.jmock.Mockery;
import org.jmock.Expectations;
import org.jmock.integration.junit4.JMock;
import org.jmock.integration.junit4.JUnit4Mockery;

@RunWith(JMock.class)
public class JMockJUnitTestExample {

    Mockery context = new JUnit4Mockery();

    private Person person;
    private ArtworkFacade artworkService;

    @Before
    public void initializeTest() {
        person = new Person();
        person.setUsername("username");
        person.setPassword("goodpassword");

        // here we use jMock to create a mock based on our Interface
        artworkService = context.mock(ArtworkFacade.class);
    }

    @Test
    public void testAuthenticationSuccess() throws AuthenticationException {

        // define expectations for authenticatePerson method
        context.checking(new Expectations() {{
            allowing(artworkService).authenticatePerson("username", "goodpassword");
            will(returnValue(person));
        }});
        artworkService.authenticatePerson("username", "goodpassword");

    }
```

```
@Test (expected=AuthenticationException.class)
public void testAuthenticationFailure() throws AuthenticationException {
    // define expectations, assuming a bad
    // username/password
    context.checking(new Expectations() {{
        allowing(artworkService).authenticatePerson("username", "badpassword");
        will(throwException(new AuthenticationException()));
    }});
    artworkService.authenticatePerson("username", "badpassword");

}

}
```

Notice that no external dependencies are required for this unit test. This not only helps to isolate the code we are testing, but also significantly speeds up the test. Recall that our `ArtworkService` façade depends on several DAOs, including `ArtEntityDao` and `PersonDao`, but there's nothing in this code that instantiates those classes before the `authenticatePerson` method is executed.

We declare that we are using the jMock framework by supplying the `@RunWith(JMock.class)` annotation. Next, we define the context instance variable, instantiating a `JUnit4Mockery` instance. We can then use the context instance variable to define the behavior and expectations of our mocked `ArtworkFacade`.

We create a mocked instance by calling the `mock` method on our context instance variable, passing in the interface for the type we wish to mock:

```
artworkService = context.mock(ArtworkFacade.class);
```

This line sets our `artworkService` instance to a mocked implementation of our `ArtworkFacade` interface. This takes care of the setup.

Now we need to delineate the behavior and expectations for the mock we just defined. This is accomplished in a few steps. Expectations are specified by calling `context.checking()` and passing in an anonymous inner class of type `Expectations`. The `Expectations` class provides most of jMock's DSL features, allowing us to more easily express the behavior of each method we intend to mock.

Things get interesting within this `Expectations` block. We can specify the behavior for each method—even defining different behavior based on different parameters or conditions. There are several options that can be defined in mocking our `ArtworkFacade`'s behavior. However, we must first set the expectations for how our method will be called. Do we expect it to be called exactly once, more than once, within a range, or a specified number of times? Or do we not care whether our method will be called at all? These details are referred to as the *invocation count*, and represent the first part of the jMock DSL.

In our example, we use the `allowing` invocation rule, which tells jMock that we don't care too much about the invocation count. If we did care, we might have used `oneOf`, which implies that we expect the method to be called only once. Or we could have used `exactly(5).of()` to require that our method be called precisely five times. Similarly, we might have used `atLeast(5).of()` to insist that our method be called at least five times. jMock will automatically fail the test if the expectations you specify are not met within the unit test.

So far, our DSL structure looks like the following:

```
Invocation-Count(mockInstance).method(expectedParams);
```

In this structure, we specify the expected parameters our mocked method should receive. You can actually define more than one rule, each specifying a different set of parameters. In fact, you don't even need to specify concrete parameters . You can instead specify *matchers*, which can be used to define more generalized conditions for a particular behavioral rule. The role of a matcher is to allow for the expression of flexible conditions for the expectations of a mocked method. Matchers must be nested within a `with` clause:

```
atLeast(5).of(artworkService).
  authenticatePerson(with(any(String.class)), with(any(String.class)));
```

This rule states that `authenticatePerson` must be called at least five times, with two parameters that must be of type `String`. In this case, we are using the `any` matcher, which allows us to specify the type that the parameter must match. There are several other matchers—such as `aNull`, `aNonNull`, `not`, and `same`—and you can even define your own matchers.

So, we've defined the basic expectation of a mocked method. But how do we express a mock's behavior? As you've probably inferred from our example, jMock allows us to define the behavior for a particular "rule" by specifying a `will` call after our expectation. We define two possible outcomes for our `authenticatePerson` method. The first expectation defines a "good" username and password. We follow this expectation with the following:

```
will(returnValue(successfulPerson));
```

This will ensure that a `successfulPerson` instance (defined earlier) will be returned whenever `pfisher` and `goodPassword` are provided to the `authenticatePerson` method in our unit test.

Similarly, we define another expectation that assumes an invalid username and password. For this variant, we specify this `will` call:

```
will(throwException(new AuthenticationException()));
```

This will ensure that an `AuthenticationException` is always thrown in our unit test, whenever an invalid username and password is provided to the `authenticatePerson` method (as long as the invalid username and password match our very stringent conditions, which require that they be `username` and `badpassword`).

A few other variations can be used with the `will` call, such as `returnIterator` and `doAll`, to provide more flexibility in defining the behavior for our mocked method given a set of conditions. There are also a few more advanced features of jMock that allow you to constrain a set of calls to a particular sequence, or to work with a state machine and verify certain assumptions about the state as it changes from one call to the next. See the JMock documentation to learn more.

■ **Note** We encourage you to explore mocking in more detail, as it is a powerful tool in the creation of an effective unit-testing strategy. Often, developers focus too much on integration testing, simply because unit testing can seem more complicated when "faking" the behavior of dependencies becomes necessary. Mocking is a pragmatic solution to easily defining behavior and expectations for dependencies, encouraging the development of more unit tests.

We've presented a cursory overview for unit testing a piece of code in isolation. However, an effective testing strategy also needs to take into consideration how a particular component works within the context of a running application. This is where integration testing comes in, and Spring serves to simplify the development of integration tests by helping to bootstrap your test suite, resolving dependencies, and handling persistence details, such as transactions.

Spring Dependency Injection and Testing

The Spring Framework provides a convenient layer of abstraction that drastically simplifies switching between these testing frameworks called the TestContext Framework. This framework, which was added as a part of Spring 3, helps to abstract away any test framework-specific details. By using Spring's TestContext Framework, you no longer need to worry about the specifics of a particular testing framework. This makes it especially easy to jump from one testing strategy to another. But more important, the TestContext Framework serves to simplify testing details, making it easier to not only write effective unit and integration tests, but also to integrate Spring dependencies and make useful assertions related to your persistence tier.

Spring testing includes a combination of XML and annotations to affect the way dependencies are injected within a test class. XML configuration works in a similar fashion to the examples you've seen earlier in this book. When defining integration tests, you can use the same XML code (more or less) that you use in your application. However, it is often desirable to override certain beans, such as your datasource, while maintaining the same wiring and implementation details for your application DAOs and service objects. Such a strategy enables you to verify the behavior of your entire persistence tier, while leveraging a specialized test database.

Quite a few Spring-specific annotations are available to get the test configuration stored in your application and the test XML into a running JUnit test. The `@RunWith` annotation allows you to specify the test framework you would like to use. As mentioned earlier, one of the primary benefits of using Spring's TestContext Framework is that it allows you to define a test class without tying your code to a particular test framework. You can specify that a particular class is in fact a test by using the `@Test` annotation. Then, to indicate which test framework should be used to run the test, you can use `@RunWith`, which allows you to specify which test framework to run. For the examples in this chapter, we're going to stick with JUnit 4. We place the following annotation at the top of our test class:

`@RunWith(SpringJUnit4ClassRunner.class)`

If we wanted to switch to TestNG, we could do that by simply changing the value of this annotation. Adding the `@RunWith` annotation to your unit test class will bring Spring into the picture for running the tests and wiring the necessary dependencies. However, there are several options for how the wiring details can be specified. The strategy you choose depends on the unique needs of your application. For instance, if you are building a simple application with only a single datasource, then you can go with an autowiring-by-type strategy, which will implicitly inject the class that matches the type specified in the setter method on which the annotation is added. However, if your application uses multiple datasources, then an autowiring-by-type approach isn't as trivial. For those scenarios, you should use the `@Resource` or `@Qualifier` annotations, in order to disambiguate the dependency you would like injected.

Though it is usually preferable to let Spring handle dependency injection via configuration or annotation, it's also possible to make your test class implement `ApplicationContextAware` or to extend `AbstractJUnit4SpringContextTests`, which gives you direct access to the `ApplicationContext`, from which you can do a lookup using the bean name:

`context.getBean("datasource");`

So now you have a handle on some of the options for injecting the layers on which your test class depends. The question that remains is how to inject. In our gallery application, we have defined Spring beans in an XML file named `spring-master.xml`, which in turn imports our `spring-persistence.xml` configuration. We can import this configuration by adding the following annotation:

```
@ContextConfiguration(locations = {"classpath:/META-INF/spring/spring-master.xml"})
```

The `@ContextConfiguration` annotation defines the locations of your configuration files. You can determine, on a test-by-test basis, whether to use the Spring configuration file for your full-blown application or to define a more specific unit-testing configuration that is tailored for the needs of a particular test.

Spring configuration via XML is handy, but now you're probably wondering how you can access some beans that are defined in your configuration or those that were picked up through component scanning. Do you remember the `@Autowired` annotation that Spring managed beans can use? You can use it in your test code to tell the Spring JUnit `Runner` that you need some Spring beans.

Here's what the `PersonDAO` test code looks like when we put all of this together:

```java
package com.prospringhibernate.gallery.test;

import org.junit.Test;
import org.junit.runner.RunWith;
import org.springframework.beans.factory.annotation.Autowired;
import org.springframework.test.context.ContextConfiguration;
import org.springframework.test.context.junit4.SpringJUnit4ClassRunner;

import com.prospringhibernate.gallery.dao.PersonDao;

@RunWith(SpringJUnit4ClassRunner.class)
@ContextConfiguration(locations = {"classpath:spring-master.xml"})
public class PersonDaoTest {

    @Autowired
    PersonDao personDao;

    @Test
    public void testPerson() {
        // insert test logic here
    }

}
```

Let's explore what's happening here. `@RunWith` tells JUnit that the test needs some extra logic in order to be set up properly. That extra logic comes in the form of an instance of a class that implements JUnit's `Runner` interface. In our case, we have a Spring `Runner` called `SpringJUnit4ClassRunner` that knows how to set up our application context and inject our test with all of the plumbing that it needs using the standard Spring dependency-injection annotations, such as `@Autowired`. `SpringJUnit4ClassRunner` also looks for some other annotations, including `@ContextConfiguration` and `@Transactional`.

As you saw in the example, `@ContextConfiguration` tells `SpringJUnit4ClassRunner` which configuration files you need to set up your testing environment. Behind the scenes, `SpringJUnit4ClassRunner` sets up and manages a Spring application context for your unit tests based on the locations you specified in the @ContextConfiguration. The TestContext Framework is responsible for actually performing the @Autowired injection. The TestContext Framework also keeps track of the results of the status of the current test, such as which method and class were run and which exception was thrown as part of the test. @RunWith and @ContextConfiguration are the essential core components of Spring JUnit4 testing.

■ **Note** The TestContext Framework has some performance optimizations to make sure that the framework will load that configuration only once for all of the tests if you run multiple test classes that use the same application context configuration. There are quite a few additional advanced features relating to the TestContext Framework that are worth exploring if you need more advanced testing.

Testing with a Database

Now that you know how to write a JUnit test class and configure it with Spring XML, you're ready to do some database testing! The simplest form of database testing can be to just reuse those fancy DAOs that you've been working on. You can also apply the usual Spring @Transactional annotations, along with another annotation: @TransactionConfiguration.

@TransactionConfiguration tells the transactional Spring testing environment information about how to get the transactionManager and whether you would like to commit or roll back the transaction after each test.

The following test takes all of those elements and puts them to work:

```
package com.prospringhibernate.gallery.test;

import java.util.List;

import junit.framework.Assert;

import org.junit.After;
import org.junit.Test;
import org.junit.Before;
import org.junit.runner.RunWith;

import org.springframework.beans.factory.annotation.Autowired;
import org.springframework.test.context.ContextConfiguration;
import org.springframework.test.context.junit4.SpringJUnit4ClassRunner;
Import org.springframework.test.context.transaction.TransactionConfiguration;
import org.springframework.transaction.annotation.Transactional;

import com.prospringhibernate.gallery.dao.PersonDao;
import com.prospringhibernate.gallery.domain.Person;
import com.prospringhibernate.gallery.exception.AuthenticationException;

@RunWith(SpringJUnit4ClassRunner.class)
@ContextConfiguration(locations = {"classpath:/META-INF/spring/spring-master.xml"})
@TransactionConfiguration(transactionManager = "transactionManager", defaultRollback = true)
```

```java
@Transactional()
public class TestContextJUnitIntegrationTest {

    Person person;
    PersonDao personDao;

    public PersonDao getPersonDao() {
        return personDao;
    }

    @Autowired
    public void setPersonDao(PersonDao personDao) {
        this.personDao = personDao;
    }

    @Before
    public void preMethodSetup() {
        person = new Person();
        person.setFirstName("First");
        person.setLastName("Last");
        person.setUsername("username");
        person.setPassword("goodpassword");
        person.setRoleLevel(Person.RoleLevel.ADMIN.getLevel());
        person.setVersion(1);
        personDao.save(person);
    }

    @After
    public void postMethodTearDown() {
        personDao.remove(Person.class, person.getId());
        person = null;
    }

    @Test
    public void testPersonPersisted() {
        final List<Person> people = personDao.getAll();
        Assert.assertEquals(1, people.size());
    }

    @Test
    public void testAuthenticationSuccess() throws AuthenticationException {
        Person p = personDao.authenticatePerson("username", "goodpassword");
        Assert.assertNotNull(p);
    }

    @Test (expected=AuthenticationException.class)
    public void testAuthenticationFailure() throws AuthenticationException {
        personDao.authenticatePerson("username", "badpassword");
    }

}
```

This example is using our web application's Spring configuration as defined in `spring-master.xml`, which means that we're using our H2 database configuration. With the `@Before` and `@After` annotations, we're ensuring that the state of the `Person` class is correct for each test method invocation. Finally, in nice discrete units, we test the behavior of our `PersonDao` when making a successful call to `getAll()` `Person` entities, a successful call to authenticate against the database, and lastly, a failed attempt to authenticate against the user data that we have scaffolded in with the `preMethodSetup()` method.

Notice also that we have set `defaultRollback = true`, which will ensure that this method is automatically rolled back after completion. Automatically rolling back your transactions within an integration test is an effective strategy for ensuring that each test method returns the database to its original, pristine state. When defining an integration test that talks to a database, it is important to reduce the potential for database "side-effects" and to ensure that each test stands alone, without being affected by or relying upon previously run methods.

Summary

This chapter introduced some testing strategies for Spring applications. Of course, you can do a lot more to test with both JUnit and Spring, not to mention the really powerful testing constructs that are made possible by the mocking frameworks we mentioned. Also, topics such as performance testing and load testing are extremely relevant to persistence.

For more advanced integration testing with databases, we recommend you check out the DbUnit JUnit extension. DbUnit provides excellent facilities for ensuring that your database is in a known state in between tests, as well as tooling to aid in assembling fixture data that can be used across an entire suite of tests.

CHAPTER 9

■ ■ ■

Best Practices and Advanced Techniques

Throughout this book, you've learned a lot about the workings of the Spring and Hibernate frameworks. In this chapter, you will learn the techniques necessary for building a performant, production-ready application. Although Hibernate and Spring are relatively easy to bootstrap, their default settings are appropriate only for simple applications. If you are building an application with significant load or performance requirements, you will likely need to do some fine-tuning in order to attain peak performance. In most scenarios, you can circumvent performance issues simply by leveraging the appropriate optimization or architectural strategies.

Lazy Loading Issues

Lazy loading has long been regarded as one of Hibernate's most valuable features, especially with respect to improving performance. By declaring a domain object's association or property to be lazy, an application can avoid undue overhead on the underlying database, which can often lead to faster response times and smaller datasets—both favorable qualities.

Without lazy loading, a simple query may be executed over and over again unnecessarily, or worse yet, a query for a single domain entity might force the loading of an entire object graph, as Hibernate attempts to traverse from one association to the next.

The problem is that lazy loading is a double-edged sword. It is vital for maintaining decent loading performance, but is also a significant risk for major performance problems. While lazy loading reduces the amount of data (as well as the potential for table joins) loaded from the database, this laziness can be very problematic for data that might need to be loaded from the database anyway.

This is not to imply that lazy loading is a bad feature or that it should be disabled. It is a misunderstood problem that is very dependent on the context.

Let's begin by looking at one of the most common and significant issues related to lazy loading that affects persistence-based applications.

The N+1 Selects Problem

Let's examine the way in which lazy loading works in a typical use case. In our sample application, our `Category` domain object contains a one-to-many association to the `ArtEntity` domain object. In other words, a `Category` contains a collection of `ArtEntity` instances:

```
@Entity
public class Category implements DomainObject {

    private Long id;
    private String categoryName;
    private String categoryDescription;
    private Set<ArtEntity> artEntities = new HashSet<ArtEntity>();

    . . .

    @ManyToMany
    public Set<ArtEntity> getArtEntities() {
        return artEntities;
    }

    public void setArtEntities(Set<ArtEntity> artEntities){
        this.artEntities = artEntities;
    }

    . . .

}
```

By default, the `java.util.Set` of `ArtEntity` entities is declared lazy. Let's consider what happens under the hood when we attempt to load all the `artEntities` for a series of `categories`.

```
entityManager.createQuery("SELECT c FROM Category c").getResultList();
```

Assuming there is at least one row in the `Category` table, the preceding statements will return a list of `Category` instances. However, because our `artEntities` association (within the `Category` class) is declared to be lazy, Hibernate will not perform a SQL join in an attempt to load data from both the `Category` table and the related rows from the `ArtEntity` table. Instead of loading these `ArtEntity` rows from the database, Hibernate populates the `artEntities` property for each of the returned `Category` instances with a proxy object.

For collections, Hibernate provides persistent collection implementations that serve as proxies for the collection associations in our domain model. For instance, our `artEntities` property is declared as a `java.util.Set`. Hibernate will set this property to an instance of `org.hibernate.collection.PersistentSet`, a special class designed to intercept attempts to access the referenced collection so that a lazy collection can be initialized.

Hibernate will generate proxies for each domain object within an application, and will use these proxies for single-ended associations that are marked as lazy. For example, we can define our many-to-one association of `commentedArt` in the `Comment` domain object to be lazy using the following annotation:

```
@ManyToOne(fetch=FetchType.LAZY)
public ArtEntity getCommentedArt() {
    return commentedArt;
}
```

This snippet will prevent a `Comment`'s reference to the associated `ArtEntity` from being loaded from the database until the property is accessed.

The goal of these proxies is to serve as placeholders of sorts. For data that is not loaded from the database, Hibernate can't simply ignore these properties. Instead, a proxy can be used to defer loading behavior. If no attempt is made to access an uninitialized, lazy property, then nothing will happen. However, if an attempt is made to access one of these proxies, then the proxy will intercept this request and trigger a callback into the database. The end result is that the lazy property is initialized with the relevant data from the database.

All of this sounds pretty ideal. But let's consider what happens if we have multiple `ArtEntity` instances associated with each `Category`. When a given `Category` instance is first loaded, the `artEntities` association is set to an instance of `org.hibernate.collection.PersistentSet`. Now imagine that we want to iterate through all the `ArtEntity` for all of the `Category` instances returned in our original query.

```
for (Category category: categories) {
    for (ArtEntity artEntity: category.getArtEntities()) {
        // implicitly initialize another collection here
        System.out.println("art:" + artEntity.getTitle());
    }
}
```

Although this code may seem innocuous, there is actually a serious performance issue hiding between the lines. Since the `artEntities` association is not yet initialized when we first retrieve each `Category` instance, we are actually initializing each `artEntities` association within each successive iteration of the loop. Because Hibernate has no way to infer what we are trying to do, it simply initializes each instance as we reference it. The result is a separate SQL query for each item within the collection. So for the preceding loop, we are actually inadvertently making (*number of categories*) + 1 queries! Suddenly, lazy loading doesn't seem like such an optimization technique anymore.

This disturbingly common scenario is known as the *N+1 selects* issue, in that a `select` query is issued *N* times (one for each item returned by the original query), plus the original query to load the entity containing the collection in the first place.

A similar predicament occurs for other associations, such as in the many-to-one reference to the `ArtEntity` domain object from the `Comment` class. In this scenario, if a list of `Comment` instances were to be loaded, an additional `select` query would be initiated each time an attempt was made to access the `commentedArt` property. Suppose a JSP page iterated through a long list of comments in an attempt to display related information about the comment and its associated art. This has the potential of requiring hundreds of additional round-trips to the database!

Understanding the potential for this problem is the first step, but how do we go about preventing the N+1 selects issue? Unfortunately, there is no single solution. (If there were, it would probably be an implicit part of Hibernate or JPA.) Each situation may require a slightly different approach. Fortunately, several strategies can help mitigate this potentially damaging scenario. The goal, of course, is to limit the number of SQL queries and attempt to load all the necessary data as efficiently as possible.

Less Lazy Mappings

One solution to the N+1 selects problem is to update your mapping configuration for the affected domain classes. The default behavior for collections is to be lazy and to initialize the collection via a SQL `SELECT` when the association is accessed. This default strategy is known as *select fetching*, as a second `SELECT` is issued in order to initialize the lazy association or property. The simplest solution is to override this default behavior, preventing the property from being lazy in the first place.

Let's refactor the mapping configuration affecting the `artEntities` association on our `Category` instance, as follows:

```
@ManyToMany
@Fetch(FetchMode.JOIN)
public Set<ArtEntity> getArtEntities() {
    return artEntities;
}
```

By adding the `@Fetch` annotation, specifying a `FetchMode` of `JOIN`, we request that Hibernate automatically initialize our `artEntities` collection by using a left outer join when a particular `Category` instance is loaded. Hibernate is affected by this `@Fetch` directive when navigating to a particular `Category` instance, loading an instance via `get()` or `load()`, or when loading `Category` instances via the Criteria API. Alternatively, you can opt to specify `FetchMode.SUBSELECT`, which will instead load the `artEntities` collection by including a SQL subselect as part of the initial query. In either case, the end result is that the `artEntities` association is no longer lazy, and an additional query is not required to initialize each `artEntities` association.

So problem solved, right? Not exactly. Remember how we mentioned that lazy loading is actually a pretty important feature, and that without it, you risk inadvertently loading too much of your entire database into memory? In other words, you may not always need the `artEntities` association, and in those circumstances, you are better off keeping the property as lazy.

So, sometimes it's good to be lazy, like on weekends and on vacation when you're catching up on rest. But other times being lazy can get you into trouble (especially at work). Hibernate is the same way. The best way of solving the N+1 selects problem is to keep your associations declared lazy by default, but override this behavior when you know the association is needed. For example, using JPQL, we could write the following query:

```
List categories = entityManager.createQuery("SELECT c FROM category c

LEFT JOIN FETCH c.artEntities

WHERE c.id = :id").getResultList();
```

As part of this JPQL query. we issue a `LEFT JOIN FETCH`. This will force Hibernate to initialize our `artEntities` association, overriding the default lazy behavior in the mapping file.

Batching for Performance

Another strategy for reducing the number of SQL queries required to load data is to use Hibernate's batching feature, which loads multiple entities or collections. Batching offers a slightly simpler solution than controlling lazy loading. You attempt to grab data in batches to prevent this data from being loaded in many more "single queries" later on. The advantage of batching is that it can help improve performance without requiring significant changes to queries or code.

The `@BatchSize` annotation can be added to a domain entity or to a particular association. Let's update our `artEntities` association in our `Category` class again to see how we might be able to use Hibernate's batching feature:

```
@ManyToMany
@BatchSize(size = 10)
public Set<ArtEntity> getArtEntities() {
    return artEntities;
}
```

Now, even though our `artEntities` association is still lazy by default, Hibernate will get ahead of us and attempt to initialize more than just a single `artEntities` collection at a time. It accomplishes this by using a SQL `in` condition, passing in ten identifiers of a `Category` instance when loading from the `ArtEntity` table.

In other words, batching works similarly to the default lazy configuration. First a `Category` is loaded, then its `artEntities` association is loaded in a separate query (when the `artEntities` property is accessed, of course). However, with batching enabled, Hibernate will attempt to load more than one `artEntities` association, querying for the number of associations specified in the `size` attribute of the `@BatchSize` annotation.

Keep in mind that `@BatchSize` doesn't attempt to load multiple items within a collection. A collection is normally initialized in entirety via a separate `select`. Rather, `@BatchSize` will load multiple associations, to preclude initialization of other associations in our other `Category` instances (using our example).

Lazy Initialization Exceptions

Another common issue is the ominous `LazyInitializationException`. You can probably infer what this exception means by its name: Hibernate is unable to initialize a lazy property. What circumstances account for such a problem?

As we discussed in Chapter 4, a domain object's persistent state is managed through Hibernate's implementation of the `EntityManager` interface. If a new domain object is instantiated, it is considered transient until it becomes associated with the `EntityManager`. Similarly, an already persistent domain object can continue to be persistent if the `EntityManager` is closed, which transitions the entity to a Detached state. However changes to this domain object will not be "recorded" until the domain object transitions back to a Managed state by being reassociated with another `EntityManager`.

A domain object that has become disassociated from an `EntityManager` is called a *detached object*. Hibernate is able to detect changes made to a detached domain object and propagate these changes to the database once the instance is reassociated. However, there are some things that are difficult to work around when an `EntityManager` is closed, and lazy properties are one of those things.

As you learned in the previous section, Hibernate implements laziness by referencing uninitialized properties with proxies—either special persistent collection implementations or proxy classes, depending on the type of association or property. These proxies are able to defer the loading of an association until an attempt is made to access them. Once that happens, the proxies will access the `EntityManager` and attempt to load the necessary data from the database. Obviously, this can't happen if the `EntityManager` is closed, so a `LazyInitializationException` is thrown.

The most common cause of a `LazyInitializationException` stems from failing to initialize a collection or lazy property in a DAO or controller method, instead leaving a JSP or other view-related technology to discover an uninitialized property. The problem is that Hibernate will close the `EntityManager` by default whenever a persistent operation completes. In the case of a DAO or service method, the `EntityManager` is normally closed when these relevant methods return.

The best way to prevent the `LazyInitializationException` is to ensure that all lazy associations and properties that are required by the view are successfully initialized before the domain objects are passed to the view layer. Fortunately, Spring provides some solutions that help to prevent the occurrence of `LazyInitializationExceptions`, even when lazy properties are not properly initialized before passing domain objects to the view. There are a couple of variations on the solution, but they both employ the same general strategy: defer the closing of the `EntityManager` until after the view has finished rendering.

Now Open Late: Keeping EntityManager Open Past Its Bedtime

Deferring the EntityManager from being closed is now typically known as the Open EntityManager In View pattern. The simplest approach for applying this strategy is to use a servlet filter, as described in the next section. However, if you are using Spring MVC, an alternative is to use an interceptor.

The interceptor technique essentially opens an EntityManager at the beginning of a servlet request and binds the EntityManager to the current thread, allowing it to be accessed by Spring's Hibernate support classes. Then, at the end of the request, the EntityManager is closed and unbound from the thread. This is a bit of an oversimplification, and the implementation details differ slightly, depending on whether you are using the servlet filter or the controller interceptor. However, the basic concepts are the same: open an EntityManager and associate it with the active thread to be used by persistence-related methods, and then ensure the EntityManager is kept open until the request completes. Because the request doesn't complete until after the view rendering has finished processing, the potential for the LazyInitializationException is significantly reduced.

Using the Open EntityManager In View pattern is relatively simple. If you are already using Spring MVC, you can define the OpenEntityManagerInViewInterceptor class as a new bean, adding it to your Spring MVC configuration, like so:

```
<bean name="openEntityManagerInViewInterceptor"
          class="org.springframework.orm.jpa.support.OpenEntityManagerInViewInterceptor"
/>
```

With your OpenEntityManagerInViewInterceptor defined, you then need to add this interceptor to your list of MVC interceptors. The interceptors defined in this list will be invoked (in order) as part of the request-processing flow of each MVC controller. Spring MVC controllers provide hooks into the life cycle of an MVC controller, such as preHandle, postHandle, and afterCompletion. Spring 3 provides an easy way to globally define interceptors. Let's take a look at an MVC configuration file.

```
<?xml version="1.0" encoding="UTF-8" standalone="no"?>
<beans xmlns="http://www.springframework.org/schema/beans"
       xmlns:context="http://www.springframework.org/schema/context"
       xmlns:mvc="http://www.springframework.org/schema/mvc"
       xmlns:p="http://www.springframework.org/schema/p"
       xmlns:xsi="http://www.w3.org/2001/XMLSchema-instance"
       xsi:schemaLocation="http://www.springframework.org/schema/beans
           http://www.springframework.org/schema/beans/spring-beans-3.0.xsd
           http://www.springframework.org/schema/context
           http://www.springframework.org/schema/context/spring-context-3.0.xsd
           http://www.springframework.org/schema/mvc
           http://www.springframework.org/schema/mvc/spring-mvc-3.0.xsd">

    <context:component-scan base-package="com.prospringhibernate.gallery"
                            use-defaultfilters="false">
        <context:include-filter type="annotation"/>
                            expression="org.springframework.stereotype.Controller"
    </context:component-scan>

    <!-- integrates MVC Controllers via @Controller -->
    <mvc:annotation-driven/>

    <!--specifies those interceptors that will be applied to all handlerMappings -->
```

```
<mvc:interceptors>
    <bean
        class="org.springframework.orm.jpa.support.OpenEntityManagerInViewInterceptor"/>
</mvc:interceptors>

. . .

</beans>
```

In this example, we use the `mvc:annotation-driven` and `component-scan` features to allow us to enable those Spring life-cycle features and to define our controllers via annotation (meaning we can add `@Controller` to the class and Spring will integrate these classes as controllers, provided they are in the appropriate package path). Also notice that we added our `OpenEntityManagerInViewInterceptor` inline within the `mvc:interceptors` block. Any interceptor beans defined here will have the appropriate methods invoked within the various stages of the request life cycle.

Applying the Open EntityManager Filter

If you aren't using Spring MVC, or just don't want to use an interceptor approach, you can instead add the `OpenEntityManagerInViewFilter` to your `web.xml` file. The approach is roughly the same as the interceptor technique, except the hooks for opening and closing the `EntityManager` occur at the servlet-request level rather than at the controller level.

Here is how you might add the `OpenEntityManagerInViewFilter` to your application's `web.xml` file:

```
<!-- binds a JPA EntityManager to the thread for the entire processing of the request -->
<filter>
    <filter-name>OpenEntityManagerInViewFilter</filter-name>
    <filter-class>org.springframework.orm.jpa.support.OpenEntityManagerInViewFilter</filter-
class>
</filter>

<!--Map the EntityManager Filter to all requests -->
<filter-mapping>
    <filter-name>OpenEntityManagerInViewFilter</filter-name>
    <url-pattern>/*</url-pattern>
</filter-mapping>
```

This snippet is an excerpt from a `web.xml` file that references the filter definition and mapping necessary for integrating the `OpenEntityManagerInViewFilter`. It is important that you set the appropriate `filter-mapping` glob pattern, as this will define to which URLs processing should be applied.

Caching

So far, we have discussed a few strategies for reducing or optimizing trips to the database. Even better than improving the ways in which data is queried is to preclude the need for accessing the database at all. Obviously, some database access is always needed, but caching can go quite a long way toward minimizing database load and improving application performance.

One of Hibernate's greatest advantages is that it gives developers many features "for free." And one of these free features is implicit caching. If you were to decide to implement a persistence layer using plain JDBC, you would need to explicitly integrate caching within your DAO methods or at some lower level of abstraction. While caching may seem trivial to implement on the surface, you will begin to perceive the complexity when you consider the rules for invalidation (the factors that cause a particular item in the cache to be expired), preventing conflicts, and handling a cached item's time to live (TTL).

So if Hibernate provides all these caching features for free, what is the benefit of understanding the mechanics of caching? Although Hibernate includes some foundational caching features, providing basic optimizations to limit any unnecessary trips to the database, tuning its default caching behavior can significantly improve your application's performance.

To be able to leverage caching for improved application performance, you need to understand the different layers of caching within Hibernate and what can actually be cached. For all domain objects, Hibernate provides two distinct caching levels:

- The first-level, or L1, cache is provided by the `EntityManager`, and therefore relates only to the limited scope of a particular user or request. The first-level cache is designed primarily as an optimization, preventing the requerying of domain objects that have already been loaded.

- The second-level, or L2, cache is scoped to the `EntityManagerFactory`, and therefore is longer-lived and can provide caching capabilities across multiple users and requests. The second-level cache provides the most utility and flexibility for optimization through caching.

So, the approach is to activate the second-level cache and integrate a cache provider to start caching. Now we need to consider what can be cached.

Hibernate caches domain objects in slightly different ways. Each top-level domain object is cached within a different region. A *region* is essentially a different section or namespace, intended to partition each entity and prevent the potential for clashes. Each domain object is persisted to a cache using its identifier as the key. So, given a cache region and an identifier, you are able to access the data for a particular domain object. Each domain object is cached by storing the values of its respective properties.

However, a domain object's references and collections are persisted *separately* from a domain object. In other words, the cached representation of a domain object will reference only the identifiers of its references. For example, many-to-one associations will be persisted as a single ID, while a collection will be persisted as a list of identifiers. Domain object collections are actually persisted within a separate cache region, intended specifically for that particular collection. The key in this case is still the parent domain object's identifier, but the region is specific to the domain object and the collection name. The value, however, is a list of identifiers, where each identifier in the list corresponds to the ID of each entity referenced in the original collection.

Hibernate uses this strategy because it is more efficient to just store the IDs of each entity within a collection, rather than the data of every entity in its entirety. The intention is that having the IDs should be enough, since the full data should be cached elsewhere, within the referenced domain object's own cache region. Furthermore, caching references as identifiers decouples the domain objects to which they relate, ensuring that changes to the referenced domain objects are cached only in a single location. This is obviously far simpler than managing a complex dependency tree—especially when you begin to consider the complexity of invalidating a particular item when it expires or when an update is made to the database.

Integrating a Caching Implementation

Hibernate provides a generic abstraction layer for caching functionality, allowing numerous caching implementations to be easily plugged in to the Hibernate infrastructure. There are a variety of excellent caching solutions, including Ehcache, SwarmCache, JBoss Infinispan, and many more. Each caching implementation differs slightly in the feature set it provides. For instance, some implementations offer clustering capability, allowing multiple nodes within a cluster to share the same caching data (which can reduce the potential for cache conflicts and stale data). Some caching solutions provide specialized features, such as transactional behavior.

■ **Note** The choice of which cache provider to use depends on your requirements. Generally, we recommend Ehcache, a flexible open source caching implementation that provides clustering capability. If your application has requirements for a transactional cache or other specific needs, you should take a look at some of the other cache provider choices.

Let's revisit our `persistence.xml` configuration and modify it to incorporate Ehcache.

```
<?xml version="1.0" encoding="UTF-8" standalone="no"?>
<persistence xmlns="http://java.sun.com/xml/ns/persistence"
                     xmlns:xsi="http://www.w3.org/2001/XMLSchema-instance"
                     xsi:schemaLocation="http://java.sun.com/xml/ns/persistence

http://java.sun.com/xml/ns/persistence/persistence_2_0.xsd"
                     version="2.0">

    <persistence-unit name="galleryPersistenceUnit" transaction-type="RESOURCE_LOCAL">
        <provider>org.hibernate.ejb.HibernatePersistence</provider>
        <properties>
            <property name="hibernate.dialect" value="org.hibernate.dialect.H2Dialect"/>
            <!--
                value='create' to build a new database on each run;
                value='update' to modify an existing database;
                value='create-drop' to create and drop tables on each run;
                value='validate' makes no changes to the database
            -->
            <property name="hibernate.hbm2ddl.auto" value="create"/>
            <property name="hibernate.show_sql" value="true"/>
            <property name="hibernate.cache.use_second_level_cache" value="true"/>
            <property name="hibernate.cache.provider_class"
                    value="net.sf.ehcache.hibernate.SingletonEhCacheProvider"/>
            <property name="hibernate.ejb.naming_strategy"
                    value="org.hibernate.cfg.ImprovedNamingStrategy"/>
        </properties>
    </persistence-unit>

</persistence>
```

Here, we enable second-level caching by setting the `hibernate.cache.use_second_level_cache` property on the persistence unit to `true`. Then we specify the cache implementation, ehcache, via the `hibernate.cache.provider_class` property.

Once you've activated the second-level cache and selected a cache provider, you have officially started caching. Next, you need to configure the caching rules.

Determining Caching Rules

To configure the caching rules for your domain model, the simplest approach is to add the `@Cache` annotation to your domain objects. As an example, let's examine the caching configuration of the `Category` domain object in our art gallery application:

```
@Entity
@Cache(region="category", usage = CacheConcurrencyStrategy.READ_WRITE)
public class Category implements DomainObject {

    private Long id;
    private String categoryName;
    private String categoryDescription;
    private Set<ArtEntity> artEntities = new HashSet<ArtEntity>();

    @Id
    @GeneratedValue
    public final Long getId() {
        return id;
    }

    public void setId(Long id) {
        this.id = id;
    }

     . . .

    @ManyToMany
    @Cache(usage=CacheConcurrencyStrategy.READ_WRITE)
    public Set<ArtEntity> getArtEntities() {
        return artEntities;
    }

    public void setArtEntities(Set<ArtEntity> artEntities){
        this.artEntities = artEntities;
    }
     . . .

}
```

Here, we have added a `@Cache` annotation in two places: at the top of the entity, which serves as the configuration for caching the domain object itself, and above our many-to-many `artEntities` association. Therefore, we have defined the caching rules for both the `Category` domain object itself and the `Category` domain object's `artEntities` collection.

In the first instance of the `@Cache` annotation, we also set the `region` attribute. This allows us to set the region within which we will be persisting our cached data. We omitted this attribute for the `artEntities` collection, which will then allow Hibernate to use the default region setting. The region default is the class name (including the package). For collections, the region default is the full class name, followed by `.<collectionname>`. So in the case of the `artEntities` collection, the default region name will be `com.prospringhibernate.gallery.domain.Category.artEntities`. Of course, we could choose to override this instead by specifying a region for the collection.

The `@Cache` annotation's `usage` attribute defines the cache strategy to use for the configured entity or collection. When using Ehcache, there are three options:

- The `read-only` setting should be used only when the data to be cached will never be updated. A `read-only` cache strategy will provide the best performance, since cached data will never need to expire or be invalidated.

- The `nonstrict-read-write` setting should be used when concurrent access of data is unlikely, as the caching implementation will not attempt to lock the cache to prevent contention or version mismatch.

- The `read-write` setting is suitable when concurrent access and updating of data is likely, as this approach provides the semantics of a read-committed isolation level.

Configuring Cache Regions

Next, you need to set up the configuration for the regions into which your data will be persisted. Ehcache employs an XML configuration file that is loaded at application startup. Typically, the file is called `ehcache.xml` and placed at the root of the classpath. However, you can override this default location by setting the following properties in your `persistence.xml` file:

```
<prop key="hibernate.cache.region.factory_class">
  net.sf.ehcache.hibernate.EhCacheRegionFactory
</prop>
<prop key="net.sf.ehcache.configurationResourceName">
  /path/to/ehcache.xml
</prop>
```

The default `ehcache.xml` file that ships with Ehcache includes a default cache configuration that contains the settings that will be used for any region that is not explicitly defined. However, it is usually a good idea to configure each cache region you plan to include in your application. Here is an example of the definition of our cache regions for our `Category` domain object and the `Category.artEntities` collection:

```
<cache name="Category"
       maxElementsInMemory="10000"
       eternal="false"
       timeToIdleSeconds="300"
       timeToLiveSeconds="600"
       overflowToDisk="true"
/>
<cache name="com.prospringhibernate.gallery.domain.Category.artEntities"
          maxElementsInMemory="10000"
          eternal="false"
          timeToIdleSeconds="300"
          timeToLiveSeconds="600"
          overflowToDisk="false"
/>
```

We have defined two cache regions, as specified by the `name` attribute. Typically, the `name` attribute for a domain object includes the fully qualified class name (including package). However, in our earlier caching configuration of the `Category` domain object (the listing in the previous section), we explicitly changed the default region attribute, using the shorter region name `Category` instead. We left the default region value for the `artEntities` collection.

These cache region settings work as follows:

- `maxElementsInMemory` specifies the maximum number of cached entities to store in this region. We used a value of `10000` for both cache regions, but it is important to consider this number very carefully. Using too high of a value can cause `OutOfMemoryException` issues, as well as degrade performance. Because object sizes and access patterns can vary so much from application to application, it is a good idea to experiment with these settings and profile your application to determine optimal values.

- `eternal` specifies whether a cache region should "live forever." This value can come in handy (along with `overFlowToDisk`) when you want to keep your cache prepopulated in between restarts. This is also valuable in situations when it might take a lot of time to populate your cache. A value of `true` for `eternal` will ensure that your cached data will persist, even when the application needs to be restarted.

- `timeToIdleSeconds` specifies how long a cached item will stay in the cache when there are no attempts to access it. For instance, if a particular `Category` instance is stored in the cache but there are no attempts to load this value from the cache for a while, then the benefit of keeping this item cached is questionable. It is a good idea to keep this setting to around half of the `timeToLiveSeconds` attribute value.

- `timeToLiveSeconds` corresponds to an entity's TTL—the amount of time before the cached entity expires and the data is purged from the cache, regardless of last access.

- `overFlowToDisk` specifies that if the `maxElementsInMemory` is exceeded, Ehcache should begin storing overflow on disk. While this setting sounds useful, keep in mind that persisting data on disk incurs significant performance penalties when compared to memory storage. You are using caching because you have a database for persisting data permanently. Of course, data cached on disk will outperform a database, but you should still consider this setting carefully.

It is very important to carefully consider your TTL values. Setting these values too high increases the potential for stale data and version conflicts. This risk is significantly increased in situations where an application is deployed in a clustered configuration (but the cache for each application server node is not shared). In a typical cluster configuration, updates made to one node will invalidate that node's cache, but these changes won't propagate to the caches of other nodes in the cluster. One solution is to use a lower TTL value for the `timeToLiveSeconds` attribute, which reduces the likelihood of stale data in the cache. A better solution is to use a clusterable caching solution, which allows all the nodes in the cluster to use a shared cache, significantly reducing the potential for conflicts and stale data. We will discuss clustered caching strategies later in this chapter.

Caching Your Queries

Much like collections caching, query caching attempts to store only the identifiers of the entities returned by a particular query's result. By default, queries are all cached within a single region, but you can override this setting by specifying a region name for a particular query, forcing the query to be cached elsewhere. The key for a particular cached query is composed of the query along with the identifiers or values of each of the query's parameters. This approach ensures that the results of each cached query are cached separately. If the same query is invoked with slightly different parameters, the cache will not be used.

While caching of your domain objects and collections is more a part of the default configuration, query caching requires a few additional steps. First, the second-level cache must be enabled, as described in the previous section. Next, the following property must be set to true in your persistence.xml file:

```
<property name="hibernate.cache.use_query_cache" value="true"/>
```

Hibernate leverages an additional cache region for powering its query cache implementation: the UpdateTimestampsCache. This cache region should also be configured explicitly in the Ehcache configuration file. Here is a sample configuration:

```
<cache name="org.hibernate.cache.UpdateTimestampsCache"
       maxElementsInMemory="5000"
       eternal="true"
       overflowToDisk="true"/>
```

Here, we specified that this cache region should be eternal. This is the recommended setting for the UpdateTimestampsCache, but at the very least, the TTL should be longer than the TTL of any of the query cache regions.

If you decide to use the default cache region for all query caches, you could configure the following in Ehcache for your query cache itself:

```
<cache name="org.hibernate.cache.StandardQueryCache"
       maxElementsInMemory="500"
       eternal="false"
       timeToLiveSeconds="120"
       overflowToDisk="true"/>
```

This configuration defines the cache region settings for the queries to be cached.

A QUERY CACHING CAVEAT

We strongly recommend doing some performance testing before attempting to use query caching, as it can actually degrade performance rather than improve it.

The reason query caching can sometimes cause worse performance than not using it at all is due to the use of the `UpdateTimestampsCache`. This region keeps track of the most recent updates for all tables within the application, storing timestamps for each table corresponding to the last time a particular table was updated. When a query is invoked, even if the result data is still stored in the cache, if Hibernate detects that a table associated with your query has changed since your query was cached, it will invalidate the query data, and you must hit the database instead of the cache. Therefore, if your application incurs frequent updates across any of your tables, the benefits of query caching become reduced. Furthermore, because any update to any table also means changes to the `UpdateTimestampsCache`, this resource becomes a potential for bottlenecks, due to lock contention. Suddenly, query caching doesn't sound so useful.

We don't want to discourage you, however. It is important to understand the way in which the query caching feature works, so that you can better evaluate your requirements and determine whether it is appropriate for your application.

Caching in a Clustered Configuration

If you are building an application that is intended to handle a high volume of requests, you will likely need to set up multiple application nodes in a clustered configuration. Although having multiple nodes will provide more resources for your application, if each node maintains its own cache, you will begin to strain the database. With each additional node added to the cluster, you will increase database load commensurately, such that the number of nodes in your cluster will represent the factor of database request volume:

(Num Nodes in Cluster) * *(Requests)* = *Load on Database*

Additionally, updates to the database by one node will not be propagated to the cache state of other nodes in the cluster, resulting in stale reads. Obviously, the load on the database will increase in proportion to the number of application server nodes in the cluster, but caching must also be taken into consideration; the more effective your caching strategy, the lesser the load on the database. That said, the database load will still be multiplied by the number of nodes, even with an aggressive caching strategy. In effect, your caching efficacy is commensurately weakened as the number of nodes in your cluster increases.

When building applications that have objects that receive high volumes of writes, the solution is to remove the redundancy of maintaining a single cache per node, and instead move to a clustered caching configuration. There are several caching implementations that provide clustering capability, including Ehcache and SwarmCache. For our discussion, we'll continue using Ehcache as our cache provider.

Cluster Caching and Replication Mechanics

Ehcache provides three different mechanisms for synchronizing each node's cache data. As data is persisted to one node's cache, the changes are broadcast to the other nodes in the cluster using a particular replication strategy. Ehcache supports replication via JMS, RMI, JGroups, or Terracotta. For all of these strategies, Ehcache does not attempt to use locking as a means to prevent data inconsistencies between nodes in the cluster. This is likely done for performance considerations, and therefore your application should be able to deal with the potential for stale data.

When used in the basic clustered configuration, Ehcache does not distribute the entirety of cached data across each of the nodes in the cluster. Rather, each node contains a complete set of the cached data. While this does increase memory overhead, it improves performance by reducing network overhead. To reduce your application's memory footprint, you should adjust the maximum number of objects stored within each cache region. You should also consider the average size of each entity that might be stored within a particular cache region, as this will impact the memory utilization. We have seen memory issues creep up in cache configurations with a low number of cached items, due to the large size of each item stored in the cache. These factors are rarely given ample consideration, but are often the cause of significant bottlenecks.

Regardless of the replication mechanism, Ehcache provides two different strategies for actually notifying different nodes in the cluster of changes:

- The default strategy is to send the key of the cached item that was updated, along with the updated value. This strategy is called `replicateUpdatesViaCopy`, as the updated value is sent to all the other nodes in the cluster. While this approach is usually the fastest way to keep the different nodes in sync, it also carries the overhead of sending the updated value over the network. In cases where the updated value is quite large, this can have performance implications.

- An alternative is to just send a notification to the other nodes that they should invalidate the data in their respective caches. Then once the particular cache key has been invalidated, it will eventually be reloaded from the database on the next attempt to access that particular entity (or collection) for each of the nodes in the cluster. Obviously, this will incur additional load on the database—when a cache miss occurs on each of the other nodes in the cluster, they will need to requery the database to populate their respective caches. The advantage of this approach is that only the cache key needs to be transmitted to the other nodes.

The default replication behavior is to notify other nodes of changes asynchronously, allowing cache propagation to happen in the background and not affect the response time of the original operation (the notifier). In high-concurrency scenarios in which data coherency is a top priority, Ehcache can perform replication synchronously instead, preventing the cache operation from returning until the other nodes in the cluster have been successfully notified. Since this will have significant performance implications, it should be used only in specialized situations.

Configuring Replication

Ehcache clustering implementation does not require any changes to an application's code or architecture. You just need to modify the Ehcache configuration.

To get rolling with a clustered caching configuration for our example, we need to update our `ehcache.xml` file. We will select the JGroups replication mechanism. The following snippet is suggested by Ehcache's documentation:

```
<cacheManagerPeerProviderFactory
        class="net.sf.ehcache.distribution.jgroups.JGroupsCacheManagerPeerProviderFactory"
        properties="connect=UDP(mcast_addr=231.12.21.132;mcast_port=45566;ip_ttl=32;
        mcast_send_buf_size=150000;mcast_recv_buf_size=80000):
        PING(timeout=2000;num_initial_members=6):
        MERGE2(min_interval=5000;max_interval=10000):
        FD_SOCK:VERIFY_SUSPECT(timeout=1500):
        pbcast.NAKACK(gc_lag=10;retransmit_timeout=3000):
        UNICAST(timeout=5000):
        pbcast.STABLE(desired_avg_gossip=20000):
        FRAG:
        pbcast.GMS(join_timeout=5000;join_retry_timeout=2000;
        shun=false;print_local_addr=true)"
        propertySeparator="::"
/>
```

These details specify the network and communication details for the JGroup implementation of Ehcache's `cacheManagerPeerProviderFactory`.

Next, we must add a `cacheEventListenerFactory` element to each of our cache regions. If we do not specify specific configuration for each cache region, we can just add this element to the default region configuration. Let's configure our `ArtEntity` cache region as follows:

```
<cache name="com.prospringhibernate.gallery.domain.ArtEntity"
        maxElementsInMemory="5000"
        eternal="false"
        timeToIdleSeconds="900"
        timeToLiveSeconds="1800"
        overflowToDisk="false">

<cacheEventListenerFactory
  class="net.sf.ehcache.distribution.jgroups.JGroupsCacheReplicatorFactory"
  properties="replicateAsynchronously=true,
              replicatePuts=true,
              replicateUpdates=true,
              replicateUpdatesViaCopy=true,
              replicateRemovals=true"/>
</cache>
```

In this configuration, we set `replicateAsynchronously` to `true`, ensuring that updates happen asynchronously. Additionally, we set `replicateUpdatesViaCopy` to `true`, ensuring that the values of updated cache elements are sent directly to all of the other cluster nodes. Most of the other attributes should be fairly self-explanatory.

USING AN EXTERNAL CACHING SERVER

Another caching solution that limits the potential for coherency issues is to use a stand-alone cache server. Memcached, a popular open source memory object caching system, uses a similar strategy.

Ehcache provides a Cache Server implementation, which is a self-contained caching server that runs inside its own JVM. Because Cache Server is not tied to any particular node within your application cluster, there isn't much of a risk of version conflicts between caches (as there is only a single, external cache). If you are concerned about the caching server being a single point of failure, you can deploy it in a clustered configuration.

Using an external caching server can reduce the potential for inconsistencies in your cached data. However, you must weigh this against the penalty of network overhead, incurred from the fact that all calls to the caching server must be made over the network (rather than in process). Again, we recommend that you experiment with the various caching options, and pick the solution that is most ideal for your application's requirements.

Summary

In this chapter, we examined several strategies for evaluating and improving application performance. One of the most common pitfalls for Hibernate developers is the N+1 selects issue. This problem typically stems from a failure to properly tune a domain object's mapping configuration or the queries within the DAO layer. Understanding how this problem can appear, as well as how to detect it, is important in ensuring decent ORM performance. Although tuning really depends on the unique requirements of an application, often the best solution is to consider what data needs to be made available within the service, controller, or view layers, and optimize your queries to load this data as efficiently as possible. You saw that using a fetch-join is often an effective approach for initializing an association without requiring multiple queries. Relying on Hibernate's batching capability can also be a decent strategy, although it isn't always as effective.

Another technique for improving performance is to leverage Hibernate's caching capabilities. Properly tuning the cache can make a dramatic difference for application performance. However, caching can also degrade performance if it is not done correctly. For example, caching too aggressively can trigger OutOfMemoryException exceptions. Understanding the different caching configuration options within Hibernate will help you select the appropriate behavior. It is also important to experiment with different TTL settings.

Hibernate provides several different caching layers. The first-level cache is scoped at the EntityManager, but rarely requires much tuning. The second-level cache provides the ability to cache domain objects, collections, and queries. Each of these cache types is managed and cached separately. Domain objects are keyed by their identifier, and the values of all an object's properties are persisted to the cache. Associations and queries, however, persist only collections of identifiers. These identifiers are cross-referenced against the entity cache to load the actual domain object data.

Some cache implementations, such as Ehcache, are clusterable, allowing updates to the cache to be persisted to other nodes in the cluster. However, without a way to keep the caches of other nodes within the cluster in sync, there is the potential for significant problems, caused by version conflicts or stale data. For instance, it is possible for an important update applied to the database to be inadvertently rolled back. This can happen when a node's cache is not notified of the initial update to the database.

Then, when a different user attempts to perform a write operation on the same entity, the user is applying his updates against stale data, which effectively rolls back the initial update once the second (stale) process is applied.

When deploying a clustered application, it is important to use a clusterable cache or a centralized cache server that all the nodes in the cluster can share. Ehcache provides a stand-alone server product called Cache Server. Additionally, Ehcache offers several configurable options for tuning its clusterable features. It is important to experiment with various settings to determine the options most suitable for your application's requirements.

In the next chapter, we will continue to investigate advanced strategies for providing specialized features for your persistence tier, improving performance, and utilizing best practices.

CHAPTER 10

■ ■ ■

Integration Frameworks

Rare will be the case in which an application will require Spring and Hibernate alone. Depending on your situation, you will likely need to integrate with multiple frameworks in order to meet your application's requirements. Sometimes these integration details will be a trivial matter. Other times, integration with another framework can present its own unique set of challenges.

Two very common requirements faced by engineers today are implementing free-text search and exposing web-based APIs. In this chapter, we'll show you how you can leverage several frameworks to attain these goals. To expose an API for our art gallery application, we'll take advantage of the RESTful web service enhancements added to Spring 3.0, as well as Dozer, Spring's Object/XML Mapping support, and the Data Transfer Object pattern for data marshaling. To implement free-text search, we'll leverage Hibernate Search, a subproject of Hibernate that provides a seamless way to integrate Lucene into a Hibernate-based application.

RESTful Web Services with Spring

These days, the requirements for web applications have become increasingly complex. As processing power and bandwidth increase, users' expectations follow along, leading to more complex architectures and more interactive and responsive features. Template-driven HTML web pages powered by controllers and JSPs are rarely adequate anymore. Instead, today's typical applications require asynchronous messaging between the client and the server—often leveraging Ajax or Flash. This shift away from pure server-side processing means that rendering the user interface is only part of the battle. A large proportion of the work in many of today's rich Internet applications (RIAs) often revolves around communicating with a web service or serializing data as part of a remoting strategy.

REST, which stands for Representational State Transfer, has become increasingly popular for implementing web services. REST is best described as an architectural style, rather than a standard or protocol. REST leverages HTTP to provide a consistent, resource-oriented approach for representing data. As opposed to a remote procedure call (RPC) style of communication, in which the metaphor is more akin to a method call, REST focuses on the representation of a particular resource, which is typically embodied as a URL. RESTful APIs leverage many of the built-in features of the Web, such as caching, proxying, and HTTP-based authentication strategies.

> ■ **Note** Roy Fielding originally coined the term REST in 2000 as a part of his doctoral dissertation. Fielding was one of the primary authors of the HTTP specification, and REST was defined in parallel with the HTTP 1.1 specification.

Nouns, Verbs, and Content-Types

RESTful APIs are usually expressed in terms of nouns, verbs and content-types:

- *Nouns* are the names of resources. These names are normally expressed as URLs.

- *Verbs* are the operations that can be performed on a resource. The verbs are the common HTTP verbs: GET, POST, PUT, and DELETE.

- *Content-type representations* refer to the data format used to enable machine-to-machine communication. Popular representations are XML, JSON, HTML, binary data such as images, or even RDF ontologies.

Nouns, verbs, and representations can be visualized as depicted in Figure 10-1.

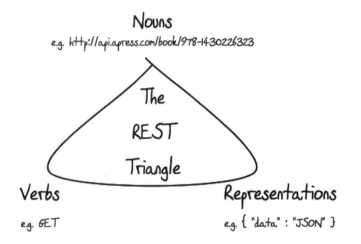

Figure 10-1. A RESTafarian's view of nouns, verbs, and content-type representations

To further illustrate the relationship between nouns, verbs, and content-type representations, let's assume that Apress has an API that is used for managing its books. To create the book you're reading, we might issue an HTTP POST on a URL like http://api.apress.com/book/. The body of that POST, as well as the format for the data returned, is completely up to the API designer. REST doesn't prescribe a particular data format, so API designers must make the right choice for their situation. The API might accept XML, JSON, or any number of data formats that can be transmitted over HTTP. The Apress API might even support multiple representations of the data, allowing consumers of the API to issue requests to a single resource URL as either XML or JSON. You would typically handle this *content negotiation* by specifying a `content-type` header (for example, `json/text`).

A well-designed API may also allow you to indicate which data representation you expect to receive in return by supplying an `Accept` header. Adhering to the semantics of HTTP, the successful addition of our book would return HTTP status code 201, created. The API would likely also provide a link to the resource representing the newly created entity by its name, `http://api.apress.com/book/prospringhibernate`, or perhaps better yet, via the ISBN-13 number, `http://api.apress.com/book/978-1430226323`.

With a resource defined, a RESTful web service can use the verbs provided by HTTP to access or manipulate the data these resources represent. For example, if you wanted to retrieve the current representation of our book, you would issue an HTTP `GET` on the resource `http://api.apress.com/book/978-1430226323`, specifying a `content-type` header as `json/text`. The JSON response might look like this:

```
{
    "book" : {
        "ISBN-13" : "978-1430226321",
        "title" : "Code Generation in Action",
        "authors" : {
            "author" : [ {
                "first" : "Paul", "last" : "Fisher"
            }, {
                "first" : "Brian", "last" : "Murphy"
            }
        ] },
        "publisher" : "Apress"
    }
}
```

Similarly, if you wanted to update the properties of this resource (to update some content related to this book), you could issue an HTTP `PUT` request targeting the URL `http://api.apress.com/book/978-1430226323`, passing in the updated state of the resource.

Here, we'll focus on the features provided by Spring that simplify developing RESTful APIs. Before we can tackle our Spring implementation though, we need to settle on a serialization strategy. In order to transmit a rich domain model over the wire, we need to be able to flatten our object graph so that it can be serialized and represented as XML or JSON.

Serializing the Object Graph

Despite the simplicity inherent in RESTful architectures, a challenge remains in the way in which your domain model is serialized into whatever format your web service chooses to provide. For instance, if you choose to represent your data as XML, there are numerous frameworks and techniques for converting an object-oriented domain model into XML. No matter which you choose to marshal your domain object, you will likely run into the problem of serializing too much of your object graph. This is a side effect of another type of impedance mismatch between the object-oriented Java realm and the flat, text-based realm of XML and JSON.

In Chapter 9, you learned about the benefits and drawbacks of lazy loading. When it comes to marshaling your data, lazy loading can flare up again, if you're not careful and attempt to marshal your domain entities after your `EntityManager` has already been closed. However, even if the `EntityManager` remains open, you are bound to initialize your object graph as the marshaling process attempts to serialize your data to the specified payload format.

Unfortunately, this is a difficult problem to solve. One solution is to plug in a specialized framework, designed to prevent the `LazyInitializationException` from popping up or too much data being inadvertently marshaled. One such solution is a framework called Gilead. Gilead attempts to clone your domain entities into a new instance in which Hibernate proxies have been filtered out. This prevents the potential for `LazyInitializationException` occurrences, as well as the likelihood of loading your entire object graph, which causes serious database overhead and performance implications.

The problem with "nulling out" all of an entity's associations so that it can be serialized into a more compact and efficient format is that if this data is read back into the application and reattached to an `EntityManager`, these nulled-out associations will cause Hibernate to remove important data, such as dropping collections on a particular entity. Gilead provides several strategies for what it calls the *merging process*, in which data returned to the Hibernate application is reassembled back into the original structure. One solution attempts to keep these details in the `HttpSession`, which requires the least intrusion into your application code, but can also come with performance and scalability penalties. Another strategy requires that your domain model extend from a base class provided by Gilead. Gilead then uses this base class as a means to stash the information required to merge the lightweight marshaled data back into the Hibernate application. You can learn more about Gilead at `http://noon.gilead.free.fr/gilead/`.

Using the Dreaded DTO Pattern

The Data Transfer Object (DTO) pattern is considered by many to be a "bad idea." This is because it has the potential to add significant code redundancy and complexity, leading to a higher potential for bugs and maintenance overhead down the road. However, there are times when the DTO pattern can serve as a viable solution, and dealing with marshaling your domain model is arguably one of those times.

The DTO pattern typically requires the creation of specialized classes intended solely for transferring your domain objects' data. Usually, you will create a separate package structure to help avoid confusion. Your DTO classes will likely be smaller and more compact than your domain objects, often replacing object references with a simple identifier, and possibly removing associations altogether. Obviously, the specifics of your DTO layer depend on your application's unique requirements. However, because your DTO classes have no dependency on Hibernate, are more compact, and have far less potential for circular references, they can help simplify the effort required by a marshaling strategy.

The primary concern raised when using DTOs is that you need to write a lot of custom code to translate from one class hierarchy to another (from your domain model to your DTOs and back). Not only does this translation effort require a lot of up-front development time, but it can also lead to bugs, especially if your domain classes are changed but your DTO translation code isn't updated accordingly.

One solution to this problem is Dozer. Dozer is a different type of mapping framework. Unlike Hibernate, Dozer doesn't attempt to map Java classes to a relational database. Dozer maps Java classes to other Java classes, and it is designed especially for the domain model-to-DTO translation requirements.

The chief advantage of a framework like Dozer is that it offloads the complex implementation details of converting one class to another. Dozer is able to make some intelligent determinations regarding how two classes relate. For instance, if two classes that are intended to be mapped to one another share properties with the same name, Dozer will attempt to automatically map these properties, unless it is told otherwise. Dozer is also able to handle conversion between types, so even if mapped properties are not of the same type, Dozer will attempt to convert from one type to another using one of its built-in converters. It is also possible to create your own converters, if you can't find an applicable converter. However, Dozer supports nested mapping behavior, so if you define the mapping behavior between two classes, these rules will be applied at any level of conversion. In other words, even if you are attempting to map two different top-level classes, Dozer will apply the mapping rules for any other defined classes as necessary. This holds true even for nested properties and collections. When Dozer is confronted with a mappable scenario, it will apply these rules automatically. These details are much clearer when examining a few examples, so let's begin integrating Dozer into our art gallery application.

Bootstrapping Dozer

To begin using Dozer, we first need to add the necessary dependencies to our Maven `pom.xml` file:

```
<!--Dozer -->
<dependency>
    <groupId>net.sf.dozer</groupId>
    <artifactId>dozer</artifactId>
    <version>5.2.2</version>
</dependency>
```

This will provide all the necessary JARs required for Dozer integration. Once this snippet is added to your `pom.xml`, you will likely need to run `mvn install` in order to download the necessary dependencies into your local Maven repository.

Building the DTO Layer

Before we can go any further, we need to define our DTO classes. Typically, DTOs are similar to their corresponding domain classes, but are simpler in nature. By removing bidirectional associations, circular references, and unnecessary properties, a DTO class can reduce the complexity in a marshaling strategy or a remoting implementation.

Let's define our `ArtEntityDTO` class:

```
package com.prospringhibernate.gallery.dto;

import java.net.URL;
import java.util.Date;
import java.util.HashSet;
import java.util.Set;
import javax.xml.bind.annotation.XmlElement;
import javax.xml.bind.annotation.XmlRootElement;

@XmlRootElement(name = "artEntity")
public class ArtEntityDTO {

    private Long id;
    private String title;
    private String subTitle;
    private Date uploadedDate;
    private String displayDate;
    private Integer width;
    private Integer height;
    private String media;
    private String description;
```

```java
    private String caption;
    private String galleryURL;
    private String storageURL;
    private String thumbnailURL;
    private Boolean isGeneralViewable;
    private Boolean isPrivilegeViewable;
    private Set<CommentDTO> comments = new HashSet<CommentDTO>();

    public Long getId() {
        return id;
    }

    public void setId(Long id) {
        this.id = id;
    }

    public String getTitle() {
        return title;
    }

    public void setTitle(String title) {
        this.title = title;
    }

    public String getSubTitle() {
        return subTitle;
    }

    public void setSubTitle(String subTitle) {
        this.subTitle = subTitle;
    }

    public Date getUploadedDate() {
        return uploadedDate;
    }

    public void setUploadedDate(Date uploadedDate) {
        this.uploadedDate = uploadedDate;
    }

    public String getDisplayDate() {
        return displayDate;
    }

    public void setDisplayDate(String displayDate) {
        this.displayDate = displayDate;
    }

    public Integer getWidth() {
        return width;
    }
```

```java
public void setWidth(Integer width) {
    this.width = width;
}

public Integer getHeight() {
    return height;
}

public void setHeight(Integer height) {
    this.height = height;
}

public String getMedia() {
    return media;
}

public void setMedia(String media) {
    this.media = media;
}

public String getDescription() {
    return description;
}

public void setDescription(String description) {
    this.description = description;
}

public String getCaption() {
    return caption;
}

public void setCaption(String caption) {
    this.caption = caption;
}

public String getGalleryURL() {
    return galleryURL;
}

public void setGalleryURL(String galleryURL) {
    this.galleryURL = galleryURL;
}

public String getStorageURL() {
    return storageURL;
}

public void setStorageURL(String storageURL) {
    this.storageURL = storageURL;
}
```

```java
    public String getThumbnailURL() {
        return thumbnailURL;
    }

    public void setThumbnailURL(String thumbnailURL) {
        this.thumbnailURL = thumbnailURL;
    }

    public Boolean getGeneralViewable() {
        return isGeneralViewable;
    }

    public void setGeneralViewable(Boolean generalViewable) {
        isGeneralViewable = generalViewable;
    }

    public Boolean getPrivilegeViewable() {
        return isPrivilegeViewable;
    }

    public void setPrivilegeViewable(Boolean privilegeViewable) {
        isPrivilegeViewable = privilegeViewable;
    }

    public Set<CommentDTO> getComments() {
        return comments;
    }

    public void setComments(Set<CommentDTO> comments) {
        this.comments = comments;
    }
}
```

At first glance, the ArtEntityDTO looks very similar to the ArtEntity domain class. On closer inspection, however, you will notice that we've removed a few references. We no longer have a dependency on any of the classes in the ArtData hierarchy. Instead, we have replaced references to a particular ArtData subclass with a String that will contain a URL to the relevant image (instead of a wrapper class that contains image metadata and the binary image data itself).

The ArtEntityDTO also omits the many-to-many association to the Category domain class. This means we won't be able to directly access the associated categories of a particular ArtEntity instance. In our application, this isn't a critical requirement. We will be able to access the ArtEntity instances associated with a particular Category by accessing a Category instance directly and navigating to its child ArtEntity instances.

Notice that our ArtEntityDTO still includes a comments property. This property is represented by a java.util.Set, but rather than containing Comment domain class instances, it holds CommentDTO instances. We haven't defined our CommentDTO class yet, but like the ArtEntityDTO, this class will serve as a simplified representation of a Comment entity.

One additional detail we added to the ArtEntityDTO is the @XmlRootElement(name = "artEntity") annotation. One use case for a DTO class is to simplify the marshaling process to XML or JSON. @XMLRootElement is a Java Architecture for XML Binding (JAXB) annotation—a standard for object-to-XML marshaling. Later in this chapter, we will leverage JAXB for rendering an XML representation of our domain classes, as part of a REST web service.

Although the differences between the `ArtEntity` domain class and the `ArtEntityDTO` are not significant, the discrepancies are intricate enough to require a fairly complex mapping strategy. For instance, consider what would be required to map a collection of `Comment` instances to a collection of `CommentDTO` instances. Luckily, Dozer is able to handle the task of mapping and converting between these classes without requiring much work.

Next, let's take a look at the `CommentDTO` class:

```java
@XmlRootElement(name = "comment")
public class CommentDTO {

    private Long id;
    private String comment;
    private Date commentDate;
    private String firstName;
    private String lastName;
    private String emailAddress;
    private String telephone;

    public Long getId() {
        return id;
    }

    public void setId(Long id) {
        this.id = id;
    }

    public String getComment() {
        return comment;
    }

    public void setComment(String comment) {
        this.comment = comment;
    }

    public Date getCommentDate() {
        return commentDate;
    }

    public void setCommentDate(Date commentDate) {
        this.commentDate = commentDate;
    }

    public String getFirstName() {
        return firstName;
    }

    public void setFirstName(String firstName) {
        this.firstName = firstName;
    }
```

```
    public String getLastName() {
        return lastName;
    }

    public void setLastName(String lastName) {
        this.lastName = lastName;
    }

    public String getEmailAddress() {
        return emailAddress;
    }

    public void setEmailAddress(String emailAddress) {
        this.emailAddress = emailAddress;
    }

    public String getTelephone() {
        return telephone;
    }

    public void setTelephone(String telephone) {
        this.telephone = telephone;
    }

}
```

The differences between the `Comment` domain class and the `CommentDTO` class are fairly trivial. We have removed the `commentedArt` property, which would create a circular reference between the `ArtEntityDTO` and the `CommentDTO` (provided that we changed the property type from `ArtEntity` to `ArtEntityDTO`).

Configuring Dozer with Spring

Now that we have defined our DTO classes, let's create the mapping configuration that instructs Dozer how to map one class to another. Dozer provides a `DozerBeanMapperFactoryBean` abstraction for Spring, which is a factory bean that will help to create the Dozer mapper. The Dozer mapper relies on an XML configuration file to learn the rules that define how the properties of one class are mapped to the properties of another class.

First, let's add the appropriate configuration to our **spring-master.xml** file:

```xml
<bean class="org.dozer.spring.DozerBeanMapperFactoryBean">
    <property name="mappingFiles" value="classpath*:/dozer-mapping.xml"/>
</bean>
```

This bean is actually quite flexible, and supports additional properties for defining custom converters, event listeners, and other Dozer extension points. You can learn more about the capabilities of the `DozerBeanMapperFactoryBean` on the Dozer website.

In the preceding configuration, we have specified that the Dozer mapping files should be located on the classpath, under the name **dozer-mapping.xml**. This XML file defines the default behavior for Dozer as well as the rules for mapping between one class and another. Let's take a look at our Dozer mapping configuration:

```xml
<?xml version="1.0" encoding="UTF-8"?>
<mappings xmlns="http://dozer.sourceforge.net"
                    xmlns:xsi="http://www.w3.org/2001/XMLSchema-instance"
                    xsi:schemaLocation="http://dozer.sourceforge.net

http://dozer.sourceforge.net/schema/beanmapping.xsd">

    <configuration>
        <stop-on-errors>true</stop-on-errors>
        <date-format>MM/dd/yyyy HH:mm</date-format>
        <wildcard>true</wildcard>
    </configuration>

    <mapping>
        <class-a>com.prospringhibernate.gallery.domain.ArtEntity</class-a>
        <class-b>com.prospringhibernate.gallery.dto.ArtEntityDTO</class-b>
        <field>
            <a>galleryPicture.url</a>
            <b>galleryURL</b>
        </field>
        <field>
            <a>storagePicture.url</a>
            <b>storageURL</b>
        </field>
        <field>
            <a>thumbnailPicture.url</a>
            <b>thumbnailURL</b>
        </field>
    </mapping>

    <mapping>
        <class-a>com.prospringhibernate.gallery.domain.Category</class-a>
        <class-b>com.prospringhibernate.gallery.dto.CategoryDTO</class-b>
    </mapping>

    <mapping>
        <class-a>com.prospringhibernate.gallery.domain.Comment</class-a>
        <class-b>com.prospringhibernate.gallery.dto.CommentDTO</class-b>
    </mapping>

    <mapping>
        <class-a>com.prospringhibernate.gallery.domain.Exhibition</class-a>
        <class-b>com.prospringhibernate.gallery.dto.ExhibitionDTO</class-b>
    </mapping>

</mappings>
```

Let's step through the important components of this configuration. First is a configuration block toward the top of the file. This section specifies the default global mapping behavior for Dozer. We define a default `date-format` and also set the `wildcard` behavior to `true`. The `wildcard` behavior determines whether Dozer will attempt to automatically map all obvious properties by default. For instance, if `wildcard` is set to `true` and both mapped classes share properties with the same name, Dozer will attempt to map these properties automatically. This feature can be overridden within specific mapping rules. If `wildcard` is left active, you can still omit certain properties from being mapped by using the `field-exclude` element. For instance, if we wanted to prevent our `subTitle` property from being mapped, we could add the following snippet to the `ArtEntity` mapping configuration:

```
<field-exclude>
    <a>subTitle</a>
    <b>subTitle</b>
</field-exclude>
```

The mapping configuration for a pair of classes is straightforward. Each mapping definition is encapsulated in a mapping XML block. Within each block, we include a `class-a` element and a `class-b` element, specifying the respective classes to be mapped. Although the configuration is sequential in nature, keep in mind that Dozer is bidirectional by default. This means that rules defining how we map from an `ArtEntity` class to an `ArtEntityDTO` class can also be applied in reverse to map from a DTO class back to a domain class. You can require that mapping rules be applied in only a single direction by adding the attribute `type="one-way"` to a mapping element.

In the case of our `ArtEntity` to `ArtEntityDTO` mapping, most of the details will be implicit since the property names are fairly consistent between the two classes. Although the `comments` collection property on the `ArtEntityDTO` contains elements of a different type, Dozer will automatically convert each `Comment` element within the `ArtEntity.comments` collection to an instance of `CommentDTO` by applying the mapping rules specified.

The only exception we need to explicitly define in our `ArtEntity` mapping rules is the conversion between the three `ArtData` references into `String` properties. In this example, the names of the properties are not in sync between the two classes, so we need to define a field element for each `ArtData` reference. Notice that we are not only mapping properties with different names, but we are also extracting the value of a subproperty and using this value for the converted DTO property. For instance, in defining the mapping rule to convert the `ArtEntity.galleryPicture` property of type `ArtData_Gallery` to the `ArtEntityDTO.galleryURL` property, we attempt to extract the `url` property from the `galleryPicture` property to use as the value for the `galleryURL`. This is accomplished by specifying a nested expression in the Dozer configuration:

```
<field>
    <a>galleryPicture.url</a>
    <b>galleryURL</b>
</field>
```

The value of element `a` specifies a nested property, and the value of element `b` simply defines the property directly. Dozer is very flexible in this regard and supports nested properties as well as indexed properties when using arrays or collections.

Making the Mapping Happen

With the configuration details out of the way, let's try to do some mapping! The easiest way to verify that everything is working properly is to start with a test. As discussed in Chapter 8, let's create an integration test. It would actually be fairly trivial to define a unit test, as our dependencies are fairly minimal. However, since we have specified some of our Dozer setup using Spring configuration, it's a little easier to let Spring take care of the details.

Here is a simple test that will help ascertain whether our Dozer mapping process is working as it should:

```
@RunWith(SpringJUnit4ClassRunner.class)
@ContextConfiguration(locations = {"classpath:/META-INF/spring/spring-master.xml"})
public class DozerMappingTest {

    private Mapper dozerMapper;
    private ArtEntity artEntity;

    public Mapper getDozerMapper() {
        return dozerMapper;
    }

    @Autowired
    public void setDozerMapper(Mapper dozerMapper) {
        this.dozerMapper = dozerMapper;
    }

    @Before
    public void preMethodSetup() {

        Comment comment = new Comment();
        comment.setComment("This is a test comment. What a cool picture!");
        comment.setCommentDate(new Date());
        comment.setEmailAddress("test@prospringhibernate.com");
        comment.setFirstName("John");
        comment.setLastName("Doe");
        comment.setTelephone("212-555-1212");

        ArtData_Thumbnail thumbnail = new ArtData_Thumbnail();
        thumbnail.setId(1L);

        artEntity = new ArtEntity();
        artEntity.setCaption("caption test");
        artEntity.addCommentToArt(comment);
        artEntity.setDescription("A very cool picture of trees.");
        artEntity.setDisplayDate("October 10th");
        artEntity.setHeight(500);
        artEntity.setWidth(300);
        artEntity.setSubTitle("This is a subtitle for a picture");
        artEntity.setTitle("This is a title of a picture");
```

```
        artEntity.setThumbnailPicture(thumbnail);

    }

    @Test
    public void testMappingArtEntity() {
        ArtEntityDTO artEntityDTO = this.getDozerMapper().map(artEntity,
ArtEntityDTO.class);
        Assert.assertEquals(artEntity.getTitle(), artEntityDTO.getTitle());
        Assert.assertTrue(artEntityDTO.getComments().size() > 0);
        Assert.assertTrue("artData_thumbnail should be a string value",
                                        artEntityDTO.getThumbnailURL().length() > 0);
    }

}
```

You should recognize much of the boilerplate detail from earlier testing examples. Notice that we specify our top-level Spring configuration file using the @ContextConfiguration annotation. Most of the code in this class is included in the preMethodSetup() method, which is annotated with the @Before annotation to ensure it is called before our test method (which is annotated with @Test). In preMethodSetup(), we instantiate an ArtEntity domain class, setting basic properties and associations. Once we have configured our ArtEntity instances, the testMappingArtEntity() method is called, which contains the code for our actual test. In this method, we call the map method on our Mapper instance, which was injected by Spring via autowiring into the dozerMapper private property. The Dozer mapper does all the real heavy lifting for us. We pass in our artEntity instance, which was set up in the previous step, along with the class type to which we want to map the instance, and Dozer converts our ArtEntity class into an ArtEntityDTO.

To ensure that all went according to plan, we assert a few properties on the mapped ArtEntityDTO instance, verifying that the correct values are present. Although the mapping process is deceptively simple, there is quite a bit going on behind the scenes. We now have an effective and reliable approach for converting Hibernate domain classes into simpler DTO classes.

Leveraging Spring 3's REST Support

Spring 3 offers numerous enhancements to MVC development. When Spring first appeared on the scene, it was praised for its elegant, interface-driven MVC approach. Things have improved significantly since then, helping to reduce configuration and simplify development effort.

By taking advantage of annotations, Spring now provides a much more intuitive approach for implementing controllers. It is no longer necessary to explicitly extract request parameters and other details from the request. Additionally, controllers are far less constrained. You have more flexibility in defining method signatures, without needing to obey a contract for parameter types. Instead, Spring lets you map method parameters to various aspects of the incoming request, such as query parameters, session attributes, and even sections of the URL. This newfound flexibility is powered by annotations—arguably a much cleaner and intuitive solution. Let's take a look at an example:

```
@Controller
public class ArtEntityRestController {

    @Autowired
    private ArtworkFacade artworkFacade;
```

```java
@Autowired
private Mapper dozerMapper;

public static final String JAXB_VIEW = "jaxbView";

@RequestMapping(method=RequestMethod.GET, value="/api/artEntities/{id}")
public ModelAndView getArtEntity(@PathVariable Long id) {
    ArtEntity artEntity = this.artworkFacade.getArtEntity(id);
    ArtEntityDTO artEntityDTO = null;
    if (artEntity != null) {
        artEntityDTO = this.getDozerMapper().map(artEntity, ArtEntityDTO.class);
    }
    ModelAndView modelAndView = new ModelAndView(JAXB_VIEW);
    modelAndView.addObject("artEntity", artEntityDTO);
    return modelAndView;
}

@RequestMapping(method=RequestMethod.GET, value="/api/category/{category}/artEntities")
@ResponseBody()
public List<ArtEntity> getArtEntities(@PathVariable Long categoryId) {
    List<ArtEntity> artEntities = this.artworkFacade.getArtworkInCategory(categoryId);
    return artEntities;
}

public ArtworkFacade getArtworkFacade() {
    return artworkFacade;
}

public void setArtworkFacade(ArtworkFacade artworkFacade) {
    this.artworkFacade = artworkFacade;
}

public Mapper getDozerMapper() {
    return dozerMapper;
}

public void setDozerMapper(Mapper dozerMapper) {
    this.dozerMapper = dozerMapper;
}
```

}

In this example, we have annotated our class with the @Controller annotation. As you'll recall, @Controller is a stereotype annotation that extends from @Component. Just as with @Service and @Repository, @Controller helps to indicate the purpose of this class and can be managed by Spring automatically through its component-scanning capability.

You will also notice that we have autowired our ArtworkFacade implementation and the Dozer mapper. The real magic happens in each of the two methods defined. Both of these methods are annotated with @RequestMapping, which tells Spring the URL mapping rules for this controller method. In both methods, we have defined the URL with which the controller will be associated. More important, however, is the use of the {} characters. Portions of the URL embedded within curly braces can be referenced in the method using the @PathVariable annotation. In this way, we have implicitly extracted portions of the URL to be injected into method parameters.

In addition to the @PathVariable annotation, Spring also offers several other options for extracting aspects of the incoming request and mapping these values to method parameters. For example, query parameters and session attributes can also be mapped to parameters through the appropriate annotation. Check out the Spring documentation to learn more about implementing MVC controllers.

Marshaling Data with Spring OXM

One important detail that we can't leave out is how we are rendering our DTOs as XML. To make this happen, we are leveraging Spring 3's Object/XML Mapping (OXM) support. Spring's OXM abstraction helps to decouple the marshaling implementation details from your application. This makes your code more portable and also simplifies the integration of multiple marshaling strategies.

Let's take a look at the Spring MVC configuration powering our REST service. The following is an abridged version of our spring-web-gallery.xml file.

```
<beans xmlns="http://www.springframework.org/schema/beans"
            xmlns:xsi="http://www.w3.org/2001/XMLSchema-instance"
            xmlns:context="http://www.springframework.org/schema/context"
            xmlns:util="http://www.springframework.org/schema/util"
            xsi:schemaLocation="http://www.springframework.org/schema/beans

http://www.springframework.org/schema/beans/spring-beans-3.0.xsd

http://www.springframework.org/schema/context

http://www.springframework.org/schema/context/spring-context-3.0.xsd

http://www.springframework.org/schema/util

http://www.springframework.org/schema/util/spring-util-3.0.xsd">

        <bean class="org.springframework.web.servlet.view.ContentNegotiatingViewResolver">
            <property name="mediaTypes">
                <map>
                    <entry key="xml" value="application/xml"/>
                    <entry key="html" value="text/html"/>
                </map>
            </property>
            <property name="viewResolvers">
                <list>
                    <bean class="org.springframework.web.servlet.view.BeanNameViewResolver"/>
                    <bean
class="org.springframework.web.servlet.view.InternalResourceViewResolver">
                        <property name="viewClass"
value="org.springframework.web.servlet.view.JstlView"/>
                        <property name="prefix">
                            <value>/WEB-INF/JSP/</value>
                        </property>
```

```xml
                        <property name="suffix">
                            <value>.jsp</value>
                        </property>
                    </bean>
                </list>
            </property>
        </bean>


    . . .


    <context:component-scan base-package="com.prospringhibernate.gallery.restapi"/>

    <bean
class="org.springframework.web.servlet.mvc.annotation.DefaultAnnotationHandlerMapping"/>
    <bean
class="org.springframework.web.servlet.mvc.annotation.AnnotationMethodHandlerAdapter"/>

    <bean id="jaxbView" class="org.springframework.web.servlet.view.xml.MarshallingView">
        <constructor-arg ref="jaxbMarshaller"/>
    </bean>

    <!-- JAXB2 marshaller. Automagically turns beans into xml -->
    <bean id="jaxbMarshaller" class="org.springframework.oxm.jaxb.Jaxb2Marshaller">
        <property name="classesToBeBound">
            <list>
                <value>com.prospringhibernate.gallery.dto.ArtEntityDTO</value>
                <value>com.prospringhibernate.gallery.dto.CategoryDTO</value>
                <value>com.prospringhibernate.gallery.dto.CommentDTO</value>
                <value>com.prospringhibernate.gallery.dto.ExhibitionDTO</value>
            </list>
        </property>
    </bean>
. . .

</beans>
```

Let's step through a few of the integral components. First, we have included a `ContentNegotiatingViewResolver`. This bean allows us to plug in multiple `ViewResolver`s (which power a particular rendering strategy), specifying which `ViewResolver` to use based on the `content-type` of the request. There are two important properties for this bean: `mediaTypes` and `viewResolvers`. The `mediaTypes` property configures the `contentTypes`. The `viewResolvers` property specifies the `ViewResolver`. The order of the items within the respective properties is key, as that is how one is associated with the other.

We've also integrated `component-scanning`, specifying the package of our REST controllers. Additionally, we have included the necessary beans for performing request mapping via annotations.

Finally, we have specified a bean for our JAXB view, using Spring's `org.springframework.web.servlet.view.xml.MarshallingView` class. This bean requires a `marshaller` as a constructor argument, which we inject using a reference to the `jaxbMarshaller` bean defined next. The `jaxbMarshaller` bean also requires a list of classes to be bound, to which we pass all of our DTO classes (which have been properly annotated with JAXB annotations).

That's all there is to it! We recommend that you take a look at the source code to get a clearer sense of how the REST service and Spring's OXM support operate.

Handling Concurrency

One of the issues we would typically run into when developing a REST web service is reliably handling concurrent attempts to modify a particular domain entity. In our earlier REST example, we examined an HTTP GET scenario, in which our web service only returned static representations of a particular entity (or entities) within our database. When dealing with HTTP PUT operations (which typically implies that a resource should be updated), things are not as simple.

Properly handling simultaneous attempts to update a particular domain entity is not always straightforward. Depending on the approach used, there can be consequences in terms of scalability risks, database deadlock potential, and data loss or conflict.

Optimistic Locking

For applications in which the likelihood that two simultaneous transactions should conflict is fairly remote, Hibernate and JPA offer support for Optimistic Locking. Optimistic Locking does not pose any constraints on accessing or writing data. Instead, the version field of the relevant domain entity is verified before the current transaction is committed. If the value of the version field does not match the value of the row (representing this particular domain entity) in the database, this implies that a concurrent transaction has modified the domain entity.

When a version field is added to a domain class (by annotating a field with `@Version`), Hibernate will automatically increment the value of this field on a particular domain entity whenever it is updated. We can then leverage this feature to help prevent entities that were modified in a concurrent transaction from having their state reverted. In other words, a typical update operation is enhanced with a SQL condition to check the version field, such that updating the name property of an `ArtEntity` domain entity would become:

```
UPDATE artentity SET name = 'foo', version = 8 where id = 4 and version = 7;
```

Optimistic Locking is beneficial in that it does not pose any significant constraints that could limit scalability, such as database locks. However, this strategy will throw an exception if a version mismatch is detected, which means that application developers must re-attempt the transaction, while trying to reconcile the conflicting data.

Pessimistic Locking

When the potential for simultaneous modifications are more likely, you may want to consider leveraging Pessimistic Locking instead. Pessimistic Locking uses database locks, and therefore poses greater risk for scalability and database deadlock. The chief advantage of Pessimistic Locking is that it limits concurrent access or modification of domain entities, which can help maintain data consistency without complicating application code. Keep in mind, however, that the longer a pessimistic lock is held, the greater the impact to scalability.

Locking an entity is relatively simple in JPA 2.0. You can acquire a pessimistic lock when loading a particular entity. You can also explicitly lock an entity after it has already been loaded, by calling lock or refresh on the `entityManager` instance.

For example, to acquire a pessimistic write lock (which is an exclusive lock) while loading a particular `ArtEntity` instance, we could do the following:

```
ArtEntity artEntity = entityManager.find(ArtEntity.class, 7, LockModeType.PESSIMISTIC_WRITE)
```

If we had previously loaded an `ArtEntity` instance, and now wanted to acquire a pessimistic read lock (which represents a shared lock), we could use the following approach:

```
entityManager.lock(artEntity, LockModeType.PESSIMISTIC_READ)
```

While it is possible to obtain multiple, concurrent read locks, there can only be a single pessimistic write lock.

Free-Text Search

As amazing as it may sound, there are some solutions that aren't in Hibernate's repertoire. It's important to recognize those situations in which a requirement might be better solved by using a different strategy altogether. These scenarios aren't always that obvious, so having a solid understanding of what other options are available can be useful.

Consider providing search-like functionality in an application. A relational database is able to handle this functionality, but only to a point. If your application is required to provide search functionality that extends far beyond what a simple "SQL-like query" will accommodate, it is time to consider an alternate solution.

Users expect search features to be intelligent. For example, if you were attempting to search for "Spring Framework" and you inadvertently typed "Sprong Framework," you would probably expect the application to work around your error and return your intended results anyway. This type of feature is often referred to as *fuzzy search*, as it reduces the strictness of the match, allowing similarly spelled terms to be included. This concept can also be extended to allow for synonyms. For example, a search for "car" can also match entries containing "automobile."

Relational databases don't typically excel at finding groups of words within blocks of text, a feature often referred to as *free-text search*. Providing this kind of search functionality within a relational database would likely incur significant performance overhead as well as additional development time.

Finding text content that begins or ends with a particular word can be implemented using a `like` condition, such as the following:

```
List<ArtEntity> blueEntities = entityManager.createQuery(
"select artEntities from ArtEntity artEntities where artEntities.description like 'blue%'"
).list();
```

Obviously, this query is a bit contrived, as we wouldn't likely have a hard-coded query, specifically one that filters items with a `description` field that starts with "blue," but it serves for demonstration purposes. While this query might be reasonably performant (since we can rely on the database index to quickly find a description that starts with an exact match of a particular word), we will begin to incur more significant performance penalties if we attempt to find those `ArtEntities` with a description containing a particular word or phrase. This sort of search operation will typically require an index scan or table scan, which can be taxing on the database.

Furthermore, we still don't have a strategy for determining the relevance of a particular match. If five `description` fields contain the word *blue*, how do we determine which match is more relevant? We could make the assumption that the more times the word *blue* appears within a particular description, the more relevant it is. However, implementing this solution with Hibernate alone will likely require a lot of extra coding, and we still have barely met the base expectations for a user's search requirements. What if we wanted to support fuzzy matching or handle synonyms?

The fundamental problem with using Hibernate alone to tackle search requirements is that a relational database is not designed to provide this type of functionality. However, this is exactly the sort of thing Apache Lucene—a powerful open source Java search framework—was intended to do.

Introducing Lucene

Lucene is a performant and full-featured information retrieval (IR) library, providing a comprehensive API for indexing and searching operations. Indexing is a strategy used by both search engines and databases to allow content to be found as efficiently as possible. A Lucene index is not all that different from the index for this book. It provides a logical and systematic way to locate and access a particular piece of data.

Indexing with Lucene

At the center of Lucene's indexing API is the `Document` class. Similar to the concept of a database table, a `Document` is composed of `Field`s, each of which contains text data extracted from the original content intended to be indexed. Unlike a database, Lucene documents are denormalized. There is no concept of joining, as data relationships are not indicative of IR. Instead, you can think of documents as containers—a means for organizing content so that it can be effectively searched against later.

Each `Field` in a Lucene `Document` typically represents a particular component of the content you wish to search. For example, if you wanted to index your personal music library, you would likely define a document with fields for an audio track, the track's album, the track's artist, the file name for the track, your notes about the track, the album's release date, and so on. To assist with the indexing process, Lucene provides a set of `Analyzers`. An `Analyzer` helps to break down and filter the content for each particular field, extracting a stream of tokens. For instance, since it's reasonable that your notes on a particular album could contain several paragraphs of text, you would need to break down this content into words. You might then want to break down these words into their roots, allowing you to be able to find notes by using the word *listen*, even if a particular note actually contained the word *listens* or *listening*. This process is called *stemming*, and helps to break down words into their root forms. An analyzer might also filter out superfluous content, such as removing *stop words*, such as *the* and *a*.

The individual tokens that an analyzer extracts are known as *terms*. Terms are the foundational elements that comprise an `Index`, and therefore are also the primary component of a search query. Lucene uses an inverted index to optimize the manner in which content is found. An inverted index uses the tokens extracted in the analyzer step of the indexing process as the lookup keys for a particular piece of content. This sort of approach is more conducive to searching, as the emphasis for lookup is placed on the individual terms or words a user might want to search for, rather than the content itself. Additionally, Lucene is able to track the frequency of a particular token, its position in relation to other tokens, and its offset within the original content from which it was extracted. This metadata is extremely valuable for a host of search features.

Lucene provides a series of options to customize how a particular field is indexed. For instance, it might be more ideal for some fields to be tokenized, while others should have their content preserved in its original form. In the music library example, you would probably want to tokenize the notes field, since you would want to be able to search for a particular word or phrase contained in your notes. However, you would not want to tokenize the track's file name, as this data makes sense only as a complete, unmodified unit.

Lucene also allows you to specify whether the original content for a particular field is stored. For instance, while you might not want to tokenize a track's file name, you would definitely want to store this data. Then when a particular document is returned as part of a search result list, you could access the file name directly so that the application could work with this data (for instance, to play the track or locate it on your file system).

Querying with Lucene

Lucene includes a powerful querying API, providing a flexible way to specify the fields and terms for which to search, along with the ability to define Boolean and grouping expressions.

The simplest Lucene query might look like the following:

```
cupcake
```

This would search for the term *cupcake* on the default field. The default field is typically specified in the QueryParser, a Lucene class used to parse a user-defined query expression into a Query instance.

More often, a Lucene query will target one or more fields, such as in the following example:

```
notes:cupcake AND album:Pepper
```

This will return all documents in which the word *cupcake* is contained in the notes field and the word *Pepper* is contained in the album field. It is also possible to define this query as follows:

```
+notes:cupcake +album:Pepper
```

As you can see, you can define Boolean AND expressions by using the + prefix or by using the AND keyword. In Lucene, a Boolean OR is the default, so you can simply specify multiple expressions together:

```
notes:cupcake album:Pepper
```

Or you can explicitly include the OR keyword:

```
notes:cupcake OR album:Pepper
```

If you want to insist that a search should not include a particular term, you can prefix it with a minus (-) character. For example, if you wanted to ensure that your search results did not contain any tracks played by the Beatles, you could use the following query:

```
notes:cupcake AND album:Pepper -artist:"The Beatles"
```

This query will look for a note containing the word *cupcake* and an album containing the word *Pepper*, but the track artist can't be The Beatles. Notice the quotes around "The Beatles" to indicate that the artist field must match the entire phrase. So, if the artist name was specified as just Beatles, you could still end up with a Beatles track in your search results. To prevent this scenario, you could just use `Beatles`, without the quotation marks.

But what if you wanted to ensure that a misspelled artist attribution on a track in your library wouldn't affect the intention of your searches? To address this problem, you can use a tilde (~) character, which lets Lucene know that you want to allow a fuzzy match:

```
(track:"Fixing a Hole" OR track:"Hey Jude") AND artist:Beatles~
```

This query expresses your intention for a fuzzy search on the `artist` field. Now, even if the artist attribution in your library is spelled as "Beetles," it will likely be included in your search results. Notice also the use of parentheses to group the first part of the query. This grouping specifies that the query should return tracks that match either title, provided they both are by the artist Beatles.

If you wanted to ensure that your results contain only tracks released within a particular date range, you could take advantage of Lucene's date-range querying capability:

```
artist:Rol* AND releaseDate:[5/18/1975 TO 5/18/2010]
```

This query will find any track with a release date between May 18, 1975, and May 18, 2010, as long as the artist name starts with *Rol*. The wildcard modifier (*) indicates that you want to match an artist given the specified prefix.

The preceding query examples should give you a sense of some of the things possible with Lucene query expressions. You will learn shortly how to parse these expressions into a Lucene `Query`. Of course, it's also possible to define queries programmatically, and doing so can often provide you with more flexibility. However, defining an expression using some of the conventions shown in these examples can give your design more clarity.

Introducing Hibernate Search

Hibernate Search is a framework that extends Hibernate in order to provide seamless integration with Apache Lucene. It is possible for developers to integrate Lucene into their applications directly. However, if your goal is to index the data within your domain classes, then it is a nontrivial problem to make this integration work reliably such that changes made to your domain model are automatically reflected in your index. Additionally, it is important that updates to the Lucene index occur within the context of a Hibernate operation.

For example, imagine if a domain class was updated as part of a DAO method, and within this method, a call was made to Lucene to trigger an update to the Lucene index. While this setup may work, what would happen if the domain class update was made within the context of a transaction, and suddenly the transaction was rolled back? Most likely, the database and the Lucene index would fall out of sync.

Hibernate Search attempts to solve these sort of problems, offering an implementation that integrates Lucene into the Hibernate life cycle and that respects the transactional boundaries to ensure the respective resources stay in sync.

Integrating Hibernate Search

Let's consider the search requirements of our image gallery application. Users will likely want to be able to find images by caption, author, title, or description, and possibly filter results by category or tag. We also want to display results in terms of relevance, not just sorted alphabetically or by date. What constitutes relevance is an important concern for search features, as ultimately, the success of search is based on how expediently users are able to find what they are looking for.

To begin integrating Hibernate Search into our art gallery application, we must first update our Maven `pom.xml` to include the necessary dependencies. This is easily accomplished by adding the following snippet to our `pom.xml`:

```xml
<!--Hibernate Search-->
<dependency>
    <groupId>org.hibernate</groupId>
    <artifactId>hibernate-search</artifactId>
    <version>3.2.1.Final</version>
</dependency>
```

Hibernate Search expects a few key configuration properties in order to define some of the basic defaults, such as the location of the Lucene index. These properties can be specified within the `persistence.xml` file. The following represents the key properties to set in order to bootstrap our Hibernate Search integration. The important new attributes are in bold.

```xml
<?xml version="1.0" encoding="UTF-8" standalone="no"?>
<persistence xmlns="http://java.sun.com/xml/ns/persistence"
                    xmlns:xsi="http://www.w3.org/2001/XMLSchema-instance"
                    xsi:schemaLocation="http://java.sun.com/xml/ns/persistence

http://java.sun.com/xml/ns/persistence/persistence_2_0.xsd"
                    version="2.0">

<persistence-unit name="persistenceUnit" transaction-type="RESOURCE_LOCAL">
        <provider>org.hibernate.ejb.HibernatePersistence</provider>
        <properties>
            <property name="hibernate.dialect" value="org.hibernate.dialect.H2Dialect"/>
            <property name="hibernate.hbm2ddl.auto" value="create"/>
            <property name="hibernate.cache.use_second_level_cache" value="true"/>
            <property name="hibernate.cache.provider_class"
                            value="net.sf.ehcache.hibernate.SingletonEhCacheProvider"/>
            <property name="hibernate.search.default.directory_provider"
                            value="org.hibernate.search.store.FSDirectoryProvider"/>
            <property name="hibernate.search.default.indexBase" value="./lucene/indexes"/>
            <property name="hibernate.search.default.batch.merge_factor" value="10"/>
            <property name="hibernate.search.default.batch.max_buffered_docs" value="10"/>
        </properties>
    </persistence-unit>

</persistence>
```

This configuration provides Hibernate Search with some of the key details required to get things rolling, such as which directory provider to use (a Lucene configuration that delineates the strategy for managing and storing the index) and where the index is located.

Adding Hibernate Search Annotations

With the configuration out of the way, we need to design our Lucene index, specifying the fields within the Lucene document and defining how these fields map to the properties within each of our domain classes. Hibernate Search is flexible in this regard, and allows you to fine-tune the requirements for every field. However, following convention over configuration, the framework includes sensible defaults, so you need to deal with only special requirements.

By default, each domain class that is indexed will be mapped to its own index. Each domain class property will map to a Lucene field of the same name, unless you choose to override this default. It is also possible to define more than one field for a particular domain class property, which is useful if you need to use multiple indexing strategies for the same domain class property. For example, you might want to have one field that is not tokenized but stores the content in its original form, while another field tokenizes the content.

To map your domain class properties to a Lucene index, Hibernate Search offers a set of specialized annotations that complement the JPA annotations we used to define our Hibernate mappings. Let's take a look at the `ArtEntity` domain class and add Hibernate Search annotations to establish our Lucene mappings:

```
@Entity
@Indexed
@Cache(usage = CacheConcurrencyStrategy.NONSTRICT_READ_WRITE)
public class ArtEntity implements DomainObject {

    private Long id;
    private String title;
    private String subTitle;
    private String uploadedDate;
    private String displayDate;
    private Integer width;
    private Integer height;
    private String media;
    private String description;
    private String caption;
    private ArtData_Gallery galleryPicture;
    private ArtData_Storage storagePicture;
    private ArtData_Thumbnail thumbnailPicture;
    private Boolean isGeneralViewable;
    private Boolean isPrivilegeViewable; // can be seen by logged-in non-administrators
(special visitors)
    private Set<Category> categories = new HashSet<Category>();
    private Set<Comment> comments = new HashSet<Comment>();

    private Integer version;

    public ArtEntity() {
    }
```

```java
@Id
@GeneratedValue
@DocumentId
public final Long getId() {
    return id;
}

public void setId(Long id) {
    this.id = id;
}

@OneToOne(cascade = CascadeType.ALL)
@JoinColumn()
public ArtData_Gallery getGalleryPicture() {
    return galleryPicture;
}

public void setGalleryPicture(ArtData_Gallery galleryPicture) {
    this.galleryPicture = galleryPicture;
}

@OneToOne(cascade = CascadeType.ALL)
@JoinColumn()
public ArtData_Storage getStoragePicture() {
    return storagePicture;
}

public void setStoragePicture(ArtData_Storage storagePicture) {
    this.storagePicture = storagePicture;
}

@OneToOne(cascade = CascadeType.ALL)
@JoinColumn()
public ArtData_Thumbnail getThumbnailPicture() {
    return thumbnailPicture;
}

public void setThumbnailPicture(ArtData_Thumbnail thumbnailPicture) {
    this.thumbnailPicture = thumbnailPicture;
}

@Field(index = Index.TOKENIZED, store=Store.YES)
@Boost(2.0f)
public String getTitle() {
    return title;
}

public void setTitle(String title) {
    this.title = title;
}
```

```
@Field(index = Index.TOKENIZED, store=Store.YES)
public String getSubTitle() {
    return subTitle;
}

public void setSubTitle(String subTitle) {
    this.subTitle = subTitle;
}

@Field(index = Index.TOKENIZED, store=Store.NO)
public String getMedia() {
    return media;
}

public void setMedia(String media) {
    this.media = media;
}

@Field(index = Index.UN_TOKENIZED, store=Store.YES)
@DateBridge(resolution = Resolution.MINUTE)
public String getUploadedDate() {
    return uploadedDate;
}

public void setUploadedDate(String uploadedDate) {
    this.uploadedDate = uploadedDate;
}


public String getDisplayDate() {
    return displayDate;
}

public void setDisplayDate(String displayDate) {
    this.displayDate = displayDate;
}

@Field(index = Index.UN_TOKENIZED, store=Store.YES)
public Integer getWidth() {
    return width;
}

public void setWidth(Integer width) {
    this.width = width;
}

@Field(index = Index.UN_TOKENIZED, store=Store.YES)
public Integer getHeight() {
    return height;
}
```

```
public void setHeight(Integer height) {
    this.height = height;
}

@Field(index = Index.TOKENIZED, store=Store.NO)
public String getDescription() {
    return description;
}

public void setDescription(String description) {
    this.description = description;
}

@Field(index = Index.TOKENIZED, store=Store.NO)
public String getCaption() {
    return caption;
}

public void setCaption(String caption) {
    this.caption = caption;
}

public Boolean getGeneralViewable() {
    return isGeneralViewable;
}

public void setGeneralViewable(Boolean generalViewable) {
    isGeneralViewable = generalViewable;
}

public Boolean getPrivilegeViewable() {
    return isPrivilegeViewable;
}

public void setPrivilegeViewable(Boolean privilegeViewable) {
    isPrivilegeViewable = privilegeViewable;
}

@ContainedIn
@ManyToMany(mappedBy = "artEntities")
public Set<Category> getCategories() {
    return categories;
}

public void setCategories(Set<Category> categories) {
    this.categories = categories;
}

@ContainedIn
@OneToMany(orphanRemoval = true, cascade = { javax.persistence.CascadeType.ALL })
@Cache(usage = CacheConcurrencyStrategy.NONSTRICT_READ_WRITE)
```

```
    public Set<Comment> getComments() {
        return comments;
    }

    public void setComments(Set<Comment> comments) {
        this.comments = comments;
    }

}
```

The Hibernate Search annotations are fairly intuitive, given the Lucene concepts introduced earlier. Let's examine the additions to this class, one at a time.

First, we need to annotate a class with the `@Indexed` annotation in order for it to be considered for indexing. Next, Hibernate Search requires that the identifier of a domain class be annotated with `@DocumentId`. The document ID is used by Hibernate Search to bridge the Lucene and Hibernate worlds. In each index, Lucene stores a Hibernate entity's full class name as well as its identifier. Together, they form the basis for querying in Hibernate Search, and allow a list of documents returned by a Lucene query to be exchanged for a list of active Hibernate entities.

Unless a domain class property is annotated with the `@Field` annotation, it will not be indexed. The `@Field` annotation specifies that a particular domain class property be included in the Lucene index. The annotation takes a few parameters, including the ability to override the name of the field. Of most importance, however, are the `index` and `store` attributes. These parameters tell Lucene how to configure the field.

As noted earlier, a field can be tokenized, which will extract the contents of a particular property into a stream of tokens, leveraging a particular analyzer to filter out superfluous words, perform stemming, insert synonyms, and possibly perform a range of other options, depending on the analyzer used. A field can also be stored, which means that the original content will be inserted into the Lucene index. Storing a field can increase the size of the index, so it is rarely a good idea for large blocks of text. However, fields containing data that may need to be displayed by the application—such as a title, file name, or a business identifier—should be marked as stored. Let's look at a few examples:

- In our `ArtEntity` domain class, we have specified that the `title` property be stored and tokenized:

```
@Field(index = Index.TOKENIZED, store=Store.YES)
@Boost(2.0f)
public String getTitle() {
    return title;
}
```

- We have specified that the `width` property be left untokenized, but still stored:

```
@Field(index = Index.UN_TOKENIZED, store=Store.YES)
public Integer getWidth() {
    return width;
}
```

- We have set the `description` property to be tokenized but not stored:

```
@Field(index = Index.TOKENIZED, store=Store.NO)
public String getDescription() {
    return description;
}
```

You probably also noticed the use of the `@DateBridge` annotation. Since Lucene typically only manages text within its index, Hibernate Search includes a bridge strategy as way to convert nontext data into a `String` (and possibly back again). Hibernate Search will use the appropriate built-in bridges for mapping fields such as integers and longs, but for more complex data types, you can leverage a custom bridge or use one of the bridges provided by the framework. For example, we can map our `uploadedDate` property in the following way:

```
@Field(index = Index.UN_TOKENIZED, store=Store.YES)
@DateBridge(resolution = Resolution.MINUTE)
public Date getUploadedDate() {
    return uploadedDate;
}
```

This mapping parameterizes the `@DateBridge` so that the date value is converted to text that can be lexicographically sorted. The date is stored within the Lucene index has a resolution of a minute. For performance reasons, you generally want to use the largest resolution setting your application can support (for instance, prefer a resolution of `Minute` over `Second`, or better yet, `Day` rather than `Minute` or `Hour`).

The `@Boost` annotation can be used to boost the weighting of a particular field within the Lucene index. For instance, to have the `title` field be twice as relevant as the `description` field, we can specify a boost factor of `2.0`:

```
@Field(index = Index.TOKENIZED, store=Store.YES)
@Boost(2.0f)
public String getTitle() {
    return title;
}
```

It is also possible to specify boost factors within a query, but in cases where you want a consistent boost weighting, the `@Boost` annotation can come in handy.

As we mentioned earlier, a Lucene index is denormalized, offering no concept of implicit relationships as found in typical relational databases. To translate some of the Hibernate association mappings into the world of Lucene, Hibernate Search offers the `@IndexEmbedded` annotation. `@IndexEmbedded` tells Hibernate Search to embed a particular association into the owning class. However, because Lucene is inherently denormalized, Hibernate Search must be made aware any time the embedded entity changes. To help track these changes, Hibernate Search provides the `@ContainedIn` annotation, to mark the other side of an embedded association.

Now that you have a clearer understanding of how to annotate a domain class for indexing, let's examine the indexing and search processes.

Putting Lucene and Hibernate in Sync

One of the primary advantages of Hibernate Search is the seamlessness of the integration between Hibernate and Lucene. Hibernate Search relies on Hibernate events to trigger the appropriate changes to the Lucene index as persistent state changes are made to your domain model.

In Chapter 4, we covered the JPA life cycle. In adhering to the JPA life cycle, Hibernate offers a fine-grained event model, broadcasting specific events based on persistent state changes to a domain object. For example, when a domain class instance is persisted, Hibernate will propagate the appropriate event. Similarly, Hibernate will broadcast numerous other events, such as delete and update notifications, providing a means to listen and respond to changes to your domain model. Event listeners are an effective design pattern for defining application behavior in a decoupled way, and Hibernate Search is able to plug in to domain life-cycle events through this powerful mechanism.

If you are building an application from scratch and are starting with an empty database, then the process of populating the Lucene index is straightforward. When your domain object is first persisted to the database, such as through `entityManager.save(artEntity)`, Hibernate Search will catch the life-cycle event and add the specified `artEntity` to the Lucene index. By default, each domain class will have its own index, and all the appropriate properties will be added to the index according to the rules specified through the Hibernate Search annotations. Because Hibernate Search takes care of keeping your database and your Lucene index in sync, the integration between the two frameworks is intuitive and simple.

However, there are circumstances under which you may need to index your domain objects more explicitly. For instance, if you are integrating Hibernate Search into an existing application or working with a legacy database, you will need to find a way to retrofit your existing data into the Lucene index. Hibernate Search provides a more direct means of indexing your domain model as well.

Hibernate Search provides an extended version of Hibernate's `EntityManager`, enhancing these core framework classes with search-specific functionality. The enhanced version of the JPA `EntityManager` is the `FullTextEntityManager`. Accessing this search-capable `EntityManager` is fairly seamless:

```
import org.hibernate.search.jpa.Search;

FullTextEntityManager fullTextEntityManager =
Search.getFullTextEntityManager(entityManager);
```

The next step is to perform the indexing. Here is how to explicitly index a single entity:

```
public void indexEntity(T object) {
    FullTextEntityManager fullTextEntityManager =
Search.getFullTextEntityManager(entityManager);
    fullTextEntityManager.index(object);
}
```

This method is intended to be added to your `GenericDaoJpa` class, in order to provide a generic means to index a domain class. If you want to implement a way to index all the entities of a particular type currently stored in the database, you could define the following method on your `GenericDaoJpa` implementation:

```
public void indexAllItems() {
    FullTextEntityManager fullTextEntityManager =
Search.getFullTextEntityManager(entityManager);
    List results = fullTextEntityManager.createQuery("from " +
type.getCanonicalName()).getResultList();
```

```
    int counter = 0, numItemsInGroup = 10;
    Iterator resultsIt = results.iterator();
    while (resultsIt.hasNext()) {
        fullTextEntityManager.index(resultsIt.next());
        if (counter++ % numItemsInGroup == 0) {
            fullTextEntityManager.flushToIndexes();
            fullTextEntityManager.clear();
        }
    }
}
```

In this method, we use the `FullTextEntityManager` to perform a standard JPA query, which simply lists all of the entities of the parameterized type. We then iterate through the results, indexing each entity. However, every ten index invocations, we call `fullTextEntityManager.flushToIndexes()`. This flushes the queued changes to the Lucene index, without waiting for the Hibernate Search batch threshold to be reached. Next, we call `fullTextEntityManager.clear()`, which clears out the JPA `persistenceContext`. This may not always be necessary, but if you are iterating through a large dataset, you want to reduce your memory footprint as much as possible.

Building a Domain-Specific Search

Now let's put together all the concepts we've covered in this chapter to offer a basic search feature that allows end users to search across several of the `ArtEntity` fields using the specified search terms. Here is an example of how this can be implemented:

```
public List<ArtEntity> searchForArtEntitiesByTerms(String searchTerms,

Integer startIndex,

Integer maxResults) {

        FullTextEntityManager fullTextEntityManager =
Search.getFullTextEntityManager(entityManager);
        String[] fieldsToMatch = new String[] {"title", "subTitle", "media", "description",
"caption"};
        QueryParser parser = new MultiFieldQueryParser(Version.LUCENE_29, fieldsToMatch,

new StandardAnalyzer(Version.LUCENE_29));

        org.apache.lucene.search.Query luceneQuery = null;
        try {
            luceneQuery = parser.parse(searchTerms);
        } catch (ParseException e) {
            log.error("Error parsing lucene query: " + searchTerms);
        }

        Query jpaQuery = fullTextEntityManager.createFullTextQuery(luceneQuery,
ArtEntity.class);
        if (startIndex != null && maxResults != null) {
            jpaQuery.setFirstResult(startIndex);
```

```
        jpaQuery.setMaxResults(maxResults);
    }
    List<ArtEntity> artEntities = jpaQuery.getResultList();

    return artEntities;

}
```

In order to search across the `ArtEntity title`, `subtitle`, `media`, `description`, and `caption` fields, we use a special Lucene query parser called the `MultiFieldQueryParser`. This query parser takes an array of field names, so that all the user-specified search terms can be equally applied to each of the fields. In other words, using the `MultiFieldQueryParser` in this way is equivalent to the following Lucene query, assuming the user searched for "test":

```
title: test OR subtitle: test OR media: test OR description:test OR caption:test
```

After parsing the Lucene query using our `MultiFieldQueryParser` and the specified `searchTerms`, we invoke the `createFullTextQuery` method on our `fullTextEntityManager` reference. This method returns a standard `javax.persistence.Query` instance, which we can use in the same manner as any JPA query. We limit our result set using `setFirstResult` and `setMaxResults` (if these parameters are specified), and then call `getResultList()` to return a `List` of `ArtEntity` instances.

One of the really interesting details here is that even though we are invoking a Lucene query, we are working with entities at the JPA level. This means that we don't need to worry about correlating the results of a Lucene query to load a series of JPA entities. Hibernate Search takes care of these details for us, providing a very powerful abstraction over Lucene to simulate a completely Hibernate or JPA-centric world.

Summary

In this chapter, we've demonstrated how to integrate and extend Hibernate in order to implement more advanced application features. We discussed some of the challenges with exposing RESTful web services on Hibernate-powered applications, and how to simplify a serialization or marshaling strategy. We examined Spring 3's new MVC capabilities, as well as its OXM abstraction for providing object-to-XML marshaling.

We also discussed the DTO pattern, and how this strategy can reduce the complexities of serializing your domain model. However, translating a domain class to a DTO class (and back again) can be a source of defects and maintenance problems. One solution is to use a framework like Dozer. Dozer handles the mapping between two different classes, using convention over configuration and mapping configuration files. By abstracting these translation details to a specialized framework, the complexities inherent in a DTO mapping layer are significantly reduced.

Providing full-text search capability is a very important and common requirement for many applications. Lucene is an open source Java framework that offers powerful indexing and search capability, but can be difficult to integrate into an application without requiring significant glue code to sync changes to the domain model with the Lucene index. Hibernate Search is a framework that bridges the gap between these two excellent frameworks, enhancing key Hibernate framework classes to offer Lucene querying and indexing capabilities. Hibernate Search allows developers to execute Lucene queries within the realm of Hibernate, so that search results return standard Hibernate entities.

Spring and Hibernate are amazing open source frameworks. However, building upon the foundations of these tools is the key to successful application development. Learning best practices for integrating your persistence tier with other frameworks is as important as learning the persistence framework itself.

CHAPTER 11

GORM and Grails

GORM is the end result of the synergistic combination of Spring, Hibernate, and Groovy. Built as one of the core components of Grails—a rapid development web framework influenced by Ruby on Rails—GORM is a different kind of ORM layer that leverages the dynamic capabilities of the Groovy language to simplify querying and persisting an application's domain model.

At the foundation of GORM lies the same strategy responsible for Ruby on Rails' success: *convention over configuration*. GORM drastically simplifies the amount of coding and effort required to define your application's persistence logic. With GORM and Grails, there is no need to define a DAO layer. Instead, the *Active Record* design pattern is employed, consolidating persistence functionality into the domain class itself without requiring up-front development to add these features. This may seem a bit like magic, but this chapter will help you understand how GORM works under the hood, by tapping into the dynamic features of Groovy.

Although GORM is the core persistence component within the Grails web framework, it can also be used outside Grails. By embedding GORM within a Spring application, you can benefit from the efficiency and terseness of Grails within a more standard architecture.

■ **Note** Some may argue that Grails does not quite fit into a book about Spring and Hibernate. However, the Grails framework and GORM rely heavily on both Spring and Hibernate for much of the flexibility and persistence they afford. The benefits of this partnership are the longevity, enterprise strength, efficiency, and flexibility offered by Spring and Hibernate. Furthermore, SpringSource, the company behind the Spring Framework, recently acquired G2One, the company behind much of the Grails and Groovy development, demonstrating a clear alignment and dedication to Spring and Grails.

A Crash Course in Groovy

Grails and GORM came onto the scene as a result of the attention brought about by the success of the Ruby on Rails framework. Ruby on Rails took the mantras of "convention over configuration" and "don't repeat yourself (DRY)" to a new level, significantly simplifying the effort required to create a new web application. Some of Ruby on Rails' success stems from the fact that Ruby is a dynamic language, which brings a level of flexibility that is not easily attainable in the Java world. For instance, the capability to dynamically generate new behavior at runtime, in order to provide customized persistence and querying functionality tailored to the specific properties of the domain model, can't be easily replicated in Java because the language doesn't natively support the dynamic creation of new methods. Luckily, Groovy came onto the scene to bring this flexibility to the Java world.

The most fundamental difference between Grails persistence and the other approaches we've discussed in this book is that Grails is the only strategy that doesn't use Java. However, Groovy code runs in the JVM and so is bytecode-compatible with Java code. This also means that Groovy can utilize Java libraries, making the myriad of open source Java libraries accessible to this new language.

Groovy is a dynamic language, which implies some significant differences from Java both syntactically and in the way Groovy can be used. Here, we'll provide a brief introduction to Groovy, to help Java developers wrap their heads around some of the core differences between the two languages.

One of the basic features of Groovy is its ability to dynamically add or modify behavior at runtime. As a brief, cursory example, let's say we want to add a new method called sayHello() to our Person instance at runtime. This could be accomplished as follows:

```
Person.metaClass.sayHello = {
    println("Hello")
}
```

Or we can make this a static method that takes a single parameter:

```
Person.metaClass.static.sayHello = {def name ->
    println("hello ${name}")
}
```

In Groovy, every class holds a reference to a corresponding metaClass instance. Method calls to a particular class or instance are delegated to that class's metaClass, which then calls a method named invokeMethod, passing along the name of the method to invoke and any corresponding parameters. So you can think of metaClass as an intermediary, or proxy of sorts, allowing more of a class's behavior to be determined at runtime.

By defining a new property on a particular class's metaClass, we are effectively implementing new behavior at runtime. Once we have defined our sayHello property to reference a closure block, future calls to Person.sayHello() will end up being delegated to the functionality specified in our closure block.

■ **Note** For a given method, constructor, or property, the Groovy compiler actually generates a call to MetaClass.invokeMethod(), passing along the object, method name, and corresponding parameters. A Groovy object's metaClass can then decide which code to invoke at runtime.

But what is a closure? A closure is an assignable block of code, similar in function to an anonymous inner class in Java. Although closures are often used in a similar context to methods, a key difference is that closures can be assigned to variables and even passed around. We will discuss closures in a bit more detail shortly.

Letting Your Types Loose

Groovy variables and references don't need to be statically typed. For instance, you can define a variable in the following way:

```
def myName = "Sam"
```

The variable `myName` can contain a `String` or can later change to an `int`. `def` defines a variable or property without delineating a specific type. It is similar to using a type of `Object` in Java, but the emphasis when using `def` is that the type isn't important and may change from one context to another.

GStrings—Strings on Steroids

Groovy supports a concept called *GString*, which is basically a Java `String` on steroids. In the earlier example, notice that we were able to create a dynamic `String` by writing `"hello ${name}"`. This strategy integrates a variable directly within a `String` without requiring concatenation. You can even invoke methods directly within a `${}` block.

Default Constructors in Groovy

Another key concept is that Groovy classes can take named parameters with just a default constructor. For instance, you can instantiate a Groovy class using the following approach:

```
Class GroovyBean {
    String name
    String favoriteColor
}
def myBean = new GroovyBean([name: 'Joe', color: 'blue']);
```

There are a few important details in the preceding example. First, notice that we defined a Groovy bean without actually defining corresponding getters and setters (and without using any semicolons!). Groovy defines these for us behind the scenes at runtime. We could reference the `name` property of the `myBean` instance with `myBean.getName()`, but `myBean.name` is more concise.

Also notice the shortcut we used for passing in a `java.util.Map` of bean properties. Maps can be defined using the following syntax: `[key: value]`. A common idiom is to define an empty map as `[:]`. Similarly, a `java.util.List` can be defined using the `[]` notation.

Closures in Groovy

One of Groovy's most significant features is its excellent support for closures. *Closures* are like methods but can also be referenced by variables or passed as parameters into methods. For instance, you can create a closure and store it in a variable called `myClosure` using the following code:

```
def myClosure = {def param ->
  println("The param is ${param}")
}
```

Notice that closure parameters appear after the first curly brace and are then followed by ->. Closures can be used to dramatically simplify code. For example, you can iterate through a list in Groovy this way:

```
List myList = ["a","b","c"]
myList.each {curItem ->
    println(curItem);
}
```

This closure will be passed to the **each** method for every element in the list. Contrast this approach with using a Java `Iterator`:

```
List myList<String> = new java.util.ArrayList();
myList.add("a"); myList.add("b"); myList.add("c");
Iterator<String> myIterator = myList.iterator();
while (myIterator.hasNext()) {
    String curItem = myIterator.next();
    System.out.print(curItem);
}
```

This is impressive, but it gets better. Imagine we wanted to iterate through a list of `String`s, returning only those items that contain the sequence *cat*. In Groovy, this can be accomplished quite simply:

```
def stringList = ["I like dogs",
        "I like cats", "I like to scat sing",
        "What is a category", "I have gas"]
def matchingStrings = stringList.findAll {curString ->
    curString.contains("cat")
}
```

Invoking a closure works in a similar way to invoking a method. You simply reference the closure property, followed by (). You can also call a closure explicitly by referencing the closure and invoking `call()`.

Now that we've covered a few basic Groovy concepts, let's move on to building our Grails persistence tier.

■ **Note** There is a lot more to learn about Groovy. We recommend you check out *Beginning Groovy and Grails* by Christopher M. Judd, Joseph Faisal Nusairat, and Jim Shingler (Apress, 2008).

Getting Grails Running

The Grails persistence solution is so dramatically different from the other DAO-based persistence solutions that we've explored so far in this book that we can't effectively build on our existing application code base, which we have been able to do up until now. Instead, we need to start over and architect our gallery application using the Grails approach. This may seem like a daunting task at first, but Grails comes with many shortcut templates and scripts designed to start stubbing out code for you. This stub code is known as *scaffolding*, in Grails speak.

Installing Grails

The first step is to install Grails. Head over to `http://www.grails.org`, and download the latest release. Unzip the downloaded archive and copy everything to a logical location on your hard drive. Next, make sure that everything under the `bin` directory is executable. If you're using a Unix-based operating system, you can run `chmod ug+x ./*` from within the `bin` directory.

Finally, make sure the `GRAILS_HOME` environment variable is set up. `GRAILS_HOME` should point to the location where you installed Grails. Also, make sure that you've added the `GRAILS_HOME/bin` directory to your `PATH`, so that you don't need to specify the full path to the Grails executables each time you want to invoke a Grails script.

If you are using a Unix-based operating system, we recommend updating your `~/.bashrc` script within your home directory so that you don't need to do this configuration more than once. On a Mac, you can append the following lines to your `~/.bashrc`:

```
export GRAILS_HOME=/opt/local/share/java/grails/
export PATH=$PATH:$GRAILS_HOME/bin
```

After you have Grails installed, the next step is to create our gallery application.

Creating a Grails Application

Grails ships with scripts that take care of generating boilerplate code to get your application started. The first of these scripts that we will introduce is `create-app`:

```
grails create-app grailsGallery
```

Here, we pass `grailsGallery` as the only argument. Grails will churn for a few seconds, and voilà! You now have a new Grails application set up and ready to go.

Part of the convention-over-configuration concept is organizing and naming key parts of your application in a standardized way. The `create-app` script makes this easy by setting up the Grails directory structure for you. After the `create-app` script completes, you will end up with the following directory structure:

```
gallery ->
    grails-app
        conf
            spring
                resources.groovy
            Bootstrap.groovy
```

```
        Datasource.groovy
        Urlmappings.groovy
    controllers
    domain
    i18n
    services
    taglib
    utils
    views

scripts
src
    java
    groovy
test
    integration
    unit
web-app
    css
    js
    images
    WEB-INF
    index.gsp
```

Most of our coding effort will be focused on the **grails-app** directory, which is where the majority of our Groovy code will live. Before we start getting our hands dirty, let's take a brief tour of the Grails application layout.

Not surprisingly, the **grails-app/conf** directory holds the application's configuration. Grails was designed to be very modular in nature, so it isn't always necessary to explicitly configure each one of your dependencies. However, since Grails is really a Spring application at its core, the **grails-app/conf/spring/resources.groovy** file can be used to configure your dependencies. Although this is a Spring configuration file, you'll notice that it isn't in XML format. Grails provides a custom domain-specific language (DSL) to configure your Spring beans, and since this file is essentially executable Groovy code, it can be a lot more flexible than a standard XML-based configuration.

■ **Note** The Groovy default application configuration approach uses a `resources.groovy` file. You can instead create a `resources.xml` file, which allows the use of the more standard XML-based Spring configuration.

Using the Spring DSL is fairly straightforward. As an example, suppose we want to create an e-mail service, so that we can notify end users via e-mail when new images are added to the gallery. We want to configure the Spring e-mail component within our **resources.groovy** file so that user can send e-mail from within our application. Here is how this configuration might look:

```
beans = {
    javaMailSender(org.springframework.mail.javamail.JavaMailSenderImpl) {
        host = 'smtp.prospringhibernate.com'
    }
}
```

The pattern is fairly intuitive. The bean name is defined first, followed by the class name within parentheses. Properties within the bean are then configured within a closure block, which is the part of the code within curly braces ({}).

If we want to inject our `javaMailSender` bean into a Grails service or controller, we can simply rely on default autowiring by name, by declaring a property named `javaMailSender` within the appropriate Grails service or controller class:

```
class EmailService {
    def javaMailSender
}
```

Similarly, if we want to reference our Grails `EmailService` within another bean configured within our `resources.groovy` file, we use its implicit bean name—in this case, `emailService`. For instance, we might define a `NotificationComponent` bean within our **resources.groovy** file as follows:

```
beans = {
    notificationComponent(com.prospringhibernate.NotificationComponent) {bean ->
        emailService = ref("emailService")
        bean.factoryMethod = "getInstance"
        bean.singleton = "false"
        defaultNotificationMethods = ["email", "sms"]
    }
}
```

Notice that we've declared a bean parameter at the top of the block using **bean ->**. By declaring a bean parameter, we are able to specify more explicit details related to the type of bean we are configuring. In this case, we specified a `factoryMethod` of `getInstance`, which ensures that new instances of this bean will be instantiated by calling `getInstance()`. We have also specified that this is not a singleton bean.

Also notice that we have injected a reference to our `EmailService` by using the convention `ref("BEANNAME")`, where *BEANNAME* is the name of our `EmailService` bean. We are able to apply most of our Spring configuration knowledge to this Groovy-based DSL. However, notice the flexibility advantage over XML in the following example:

```
beans = {
  javaMailSender(org.springframework.mail.javamail.JavaMailSenderImpl) {
    if (Environment.getCurrent() == "production") {
      host = "smtp.prospringhibernate.com"
    } else {
      host = "smtp.dev.prospringhibernate.com"
    }
  }
}
```

Clearly, interpretable code has its benefits over static XML.

This overview only touches on some of the configuration options for Grails. It is also possible to configure dynamic bean names, as well as specify property placeholders and override configuration.

■ **Note** The `grails-app/conf/Bootstrap.groovy` file provides simple hooks (`init()` and `destroy()`) for handling application startup and shutdown events. During development, `Bootstrap.groovy` is an effective means for seeding your application's database with default data.

Configuring Your Application

The `grails-app/conf/Config.groovy` file is a centralized location for specifying key configuration details about your Grails application. This file contains information about the character encoding your application should use, as well as logging details (using log4j).

Grails leverages the innate concept of environments to facilitate the creation and separation of different development and deployment scenarios. For instance, you will likely need to use a different database (requiring variant configuration details) for development or testing than you would for your production deployment. These concepts are built into the Grails core, making it easy to test with a development database and then deploy your application to production for use with the live database, without needing to remember to swap out the configuration. Environment-specific details are present in several key configuration files.

The `Config.groovy` file contains an initial block of code to specify the default server URL for production:

```
environments {
  production {
    grails.serverURL = "http://www.changeme.com"
  }
}
```

If you want to specify a different URL for development, you can modify the configuration snippet accordingly:

```
environments {
  production {
    grails.serverURL = "http://www.prospringhibernate.com"""
  }
  development {
    grails.serverURL = "http://www.prospringhibernate.com"
  }
}
```

There are no constraints on the kinds of environments your application defines or uses. You can add as many environments as you see fit. This can come in handy for your organization's development process, build cycle, or testing strategy.

Configuring Your Datasource

Since most web applications require a database, Grails defines a file specifically for configuring datasource-related details: `grails-app/conf/DataSource.groovy`. This file also uses a custom Groovy-based DSL, making this configuration clear and concise. The environment concept is built into this file as well. Properties can be configured at a global level if they apply to all environments. Environment-specific configuration, however, should be nested within the appropriate environment block.

In the case of our gallery application, here's what our `DataSource.groovy` file might look like (keep in mind that most of this file is already created for you, so you need to configure only the details that are specific to your application):

```
dataSource {
    pooled = true
    driverClassName = "org.hsqldb.jdbcDriver"
    username = "sa"
    password = ""
}
hibernate {
    cache.use_second_level_cache = true
    cache.use_query_cache = true
    cache.provider_class = 'net.sf.ehcache.hibernate.EhCacheProvider'
}
// environment specific settings
environments {
    development {
        dataSource {
            dbCreate = "create-drop"
              // one of 'create', 'create-drop','update'
            url = "jdbc:hsqldb:mem:devDB"
        }
    }
    test {
        dataSource {
            dbCreate = "update"
            url = "jdbc:hsqldb:mem:testDb"
        }
    }
    production {
        dataSource {
            dbCreate = "update"
            url = "jdbc:hsqldb:file:prodDb;shutdown=true"
        }
    }
}
```

Notice that the `dataSource` property is specified at the top of the file as well as within the `environments` block. Global details, such as database connection pooling settings and the JDBC driver, are configured globally by placing these details within a top-level `dataSource` block. Environment-specific details, such as the database URL for the `development`, `test`, and `production` environments, are configured in the `dataSource` blocks within their respective environments. If you need to use a different JDBC driver for production, you could either move these details within the appropriate environment blocks or simply override the globally configured details within the appropriate environment. Again, the types of environments you can configure are not restricted: `development`, `test`, and `production` are just default environments created by the Grails templates.

Mapping URLs

The last file we need to cover in the `grails-app/conf` directory is `UrlMappings.groovy`. This file provides an amazingly flexible construct for associating URL patterns with a particular controller and action. For example, here's how we might relate the pretty URL `/category/panoramas` with the `CategoryController`, specifying that the `panaromas` category be displayed:

```
class UrlMappings {
  static mappings = {
      "/$controller/$action?/$id?"{
          constraints {
          }
      }

      "/category/$categoryName"(controller: CategoryController, action: "displayCategory")

      "/"(view:"/index")

      "500"(view:'/error')
  }
}
```

The mapping we described is actually the second block in this example. The first component of the mapping is the part in quotes. We are essentially defining a regular expression that starts with `/category/`. The `$categoryName` defines a parameter name that will be passed to your controller automatically, using the specified chunk of the URL where the parameter name resides. In our example, the part of the URL after `/category/` will be extracted and then stored in the parameter named `categoryName`.

If you look at the first block in the example, you will notice the default `URLMapping`. In this scenario, we are defining `$controller` and `$action` parameters. These are special keywords; instead of denoting a particular parameter, they define the controller to which the matching request should be directed, as well as the corresponding action. In our category listing page example, we haven't defined a `$controller` within our mapping expression, so we instead specify this explicitly, as follows:

```
(controller: CategoryController,action: " displayCategory")
```

Now that we've looked at the Grails application directory structure, let's move on to defining our Grails domain model.

Defining the Grails Domain Model

By default, Grails generates three core layers, which resemble the tiers we've discussed earlier in this book: domain, controller, and service. To provide consistency and better enforce convention, Grails enforces a directory structure to help organize and sequester classes from each respective layer. The domain model typically serves as the foundation for a Grails application, so it is usually the first layer to be defined.

As you probably already guessed, the domain model classes all go into the `grails-app/domain` directory. By default, all domain classes will live in the default Grails package. However, you are free to define your own package structure, and for larger applications, this is recommended. Additionally, if you will need to access any of your Grails code from Java, you must keep your Grails classes within a package, or it will be difficult to access them outside the Grails/Groovy world. You can also have your Groovy classes implement an interface that is accessible to Java, as a means to better integrate your Grails code with Java.

Let's begin our Grails-based gallery application by defining our `Person` domain entity. Grails provides scripts to help create most of the core Grails archetypes, each corresponding to a particular template. You can edit these templates if you want to change the way your default views or domain and service classes are created. To do this, you will need to run `grails install-templates`. You will then be able to access (and modify) the templates from within the `src/templates` directory. For most Grails development, the default templates are just fine.

To create our `Person` domain class, run the following:

```
grails create-domain-class Person
```

Once this script completes, you will find a `Person.groovy` class within the `grails-app/domain` directory. Grails uses Hibernate behind the scenes to persist `Person` instances to, and retrieve them from, the database. Unlike Hibernate, Grails does not require any mapping files or annotations , since convention helps Grails infer most of what it needs to handle persistence for your domain model.

Now that we've created our stub for our `Person` domain entity, let's define the rest of the properties:

```
class Person {

    String firstName;
    String lastName;
    String username;
    String password;
    String email;

    Integer roleLevel;

    public static final USER_ROLE = 1;
    public static final ADMIN_ROLE = 2;
    public static final SUPERUSER_ROLE = 4;
    public static final CONTACT_USER = 16;
    public static final COMMENT_USER = 64;

    static constraints = {
        firstName(maxSize:255, unique: false, blank: false)
```

```
        lastName(maxSize:255, unique: false, blank: false)
        username(maxSize:255, unique: true, blank: false)
        password(maxSize:25, unique: false, blank: false)
        email(email:true, blank: false, unique: false)
        roleLevel()
    }

    static mapping = {
        cache true
    }

}
```

The first thing you will probably notice in this class is just how concise this code is. Most of the properties should be self-explanatory. Since we are using Groovy, there is no need to define getters or setters (these are implicit within Groovy). Also notice that there are no properties specified for id or version; these fields are created by Grails automatically.

Adding Constraints and Validation

Let's now look at the constraints block. Constraints allow you to better define each field within your domain model, providing clues and requirements to Grails as to how your database schema should be modeled. A number of constraint options are available, but here are some of the most useful:

- blank
- minSize
- maxSize
- range
- unique
- size
- range
- inList
- email
- creditCard
- matches
- nullable

Some of these constraints can be extremely powerful. For example, the matches constraint allows you to specify a regular expression that will be used to validate the value in the specified field, ensuring it matches the specified regular expression.

The domain-specific constraints, such as email and creditCard, will help to ensure that a field conforms to a valid e-mail address or credit card number, respectively.

If you need a custom constraint, Groovy includes a construct that allows you to define your own. You specify the property, followed by a mapping of constraint types and their corresponding values. Here is an example:

```
username(blank: false, maxSize: 255, unique: true)
```

This will ensure that the `username` value cannot be left blank and that the database field has a maximum size of 255 characters. Additionally, a `unique` constraint will also be added to the `username` database field.

Constraints come into play when you attempt to save a domain entity to the database. If a particular field is not validated, an error will be attached to a dynamic `errors` property on your domain instance.

Additionally, the constraints defined for each property, coupled with a consistent naming convention, are assembled into error message codes that are automatically used within the default Grails Groovy Server Pages (GSP) templates. For example, if you attempt to save a `Person` entity without specifying a `username`, a validation error will be raised and associated within the instance's `errors` property. Afterward, this error will be properly rendered within the default GSP template, using an error code that is defined in the application's `messages.properties` resource bundle.

When a validation error code is found, Grails will attempt to look for the appropriate code within the `messages.properties` file, starting with the most specific naming convention and moving toward the more generic conventions until a match is found. This ensures that if you don't bother adding a specific error code in your `messages.properties` file, users will still see a sensible error (something to the effect that the `blank` constraint for the `username` field has been violated). However, you can easily override this default message by specifying a `blank` constraint error code that's specific to the `Person` class.

Defining Associations and Properties

The `Person` domain entity is a fairly simplistic example, as it doesn't really contain any associations or customized mappings. Let's take a look at a more complex entity to see how Grails addresses a typical scenario. Update your domain model, and then we'll dive deeper. Use the `grails create-domain-class` script to stub out the `ArtEntity`, `Category`, and `Comment` classes, respectively. The `Comment` class would then be modified as follows:

```
class Comment {

  String comment;
  Date commentDate;
  Person person;

  static belongsTo = [commentedArt: ArtEntity]

  static constraints = {
    comment(maxSize: 2000, blank: false)
    commentDate(nullable: false)
  }

  static mapping = {
    cache true
  }

}
```

This class is similar to the `Person` entity we defined earlier. We've defined a few properties, as well as a `constraints` block. One addition is the `belongsTo` field, which provides clues to Grails about the relationship between two entities. In this example, we are defining a parent-child relationship between a `Comment` and an `ArtEntity`. We are also defining a property called `commentedArt` and declaring that this property is of type `ArtEntity`. We could specify additional `belongsTo` relationships by appending them to this map. In each case, the `key` represents the property name, and the `value` represents the type.

■ **Note** The `belongsTo` property defines the owning side of an association. When a domain class specifies a `belongsTo` property, it is not the owner of the association. The association owner is the class referenced by the `belongsTo` property.

The use of `belongsTo` also asserts cascading rules. In the previous example, we are declaring that `ArtEntity` is the parent in this relationship, meaning save and delete operations (on `ArtEntity`) will cascade appropriately to related `Comment` instances. This relationship will become clearer after we examine the opposing side, which is the `ArtEntity` domain class.

```
class ArtEntity {

    String title;
    String subTitle;
    Date uploadedDate;
    Date displayDate;
    int width;
    int height;
    String media;
    String description;
    String caption;
    ArtData_Gallery galleryPicture;
    ArtData_Storage storagePicture;
    ArtData_Thumbnail thumbnailPicture;
    boolean isGeneralViewable;
    boolean isPrivilegeViewable;

    static hasMany = [categories: Categories, comments: Comment]
    static belongsTo = Category

    static constraints = {
        title(blank:false, maxSize: 255)
        subTitle(blank:true, maxSize: 255)
        uploadedDate(nullable: true)
        displayDate(nullable: false)
        width(nullable: true)
        height(nullable: true)
        media(nullable: true, maxSize: 255)
        description(nullable: false, blank: false, maxSize: 2000)
```

```
        caption(nullable: true, maxSize: 2000)
    }

    static mappings = {
        cache true
    }

}
```

This class follows a similar pattern, but uses the `hasMany` property, which defines a one-to-many association to another class. It can also be used to declare a many-to-many association, as long as one side of the relationship is deemed the owner of the association (through the use of `belongsTo`).

The `hasMany` relationship works in a similar fashion to the `belongsTo` convention. You are defining a map in which the `keys` correspond to the property (that is, collection) names and the `values` correspond to the domain class. In our example, we are defining two associations: `comments` and `categories`. When Grails deciphers this property, it will create corresponding collections to be used to hold these associations. We can define the type of collection we would like to use by explicitly declaring the collection as a property. For instance, we define our `categories` association (in our `ArtEntity` domain class) as a `java.util.Set` by explicitly defining this property:

```
Set categories = new HashSet();
```

■ **Tip** If you need to ensure that a collection is logically ordered, you can define a property of type `SortedSet`, and then have your collection class implement the `Comparable` interface, in which the ordering logic is specified. For instance, if we wanted our categories to be ordered alphabetically, we would have our `Category` class implement `Comparable` and define a `compareTo(def obj1, def ob2)` method in which the ordering is based on the category name.

Customizing Domain Class Hibernate Mappings

You probably noticed the static `mappings` property defined in each of our example domain classes. This field can be used to enhance the Hibernate mapping that Grails creates and manages behind the scenes. In our example, we just assert that the domain entity be cached, using the `CacheManager` specified in the `Config.groovy` file. However, the mapping construct is extremely flexible and can be used to modify many areas of the default Hibernate mapping for a particular domain class. For instance, if you need to override the table name or the default column name or type, the mapping DSL provides a means for this to be accomplished. It is also possible to add caching rules for collections or override the default fetching policy for a collection, specifying whether a particular collection will be lazily or eagerly fetched. You can even specify that one or more columns map to a particular Hibernate `UserType`.

In our earlier Hibernate example, we defined a hierarchy of `ArtData` classes (each extended from the `ArtData` base class). In Grails, implementing polymorphic domain classes is even simpler. Here is our `ArtData` class:

```
class ArtData {

  byte[] picture;

  static mapping = {
    cache true
  }

}
```

And here is the `ArtData_Storage` class (which extends `ArtData`):

```
class ArtData_Storage extends ArtData {

}
```

That's really all there is to it. By default, Grails uses the table-per-hierarchy strategy, meaning it persists the sum of all the properties across the entire hierarchy into a single table.

Unlike with Hibernate, there is no need to explicitly define a discriminator (to help differentiate between types), as Grails will take care of this. However, Grails is flexible enough to allow you to use a different polymorphic strategy. For example, you could use the custom mapping DSL described earlier like so:

```
static mapping = {
  tablePerHierarchy false
}
```

Now that we've defined our Grails domain model, let's move on to persisting and retrieving this data.

Using Active Record As an Alternative to DAOs

Throughout this book, you've learned how Spring simplifies the development of a persistence tier by enforcing several key design patterns, most notably the DAO, Template, and Facade patterns. Although Grails is built on the foundations of Spring and Hibernate, it provides an alternative to the DAO pattern typical of most Spring applications. Following the lead of other rapid development frameworks, such as Ruby on Rails, Grails utilizes the Active Record design pattern as the approach for handling database persistence operations.

In keeping with the Active Record pattern, a table in the database is represented directly by a domain class. For instance, in our gallery example, we have already defined a `Person` class that describes a corresponding `Person` table in our database, meaning table fields and associations are represented by properties within our `Person` class.

This approach doesn't seem too different from the domain models we've used throughout this book. However, the key distinction is that the domain class also serves as the wrapper around database operations. Dynamic static methods are injected into each domain class, providing a means for querying for instances of that class's type. As in Hibernate, each row in our database is represented by a corresponding instance of the appropriate domain class. However, `save()` and `update()` methods are injected into each domain class instance, allowing newly created or retrieved instances to be persisted by invoking `save()` or `update()` directly on that instance.

For example, if we want to create or update a particular row in the `Person` table, we just call `person.save()` directly on the `person` instance we wish to save. If we want to load a particular `Person` record from the database, we simply call the static method `Person.get(id)`, passing in the primary key for the record we wish to retrieve.

Contrast this approach with the DAO pattern, in which we need to create a separate abstraction layer for all database operations related to a particular domain entity. The Active Record pattern dramatically simplifies our effort for retrieving and persisting data, since there is no need to define any DAO classes or methods. Instead, this functionality is implicit within our domain model through dynamic behavior that is injected into each domain class.

If we don't need to define a DAO implementation, where do the implementations for methods like `Person.get(id)` and `Person.save()` come from? The Active Record pattern states that we should simply be able to define a domain model and begin calling methods on these classes to achieve the persistence logic we are trying to build. The question remains, however: if we can simply call `save()` on our `Person` instance, where do we define the behavior for this method? Let's take a look under the hood of GORM to get a better sense of how this works.

Looking Under the Hood of GORM

One of the key advantages to languages like Groovy is that they are dynamic, which means, among other things, that you are able to define new behavior for your classes at any time. In the case of Grails and the Active Record pattern, the framework is able to enhance your domain model with new functionality related to persistence. This strategy is a key Groovy concept and is enabled through the use of Groovy's `metaClass` construct, as discussed earlier in this chapter.

Working with Dynamic Finder Methods

Grails injects new functionality into every domain model class to facilitate the Active Record pattern. Unlike with the DAO approach, no methods need to be defined up front. Instead, Grails uses naming conventions to interpret how to interact with the database. Using the name of the method invoked, Grails intuits what type of operation to perform. This is best explained through a few examples.

Getting back to our gallery application, let's define a simple unit test that illustrates saving and loading our `Person` domain class. Since we want to demonstrate how Grails behaves within a running application, we need to create an integration test, which actually bootstraps a Spring `ApplicationContext`, so we can test functionality that relies on core Grails features such as persistence. Grails ships with a script that creates the integration test scaffolding for us:

```
grails create-integration-test Person
```

After running this command, you will find an integration test stub under `test/integration/grailsGallery/PersonTests.groovy`. In our test, we are going to verify that we can instantiate, save, and load a `Person` domain entity:

```
class PersonTests extends GroovyTestCase {

  ...

  void testSavePerson() {

    Person person = new Person(
        [firstName: "Sam", lastName: "Smith",
         username: "ssmith", password: "1234",
         email: "sam@notarealaddress.com",
         roleLevel: Person.ADMIN_ROLE])

    assertTrue("Person entity is valid and can be saved",
        (person.validate() && person.save()))

    assertNotNull ("person id is null", person.id)

    def loadedPerson = Person.get(person.id)

    assertTrue(
        "Person was successfully loaded",
            loadedPerson != null &&
                loadedPerson.username != null)
  }
}
```

This is a very straightforward test. Notice that we instantiate our **Person** entity using a **java.util.Map** containing default properties for our Groovy class. After our **Person** instance is instantiated, we verify that the instance validates and saves successfully. **validate()** verifies all the requirements specified within our domain model's **constraints** block. If our domain model does not validate successfully, Grails will set an **errors** property on our **Person** instance. The **errors** property contains details on each validation failure and is an implementation of the **org.springframework.validation.Errors** interface. This interface is quite useful for tracking and managing form submissions, and should be familiar to users of Spring MVC.

In the event of a validation error, we can iterate through each error to find out exactly what went wrong:

```
person.errors.allErrors.each {curError ->
    log.error("Error saving Person instance: ${curError}");
}
```

We can also get an error count this way:

```
person.errors.errorCount()
```

■ **Note** A `log` instance variable is automatically injected in all controller and service classes, allowing you to easily emit logging messages. This is an instance of log4j's `Logger` class, and is configured in the `Config.groovy` file described earlier in this chapter.

Grails ships with a tag library that helps to render errors within a typical form submission. Additionally, the default Grails templates will create GSP views that will automatically render clear error messages in the event of any validation or save failures. Of course, default error messages can be easily overridden by updating the `messages.properties` file.

At this point, you should have a solid understanding of how to go about saving and loading a domain entity. Unfortunately, that won't get you very far. You'll want to be able to query the database. To demonstrate how that works, we first need to add some data to our database.

Let's return to the `PersonTests.groovy` file and define a `setup()` method that will be executed before each of our tests are run and allow us to populate the database with some sample data:

```
void setUp() {
  def baseNames = [
    "Sam", "Bob", "Heather",
    "Steve", "Sofia"]
  baseNames.each {curName ->
    def person = new Person(
      [firstName: curName,
       lastName: curName,
       username: curName,
       password: "1234",
       email: "${curName}@apress.com",
       roleLevel: Person.USER_ROLE])
    assertTrue (
      "Person entity is valid and can be saved",
      (person.validate() && person.save()))
    assertFalse(
      "There should be no errors on the saved entity",
      person.hasErrors())
  }
}
```

This method is a little archaic, as we simply iterate through a `java.util.List` of names and create new `Person` entities using these names as seed data for each field. Also notice that we've added a new assertion to verify that `person.hasErrors()` is false. After a `save` operation, calling `hasErrors()` is a useful idiom to ascertain that there were no errors preventing the entity from being persisted to the database. You will see this approach used frequently within the default Grails controllers.

Now that we have a way to seed our database with some sample data, let's see how Grails makes querying the database very intuitive.

```
void testFinders() {

  def foundPeople = Person.findAllByUsername("Sam");

  /* foundPeople should reference a List
          containing one Person entity */
  assertEquals("One person found", 1, foundPeople.size())

  /* singlePerson should refer to a single Person
     entity, and the lastName property
     should be equal to Sam*/
  def singlePerson = Person.findByUsername("Sam")
```

```
assertEquals(
  "Lastname is Sam", "Sam", singlePerson.lastName)

def allPeopleSorted =
  Person.list(max: 3, order: "asc",
      sort: "username", offset: 0);

assertTrue(
    "Three people returned", allPeopleSorted.size())

assertEquals(
    "First person in list is Sam", "Sam",
        allPeopleSorted[0].username)
}
```

This new method helps to illustrate a lot of the flexibility for querying data using Grails' dynamic finder concept. Notice that the way each method name is formatted determines the query that eventually is generated on the database.

In our first example, we run `Person.findAllByUsername("Sam")`. This type of structure returns *all* data that matches the field `username`. Notice that we use camel casing. The format might be better expressed using the following structure:

`DOMAIN.findAllBy<PROPERTYNAME>`

If you look at the assertions, you will notice that this type of method will always return a collection of objects. Conversely, our next assertion uses the format:

`DOMAIN.findBy<PROPERTYNAME>`

This method works in a similar fashion but will return only a single object. This claim is validated on our assertion, as we demonstrate that the returned value is a single `Person` instance, instead of a collection.

Both the `findAllBy` and `findBy` dynamic methods can also be expanded, in order to specify modifiers on the property name or provide further constraints. For example, if we wanted to find all users that have first and last names that start with the letter *p*, this could be expressed in the following method:

`Person.findAllByFirstNameIlikeAndLastNameIlike("P%", "P%");`

In this example, we first specify a conditional property of `firstName` and then modify the condition using `Ilike`. The `Ilike` modifier is similar to the `like` modifier but is case-insensitive. Next, we append `And` to the method name to further constrain the query with an additional property condition.

A similar approach may be taken to find out the number of rows in the database that match a specified set of conditions by using the `countBy*` dynamic finder method. Based on this example, we can define a method-naming structure that delineates the way in which a dynamic-finder method is formatted:

`countBy/findBy/findAllBy<PROPERTYNAME><MODIFIER>AND/OR<PROPERTYNAME><MODIFIER>`

The following are some of the modifiers that can be used:

- Between
- GreaterThan
- GreaterThanEquals
- LessThan
- LessThanEquals
- Like
- Ilike
- Not
- Equal

Our next example simply calls `Person.list()`, which returns all the instances of the `Person` domain class. However, we also pass in a `Map` of options that help to define constraints and sorting options on our returned data. These options can also be used for pagination, since you can set the maximum number of items to return (`max`), as well as an `offset`. Table 6-1 summarizes the options that can be passed to the `list()` method.

Table 6-1. *Options for Sorting and Paginating a Result Set*

Option	Purpose
sort	Field to sort on
order	Direction of sort (ascending or descending)
max	Maximum number of items to return
offset	Offset within total result set for first item returned

A `Map` containing the options listed in Table 6-1 will also work with the `findAllBy*` methods. For instance, we could request the second page (assuming each page contains ten objects) of `Person` instances, sorted by name in descending order:

```
def people = Person.list(sort: "name", order: "desc", max: 10, offset: 10);
```

Creating Advanced Query Methods

The dynamic finder approach described in the previous section works well for most types of queries. However, sometimes having a little more flexibility is important. Grails also provides the `find()` and `findAll()` methods, which allow you to utilize arbitrary HQL queries. `Find()` returns a single entity, and `findAll()` will return multiple entities. Alternatively, an even more flexible `executeQuery()` method allows you to define queries that don't return a specific domain entity.

Let's look at an example using HQL. Suppose we want to query for all `ArtEntity` objects that fall within a particular category. This could be represented using the following query:

```
List artEntities = ArtEntity.findAll(
 "from ArtEntity artEntity left join
     artEntity.categories as category with
         category.id = :categoryId",
             ["categoryId": category.id])
```

Notice that we use a left join on the `Category` domain object, specifying a `with` constraint for those categories matching the specified category ID.

We use named parameters in this query. As in a typical HQL query, parameter names are represented in the query by prefixing the name with a colon. The parameter name-value mappings are then passed in as a `Map` (as the second parameter to the `findAll` query).

Using the Criteria API

Just like standard Hibernate, Grails provides a means to express queries using the Criteria API. However, because we are using Groovy instead of Java, we can take advantage of a Criteria DSL, allowing us to define our query criteria in a more concise and readable way. For instance, we could query for all `ArtEntity` instances within one of two specified categories that also fall within a particular date range using the following query:

```
def criteria = ArtEntity.createCriteria()
def currentDate = new Date()
def earlierDate = currentDate - 3
def catName1 = "autumnPicts"
def catName2 = "summerPicts"
def results = criteria.list {
    between('displayDate', earlierDate, currentDate)
    categories {
        or {
            equals("name", catName1)
            equals("name", catName2)
        }
    }
}
```

The preceding example uses the Grails Criteria Builder, allowing us to express a fairly complex set of restrictions in a very intuitive manner. If you recall the standard Hibernate Criteria API, you should be able to infer most of what is occurring in our example. Criteria disjunctions and conjunctions can be specified using **or** and **and** blocks, respectively. Similarly, association criteria may be expressed by defining a block with the association name, which is what our **categories** block does in the preceding example. Within our **categories** block is a nested **or** disjunction, and within that block are our **equals** restrictions, allowing us to filter those categories that match either of the category names we've specified.

Handling Associations in Grails

We have described how associations can be defined by using the `hasMany` and `belongsTo` conventions. These constructs are effective for indicating how our domain entities relate to each other. Once our domain model is defined, we need to manipulate it.

Recall that in the Hibernate world, it is important to write code to ensure that bidirectional associations are properly managed. For instance, it is common practice to define **add*** and **remove*** methods within a Hibernate domain class that ensure both ends of an association are properly set or removed. Grails helps to ensure that both sides of an association are properly referenced (or dereferenced) by providing dynamic **addTo*** and **removeFrom*** methods. For instance, if we want to add new `Comment` instances to an `ArtEntity`, we could do so using the following code:

```
def loadedArtEntity = ArtEntity.findByName("Awesome Panorama");
def loggedInUser = Person.findByUsername("Sam");
Comment newComment = new Comment(
                        comment: "Cool pict!",
                        commentDate: new Date(),
                        person: loggedInUser);
loadedArtEntity.addToComments(newComment);
if (!loadedArtEntity.hasErrors() && loadedArtEntity.save()) {
    println("new comment saved");
} else {
    println("Error saving new comment");
}
```

In our example, we define a new `Comment` and then add it to the `ArtEntity comments` association using the `addToComments` method. We could also choose to remove a particular comment reference using the `removeFromComments` method. Notice that we did not invoke **save()** on our new `Comment` instance directly. Instead, we saved our `ArtEntity` instance, allowing the save operation to cascade to the `comments` association since we have specified that `ArtEntity` is the owner of the association. This association ownership is expressed in this line within the `Comment` domain class:

```
static belongsTo = [commentedArt: ArtEntity]
```

Scaffolding and Building Your Grails Application

With our domain model defined, we can rely on Grails' generation scripts to create scaffolded functionality for our gallery application. You can download the full Grails-based gallery application from this book's web site.

To generate controllers and views for a particular domain class, make sure you are at the root of our Grails gallery application and then run the following:

```
grails generate-all <<domain-class>>
```

Be sure to swap *domain-class* for the name of the domain entity for which you would like to generate controllers and GSPs. You can also generate just the controllers or just the GSPs by calling the following scripts, respectively:

```
grails generate-controller <<domain-class>
grails generate-views <<domain-class>>
```

We strongly recommend examining the generated controllers and views to get a better sense of how a typical Grails application works. Keep in mind that the generated code is based on scaffolding designed to work in a very generic way (so that it works for all types of domain models). Therefore, it is also useful to examine the sample Grails gallery application for a slightly different perspective.

■ **Note** For details on Grails development, including building controllers and GSPs, see *The Definitive Guide to Grails, Second Edition*, by Graeme Rocher (Apress, 2009).

You can easily start up your Grails application using a particular environment, by passing the `grails.env` environment variable into the **grails run-app** script:

```
grails -Dgrails.env=development run-app
```

This command will automatically start up our application using the **development** environment configuration. You wouldn't normally want to run a production or staging application this way, but it is convenient for testing purposes. Internally, Grails uses an embedded Jetty server to run your application when you use the **run-app** command.

You can deploy Grails to any application server if you create a WAR file using the Grails **war** command. If you want to create an application for deploying into your own application server, you would instead run this:

```
grails -Dgrails.env=production war
```

We recommend explicitly using **-Dgrails.env** to specify an environment, as it supports both default and custom environments. However, if you are using the default Grails environments, you can use this shortcut:

```
grails prod war
```

Defining a Transactional Service Layer in Grails

You've learned about transactional support throughout this book. You know how important it is to ensure that operations within a particular method all complete (or roll back) as a single, atomic unit of work. Grails also encourages the use of the service facade pattern, and makes defining transactional requirements extremely easy. However, in the name of flexibility, Grails provides a couple of options for ensuring persistent operations occur within a transactional context.

If you don't want to create a service class, an alternative approach for ensuring persistence operations occur within a transactional context is to enclose a block of code inside a closure and pass this to the dynamic `withTransaction` method, injected to each domain class. For instance, we could ensure an update to a category and an `ArtEntity` occurs within a transaction by doing the following:

```
Comment.withTransaction {txStatus ->
    def comments = Comment.findAllByCommentDateGreaterThan(lastWeek);
    comments.each {Comment curComment ->
      if (Comment.hasSpam(curComment)) {
        curComment.delete()
      }
    }
}
```

Here, we are actually defining an anonymous closure block and passing this closure to the `Comment` domain object's dynamic `withTransaction` method. This is a trivial example, but it illustrates how simple defining a transaction can be using Grails.

■ **Note** The `txStatus` closure parameter is an `org.springframework.transaction.TransactionStatus` object, which allows you to get information about the currently executing transaction and trigger a rollback programmatically by calling `txStatus.setRollbackOnly()`.

A cleaner approach is to implement a service layer and organize your transactional operations within a service method. In Grails, you can create a new service method by running the following command:

```
grails create-service servicename
```

This will create a new service within the **grails-app/services** directory. Grails has a fairly simplistic way of declaring whether a particular service class should be transactional. Just add the following to the top of your service class:

```
static transactional = true;
```

If `transactional` is set to `true`, your methods will all run within a transactional context. If the static property is `false`, a transaction will not be used.

Summary

In this chapter, we've covered some of the fundamentals for developing a web application using Groovy and Grails. Grails provides an interesting contrast to the topics covered in the previous chapters. Although based firmly on Spring and Hibernate, Grails utilizes Active Record as an alternative to the DAO design pattern. This approach is more practical in Grails due to its use of the dynamic language Groovy, allowing new behavior and methods to be dynamically defined. Through the use of convention-over-configuration, Grails can significantly reduce the amount of effort required to get a working application up and running.

Despite some of these differences, Spring's profound influence is clearly present, and most of the lessons and patterns utilized with other persistence frameworks can still be applied to Grails. You've seen how some of the fundamental Spring concepts, such as dependency injection, can be further enhanced through Groovy-based configuration and implicit, convention-based wiring.

CHAPTER 12

■■■

Spring Roo

SpringSource has a growing track record of delivering software that removes impediments that plague enterprise software engineers. Spring Roo is its latest ambitious attempt to bring rapid application development (RAD) to Java developers.

In this chapter, we're going to rebuild our art gallery application from scratch so that you can see just how quickly Roo can jump-start a project. This will also provide you with an excellent opportunity to compare and contrast what we've done by hand up to this point with everything that Roo generates automatically. The productivity gains will be immediately obvious.

What Roo Is (and What It Is Not)

Roo's architecture revolves primarily around Spring and AspectJ, the AOP framework that Spring uses to express pointcuts throughout the various Spring modules. AspectJ provides a feature called *inter-type declaration* (ITD), which Spring Roo uses as a part of its code-generation process. ITD allows for a clean separation of your source code (`.java` files) and Roo's generated source code (`.aj` Aspect ITD files). These two source files are then combined during a compilation step to fabricate bytecode representing all of the intended functionality.

This clean separation provides exactly what you would expect from a RAD framework: convention over configuration is realized via the generated `.aj` source files, and you may code your normal `.java` classes, overriding the conventions as you deem appropriate, without extending or implementing any Roo-specific classes or APIs. As a result of this clever approach, all Roo code will look and feel completely natural for Java developers.

While an IDE isn't required to use Roo, IDEs like Eclipse and SpringSource Tool Suite (STS) can take advantage of Java's static typing to provide full integration for the conveniences like code completion.

Because of the compilation approach Roo takes, the framework imposes absolutely no requirements on your runtime at all! It's a simple, effective vehicle for speeding up development and empowering developers to be productive with Java, without the learning curve associated with picking up new languages and runtime frameworks.

The core infrastructure of Roo delivers capabilities like file monitoring, metadata management, and type introspection. One of Roo's greatest assets is its add-on infrastructure. Roo is a very young project, but its library of add-ons is already impressive. Roo 1.0.*x* was implemented as a single classloader. As of 1.1.0, however, Roo is entirely based on OSGi.

OSGi (formerly known as the Open Services Gateway initiative, now an obsolete name) is a module system and service platform for the Java programming language that implements a complete and dynamic component model. These modules, referred to as *bundles* in OSGi parlance, can be installed, started, updated, and uninstalled without restarting the application. Each bundle has its own classloader, and bundles may interact with each other through a service registry. The modularity provided by OSGi offers an extensible platform for Roo. All of the key components that you interact with, such as Hibernate and automated integration testing, are actually built as OSGi bundles. This architecture enables the community to continue to extend Roo.

At first blush, it might seem a bit strange that SpringSource has two distinct RAD frameworks in its stable: Grails (covered in the previous chapter) and Roo. But we believe that the two are sufficiently different to coexist. On green field projects where a team is afforded the luxury of time to learn something new and open to using dynamically typed languages, we would be hard-pressed not to recommend using Groovy and Grails. But if you're working in the context of a legacy application, or just want to stick with the tools and language you know best, Roo is a fantastic alternative. In this chapter, we hope to show you why.

JAVA, GRAILS, AND ROO

Java enjoys a very strong foothold in the enterprise, and for good reason. Java was created by James Gosling and first released by Sun Microsystems in 1995. Fifteen years later, its ecosystem is enormous! Java has been used to program everything from cell phones to kitchen appliances to incredibly complex global trading systems that require submillisecond response times. It's frequently taught as a part of computer science curriculums, and there are legions of engineers with extensive experience using Java in the enterprise. This ensures easy access to talented engineers at all experience levels. Additionally, there are many frameworks and libraries to choose from, both open source and commercial, so that you don't need to reinvent the flat tire every time you are presented with commonly faced problems for which design patterns and best practices are well studied and understood. Development teams can reap prodigious time and cost savings by reusing or extending existing software. Such system scaffolding enables you to focus on writing code that truly differentiates your organization. All of these reasons make selecting Java as the platform that powers a business very attractive.

Despite Java's promise in the enterprise, all is not rosy for the individual Java programmer. As web development in general, and open source software in particular, has blossomed over the past decade, we've seen a tremendous influx of new programming languages and web frameworks (and interestingly enough, we're seeing old languages finding new niches as well). If you've spent any time exploring some of these alternate technologies, Java's productivity shortcomings become readily apparent. There are many technical hurdles when programming in a Java environment that can slow down a developer. Among them are compilation steps, a need to restart your application server to see the effect of changes, and what many cite as the "high ceremony" aspect of Java, whereby engineers lose precious time writing and maintaining an inordinate amount of boilerplate code.

Within the Java community, we've seen frameworks that employ newer scripting languages emerge, aiming to deliver faster development models on top of the battle-tested JVM. Grails is one such framework, written in the Groovy language, which rose to prominence under the stewardship of Graeme Rocher and was later acquired by SpringSource.

As you learned in Chapter 11, Grails delivers increased productivity through the software design paradigm known as convention over configuration (sometimes referred to as coding by convention). Frameworks that apply this paradigm are often said to be "very opinionated." They strive to reduce the number of decisions that a developer must make in building an application, while still providing ample hooks for you to specify or override behavior where your application deviates from convention. For example, in our art gallery application, a framework using convention over configuration would ensure that the `Person` domain class maps to a corresponding database table named `person` by default. The framework would also provide a means to override such behavior if we knew that our database table was actually named `user` rather than `person`.

The very nature of Groovy as a dynamically typed scripting language obviates the need for compilation steps and, in many cases, even application server restarts. Grails further lessens the burden on developers and addresses the hurdles mentioned earlier through heavy use of reflection and Groovy's metaprogramming model in order to dynamically generate code at runtime, thereby alleviating much of the boilerplate code required for typical web applications.

Conversely, under the direction of Ben Alex, Spring Roo lets engineers leverage pure Java, complete with all the tooling they know and love, while speeding up the development life cycle through extensive code generation.

Creating a Domain Model with Roo

Domain-driven design (DDD) is a methodology for developing software popularized by Eric Evans in his exceptional book *Domain-Driven Design: Tackling Complexity in the Heart of Software* (Addison-Wesley Professional, 2003). DDD attempts to model real-world systems or processes in software by focusing on and refining your application's domain layer throughout the entire development process. To achieve this, Evans advocates that you begin your work in a highly iterative and interactive manner with a domain expert to define a *ubiquitous language*. This ubiquitous language provides consistent terminology and definitions so that engineers and domain experts can effectively communicate about entities in the system.

Spring Roo doesn't explicitly advocate DDD, but since Roo places so much emphasis on your entity layer, the principles of DDD are a natural fit. As an introduction to Roo, we'll walk through using it to create our art gallery applications domain, shown in Figure 12-1.

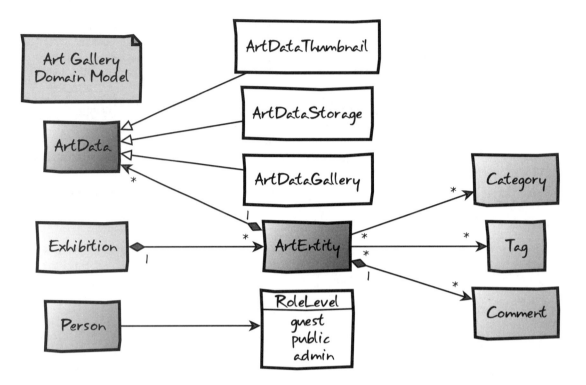

Figure 12-1. The art gallery domain model

Getting Started with Roo

Be sure that you have the prerequisites, Java 5 or higher and Maven 2.0.9 or higher, configured on your system. Then download and follow the installation instructions for the stand-alone version of Roo available at `www.springsource.org/roo` to ensure that `roo` is available on your path.

Next, create a directory on your machine for your new project, named `rooGallery`. Change into this new directory and execute `roo`. You'll enter the Roo shell environment and be presented with a Roo welcome screen, as shown in Figure 12-2.

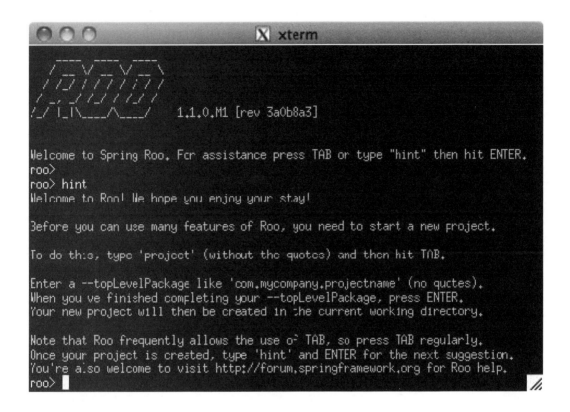

Figure 12-2. The Roo shell

■ **Tip** As you explore Roo, you can use hint and tab completion liberally to get contextual help from Roo. Each Roo command has an extensive list of options that you may specify. Be sure to fiddle with the intelligent tab completion in the Roo shell as you tinker with commands to see how Roo steers you down the right path, eliminating any need to memorize the Roo commands.

Before we create a new project, in the Roo shell, type in the osgi command and use tab completion to see all of the options that Roo provides. One of the most basic OSGi commands supported by the Apache Felix runtime upon which Roo is based is ps. Executing osgi ps will list all of the OSGi bundles in the Roo runtime, along with version information and the status of the bundle, such as ACTIVE, STARTING, and so on

Creating a New Project

Let's get down to business. First, create your project using the **project** command at the Roo shell, as follows:

```
roo> project --topLevelPackage com.prospringhibernate.gallery

Created ~/rooGallery/pom.xml
Created SRC_MAIN_JAVA
Created SRC_MAIN_RESOURCES
Created SRC_TEST_JAVA
Created SRC_TEST_RESOURCES
Created SRC_MAIN_WEBAPP
Created SRC_MAIN_RESOURCES/META-INF/spring
Created SRC_MAIN_RESOURCES/META-INF/spring/applicationContext.xml
Created SRC_MAIN_RESOURCES/log4j.properties
```

This command creates all of the necessary directories for a Maven project. Additionally, it sets up your Maven **pom.xml** file and creates a Spring **applicationContext.xml** file.

From the Roo shell, execute **hint** to see how the messaging has updated to reflect the current context of your application. You'll see that you have the basic structure, but no mechanism for persistence. So we'll follow Roo's suggestion and configure our JPA provider and associated database using Hibernate and the H2 in-memory database, as follows:

```
roo> persistence setup --provider HIBERNATE --database H2_IN_MEMORY
```

You'll notice in the resulting output that Roo creates a JPA **persistence.xml** configuration as well as a **database.properties** file. It also modifies the **applicationContext.xml** file and introduces a handful of dependencies to the **pom.xml** file.

After just two commands in Roo, you now have a completely configured Spring 3 and Hibernate 3.5 application. Roo has created many of the constructs we covered earlier in this book automatically with sensible defaults, including all the Spring beans necessary for JPA and declarative transaction management.

■ **Note** As someone who has been using Unix variants for almost two decades, it's hard not to fall in love with Roo's interactive shell. The Roo shell is so much more than just an interface for executing commands. Whenever you start up a Roo shell, whether it's from a Unix prompt or within an IDE, Roo keeps tabs on the files in your project and seamlessly makes modifications to your project on the fly in the background as you make changes to the code. This may sound a little disturbing at first, but those ITD files we mentioned earlier localize Roo's changes. Roo won't touch your Java files unless you explicitly issue commands to do so. And you, as a developer, just need to respect Roo's turf and shy away from editing the ITD files themselves.

As we'll demonstrate later in this chapter, it is incredibly easy to override Roo's automatically generated behavior. All of these considerations give you a lot of choice when developing an application. You may modify your code within your IDE as you normally would (for instance, to add fields to entities), or you can hop into your Roo shell and create your code in a command-line savvy way. This automation and flexibility of choice frees up precious development time to focus on what matters: the business problem at hand.

Adding Entities

Now we've created a project and configured our persistence layer. Again, execute the `hint` command within the shell, and you'll see that Roo is suggesting that we begin fleshing out our domain with the `entity` command. The `entity` command generates a simple JavaBean with JPA annotations. We'll start by creating our `ArtEntity` type using the `entity` command, as follows:

```
roo> entity --class com.prospringhibernate.gallery.domain.ArtEntity --testAutomatically

Created SRC_MAIN_JAVA/com/prospringhibernate/gallery/domain
Created SRC_MAIN_JAVA/com/prospringhibernate/gallery/domain/ArtEntity.java
Created SRC_MAIN_JAVA/com/prospringhibernate/gallery/domain/ArtEntity_Roo_Entity.aj
Created SRC_MAIN_JAVA/com/prospringhibernate/gallery/domain/ArtEntity_Roo_ToString.aj
Created SRC_MAIN_JAVA/com/prospringhibernate/gallery/domain/ArtEntity_Roo_Configurable.aj
Created SRC_TEST_JAVA/com/prospringhibernate/gallery/domain
Created SRC_TEST_JAVA/com/prospringhibernate/gallery/domain/ArtEntityDataOnDemand.java
Created SRC_TEST_JAVA/com/prospringhibernate/gallery/domain/ArtEntityIntegrationTest.java
Created SRC_TEST_JAVA/com/prospringhibernate/gallery/domain/↪
  ArtEntityDataOnDemand_Roo_Configurable.aj
Created SRC_TEST_JAVA/com/prospringhibernate/gallery/domain/↪
  ArtEntityDataOnDemand_Roo_DataOnDemand.aj
Created SRC_TEST_JAVA/com/prospringhibernate/gallery/domain/↪
  ArtEntityIntegrationTest_Roo_Configurable.aj
Created SRC_TEST_JAVA/com/prospringhibernate/gallery/domain/↪
  ArtEntityIntegrationTest_Roo_IntegrationTest.aj
```

The `entity` command gives you your first real glimpse into Roo's impressive code generation. It automatically created an `ArtEntity.java` entity bean with JPA and Roo annotations. It also created the folder structure that corresponds to our Java packaging scheme.

At this juncture, you also get your first taste of those AspectJ ITD files we mentioned earlier. The generated `ArtEntity` class itself is pretty lean, as Roo has tucked as much of the classic boilerplate code required in a series of ITD files. Remember that everything in the `.aj` files will be combined with the code you place in your `.java` source files at compile time.

Let's take a look at some of what was created. Our `ArtEntity.java` class follows.

```
package com.prospringhibernate.gallery.domain;

import javax.persistence.Entity;
import org.springframework.roo.addon.entity.RooEntity;
import org.springframework.roo.addon.javabean.RooJavaBean;
import org.springframework.roo.addon.tostring.RooToString;
```

```
@Entity
@RooJavaBean
@RooToString
@RooEntity
public class ArtEntity {

}
```

By now, the @Entity annotation and its behaviors should be quite familiar to you. The @Roo annotations warrant some explanation:

- @RooJavaBean tells Roo to generate accessors and mutators for each field present in the ArtEntity. Those getters and setters will show up in a file named ArtEntity_Roo_JavaBean.aj once we add some fields.

- The ArtEntity_Roo_ToString.aj source file corresponds with the @RooToString annotation. This source file will construct a toString() method representation for our entity by concatenating all of the field names and their values.

- @RooEntity is responsible for the majority of the generated code related to persistence.

- The ArtEntity_Roo_Configurable.aj source file created adds Spring's @Configurable annotation to our ArtEntity type. This annotation allows you to inject any types from the Spring bean factory, such as a JPA EntityManager, into the ArtEntity type.

At this juncture, the most interesting ITD file is probably ArtEntity_Roo_Entity.aj. It contains all of the boilerplate code you would expect to find in JPA entities. In the following listing, notice the code that has been automatically created contains an autogenerated id, a proper version field, and an EntityManager reference, as well as methods for operations (like persist, remove, merge, and flush) and several convenience finders.

```
package com.prospringhibernate.gallery.domain;

import com.prospringhibernate.gallery.domain.ArtEntity;

import java.util.List;
import java.lang.Integer;
import java.lang.Long;
import java.lang.SuppressWarnings;

import javax.persistence.Id;
import javax.persistence.Column;
import javax.persistence.Version;
import javax.persistence.EntityManager;
import javax.persistence.GeneratedValue;
import javax.persistence.GenerationType;
import javax.persistence.PersistenceContext;

import org.springframework.transaction.annotation.Transactional;

privileged aspect ArtEntity_Roo_Entity {
```

```java
@PersistenceContext
transient EntityManager ArtEntity.entityManager;

@Id
@GeneratedValue(strategy = GenerationType.AUTO)
@Column(name = "id")
private Long ArtEntity.id;

@Version
@Column(name = "version")
private Integer ArtEntity.version;

public Long ArtEntity.getId() {
    return this.id;
}

public void ArtEntity.setId(Long id) {
    this.id = id;
}

public Integer ArtEntity.getVersion() {
    return this.version;
}

public void ArtEntity.setVersion(Integer version) {
    this.version = version;
}

@Transactional
public void ArtEntity.persist() {
    if (this.entityManager == null)
        this.entityManager = entityManager();
    this.entityManager.persist(this);
}

@Transactional
public void ArtEntity.remove() {
    if (this.entityManager == null)
        this.entityManager = entityManager();
    if (this.entityManager.contains(this)) {
        this.entityManager.remove(this);
    } else {
        ArtEntity attached = this.entityManager.find(this.getClass(), this.id);
        this.entityManager.remove(attached);
    }
}

@Transactional
public void ArtEntity.flush() {
    if (this.entityManager == null)
        this.entityManager = entityManager();
```

```
        this.entityManager.flush();
    }

    @Transactional
    public ArtEntity ArtEntity.merge() {
        if (this.entityManager == null) this.entityManager = entityManager();
        ArtEntity merged = this.entityManager.merge(this);
        this.entityManager.flush();
        return merged;
    }

     public static final EntityManager ArtEntity.entityManager() {
        EntityManager em = new ArtEntity().entityManager;
        if (em == null) throw new
            IllegalStateException(
                "Is the Spring Aspects JAR configured as an AJC/AJDT aspects library?)
            ");
        return em;
    }

    public static long ArtEntity.countArtEntitys() {
      return ((Number) entityManager().createQuery(
        "select count(o) from ArtEntity o"
      ).getSingleResult()).longValue();
    }

    @SuppressWarnings("unchecked")
    public static List<ArtEntity> ArtEntity.findAllArtEntitys() {
        return entityManager().createQuery("select o from ArtEntity o").getResultList();
    }

    public static ArtEntity ArtEntity.findArtEntity(Long id) {
        if (id == null) return null;
        return entityManager().find(ArtEntity.class, id);
    }

    @SuppressWarnings("unchecked")
    public static List<ArtEntity> ArtEntity.findArtEntityEntries(int firstResult,
                                                      int maxResults) {
      return entityManager().createQuery(
        "select o from ArtEntity o"
      ).setFirstResult(firstResult).setMaxResults(maxResults).getResultList();
    }
}
```

As with the @Entity annotation, this code should feel very familiar and natural. Therein lies Roo's beauty. It is just normal Java code. It's no different than the code you would have needed to write on your own. It is already adhering to best practices, and will be upgraded to apply newer Spring and Hibernate conventions as you upgrade to newer versions of Roo. This alone is likely to save developers countless hours. It will also save your company a large amount of money in reduced costs to upgrade and fewer defects introduced by silly oversights and mistakes.

Adding Fields

The utility of the `field` command is fairly self-evident. With it, you can add members to a given entity. The `field` command allows you to specify attributes that are translated into JPA and JSR-303 annotations.

In the series of commands that follows, we'll add a few fields of type **string** and **date**, with some validation checks for field sizes and whether a given column in the database should allow null values.

```
~.domain.ArtEntity roo> field string --fieldName name --sizeMax 50 --notNull
~.domain.ArtEntity roo> field string --fieldName title --sizeMax 255 --notNull
~.domain.ArtEntity roo> field string --fieldName subtitle --sizeMax 255 --notNull
~.domain.ArtEntity roo> field string --fieldName description --sizeMax 255 --notNull
~.domain.ArtEntity roo> field string --fieldName caption --sizeMax 255 --notNull
~.domain.ArtEntity roo> field date --fieldName createDate --type java.util.Date --notNull
~.domain.ArtEntity roo> field date --fieldName displayDate --type java.util.Date
```

After executing each of those commands, you should see output like the following in your Roo shell. Each field is added to our Java class, and the ITD files are updated accordingly.

```
Managed SRC_MAIN_JAVA/com/prospringhibernate/gallery/domain/ArtEntity.java
Managed SRC_MAIN_JAVA/com/prospringhibernate/gallery/domain/ArtEntity_Roo_JavaBean.aj
Managed SRC_MAIN_JAVA/com/prospringhibernate/gallery/domain/ArtEntity_Roo_ToString.aj
Managed SRC_TEST_JAVA/com/prospringhibernate/gallery/domain/↦
    ArtEntityDataOnDemand_Roo_DataOnDemand.aj
```

Now our entity looks like this, complete with annotations for JSR-303 bean validation:

```
package com.prospringhibernate.artgallery.domain;

import java.util.Date;
import javax.persistence.Entity;
import javax.persistence.Temporal;
import javax.persistence.TemporalType;

import javax.validation.constraints.NotNull;
import javax.validation.constraints.Size;

import org.springframework.roo.addon.entity.RooEntity;
import org.springframework.roo.addon.javabean.RooJavaBean;
import org.springframework.roo.addon.tostring.RooToString;
import org.springframework.format.annotation.DateTimeFormat;

@Entity
@RooJavaBean
@RooToString
@RooEntity
public class ArtEntity {
```

```
@NotNull
@Size(max = 50)
private String name;

@NotNull
@Size(max = 255)
private String title;

@NotNull
@Size(max = 255)
private String subtitle;

@NotNull
@Size(max = 255)
private String description;

@NotNull
@Size(max = 255)
private String caption;

@NotNull
@Temporal(TemporalType.TIMESTAMP)
@DateTimeFormat(style = "S-")
private Date createDate;

@Temporal(TemporalType.TIMESTAMP)
@DateTimeFormat(style = "S-")
private Date displayDate;
}
```

Of course, Roo can't do everything for us. In the interest of simplicity, the framework designers needed to pick and choose which conventions they could realistically support. As an example, in our gallery application, we want the name field to be unique. Although this is a manual step, it can be accomplished quite simply. As you would on any project using a bean validation implementation, just apply the JSR-303 annotation to declare the value of the column as unique, like so:

```
@NotNull
@Size(max = 50)
@Column(unique=true)
private String name;
```

Exploring the Automatically Generated Testing Infrastructure

Now it's time to take a look at the --testAutomatically parameter used when we created our ArtEntity class earlier.

As we stressed in Chapter 8, unit and integration testing are essential for enterprise development projects. Roo's approach to configuring everything you would need in your test harnesses is another boon for productivity. Roo created fixture data in the ArtEntityDataOnDemand_Roo_DataOnDemand.aj source file and an integration test in ArtEntityIntegrationTest_Roo_IntegrationTest.aj. In addition, two Java source file stubs were generated for us to enhance the data fixtures further and to write our own integration tests that exercise business logic that Roo couldn't hope to infer. This gives us some basic test coverage with zero effort, as well as all the plumbing required to flesh out the tests on our own. You'll notice this exceptional attention to detail throughout your Roo experience.

Here is a snippet from the Data On Demand ITD:

```java
package com.prospringhibernate.gallery.domain;

...

privileged aspect ArtEntityDataOnDemand_Roo_DataOnDemand {

...

    public ArtEntity ArtEntityDataOnDemand.getNewTransientArtEntity(int index) {
        ArtEntity obj = new ArtEntity();
        obj.setCaption("caption_" + index);
        obj.setCreateDate(new java.util.Date());
        obj.setDescription("description_" + index);
        obj.setDisplayDate(new java.util.Date());
        obj.setName("name_" + index);
        obj.setSubtitle("subtitle_" + index);
        obj.setTitle("title_" + index);
        return obj;
    }

    ...

    @Transactional(propagation = Propagation.REQUIRES_NEW)
    public void ArtEntityDataOnDemand.init() {
        if (data != null) {
            return;
        }

        data = com.prospringhibernate.gallery.domain.ArtEntity.findArtEntityEntries(0, 10);
        if (data == null)
            throw new IllegalStateException(
                "Find entries implementation for 'ArtEntity' illegally returned null"
            );
        if (data.size() > 0) {
            return;
        }

        data = new java.util.ArrayList<com.prospringhibernate.gallery.domain.ArtEntity>();
        for (int i = 0; i < 10; i++) {
            com.prospringhibernate.gallery.domain.ArtEntity obj =
            getNewTransientArtEntity(i);
            obj.persist();
            data.add(obj);
        }
    }

}
```

This is a nice, simple approach for generating a small amount of data for each entity in a given application, and it provides the perfect springboard to strive for complete test coverage. You may verify that all of the generated tests are working by executing `perform tests` within your Roo shell or by running `mvn test` from your command prompt.

Mapping Associations

The `field` command has some special properties that deliver support for associations between entities as well. From the shell, you can specify one-to-many or one-to-one relationships with the `reference` attribute, or you can build many-to-many mappings via the `set` property.

In the following example, we re-create our `Category` entity, and then establish a many-to-many relationship between our `ArtEntity` and `Category` types.

```
~.domain.ArtEntity roo> entity --class com.prospringhibernate.gallery.domain.Category↪
                --testAutomatically

~.domain.Category roo> field string --fieldName name --notNull --sizeMax 50

~.domain.Category roo> field string --fieldName description --notNull --sizeMax 2000

~.domain.Category roo> field set --fieldName artEntities↪
                --element com.prospringhibernate.gallery.domain.ArtEntity

~.domain.Category roo> focus --class ~.domain.ArtEntity

~.domain.ArtGallery roo> field set --fieldName categories↪
                --element com.prospringhibernate.gallery.domain.Category
```

Creating the `Category` type is nearly identical to what we did previously to create `ArtEntity`, until the last property, `artEntities`, which establishes a collection of `ArtEntity` objects. We then use the `focus` command to change the context of our shell over to the `ArtGallery` type, and we add a collection of `Category` objects, again using the `set` command. The tilde (~) character offers a shorthand reference for the `topLevelPackage` we defined when we initiated the project.

Here's how the many-to-many association appears within the `ArtEntity` class:

```
@ManyToMany(cascade = CascadeType.ALL)
private Set<com.prospringhibernate.gallery.domain.Category> categories =
    new java.util.HashSet<com.prospringhibernate.gallery.domain.Category>();
```

This, too, should be quite familiar to you by now, and Roo makes the setup trivial.

Modeling Inheritance

Now we will walk through setting up an aspect of our domain that requires inheritance. Here too, the framework designers have elected to keep Roo simple, rather than allow enormous complexity to bleed into the syntax in the Roo shell. Having a strong grasp of the inner workings of Spring and Hibernate becomes vital on any real project, whether or not you're using a RAD framework. As you'll see, Roo will help you stub out these classes, but you'll still need to do a small amount of work on your own to actually make the associations work.

First, the following commands create our entity and establish a one-to-many relationship between ArtData and ArtEntity.

```
~.domain.ArtGallery roo> entity --class com.prospringhibernate.gallery.domain.ArtData↳
                         --testAutomatically

~.domain.ArtData roo> field set --fieldName artEntities↳
                      --element com.prospringhibernate.gallery.domain.ArtEntity
```

In order to introduce single-table inheritance between **ArtData** and its three subclasses—**ArtDataThumbnail**, **ArtDataStorage**, and **ArtDataGallery**—we need to manually add several annotations via either an IDE or text editor. The code in bold should be added manually.

```
package com.prospringhibernate.gallery.domain;

import java.util.Set;

import javax.persistence.Lob;
import javax.persistence.Basic;
import javax.persistence.Entity;
import javax.persistence.ManyToMany;
import javax.persistence.CascadeType;
import javax.persistence.Inheritance;
import javax.persistence.InheritanceType;
import javax.persistence.DiscriminatorType;
import javax.persistence.DiscriminatorValue;
import javax.persistence.DiscriminatorColumn;

import org.springframework.roo.addon.javabean.RooJavaBean;
import org.springframework.roo.addon.tostring.RooToString;
import org.springframework.roo.addon.entity.RooEntity;


@Entity
@RooJavaBean
@RooToString
@RooEntity
@Inheritance(strategy=InheritanceType.SINGLE_TABLE)
@DiscriminatorColumn(discriminatorType = DiscriminatorType.STRING)
@DiscriminatorValue("GENERIC")
public class ArtData {

    @Lob
    @Basic(fetch=javax.persistence.FetchType.LAZY)
    private byte[] file;

    @ManyToMany(cascade = CascadeType.ALL)
    private Set<com.prospringhibernate.gallery.domain.ArtEntity> artEntities =
        new java.util.HashSet<com.prospringhibernate.gallery.domain.ArtEntity>();

}
```

You'll also likely recall that our `ArtData` class and its subclasses had a BLOB field for storing the binary representation of the images. Roo doesn't yet support `byte[ ]` fields, but they're simple enough to add and annotate on our own via the adjustments shown in the preceding listing. We also need to add a Spring bean to our application context for LOB handling.

Now let's create the `ArtDataThumbnail` type, which extends `ArtData`.

```
~.domain.ArtData roo> entity --class com.prospringhibernate.gallery.domain.ArtDataThumbnail
                         --extends ~.domain.ArtData --testAutomatically
```

The `--extends` parameter sets up our class hierarchy. But again, since Roo doesn't have built-in support for JPA entity inheritance, we need to add a `@DiscriminatorValue` annotation ourselves.

```
package com.prospringhibernate.gallery.domain;

import javax.persistence.Entity;
import javax.persistence.DiscriminatorValue;

import org.springframework.roo.addon.entity.RooEntity;
import org.springframework.roo.addon.javabean.RooJavaBean;
import org.springframework.roo.addon.tostring.RooToString;

@Entity
@RooEntity
@RooJavaBean
@RooToString
@DiscriminatorValue("THUMBNAIL")
public class ArtDataThumbnail extends ArtData {

}
```

Creating the `ArtDataGallery` and `ArtDataStorage` types involves the same steps. The other entities in our model have some nuances as well. Check out the `rooGallery` code that accompanies the book to see the details.

Adding Spring MVC

Once your model is in place, the next logical step is to add Spring MVC to the mix to provide a HTML or RESTful front end for your application. Roo makes this ridiculously easy. If you don't need fine-grained control over each generated class, you can scaffold out the entire web front end in a single command.

```
controller all --package ~.web
```

And that's it! In another shell or within your IDE, execute `mvn tomcat:run` or `mvn jetty:run` and point your browser at `http://localhost:8080`. You should see something like the page shown in Figure 12-3.

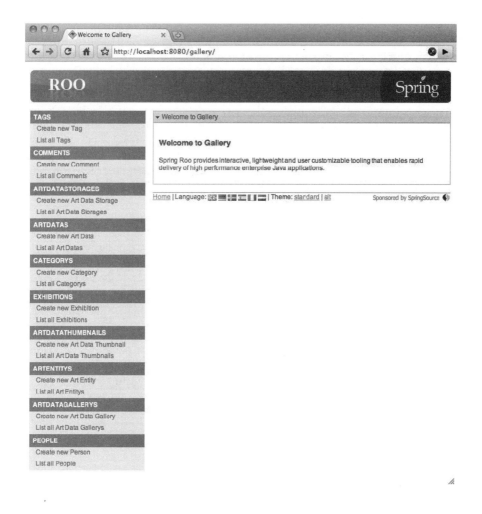

Figure 12-3. Running our Roo application

Of course, this is only very basic scaffolding for a web application, but it proves that everything you need for a Spring MVC web application is in place. From here, you would create more controllers or edit the generated ones to tailor the application to the needs of your business.

Adding Service Layers and DAOs

In the pursuit of simplicity, Roo will generate only the classes that are *strictly necessary*. When building a truly simple application, you can place business logic in either your controller or your domain class.

For nontrivial applications, we harbor strong preference for creating a service layer. This way, your controllers can strictly revolve around the management of HTTP semantics and view resolution. Your business logic is kept within your domain model and wrapped with a nice service layer façade as appropriate. This is especially important when modeling code that manipulates multiple entities in the same transaction.

Roo can't reasonably be expected to predict the intent of your application well enough to generate service layer classes for you. Fortunately, because Roo applications are just normal Spring projects, you can create a service layer class, annotate it with the @Service stereotype annotation, and your Roo application will automatically detect it and incorporate it into your application context.

As with a service layer, there's nothing about Roo that would prevent you from wiring DAOs into your application. The biggest shortcoming would be that the Roo add-on infrastructure doesn't support them, so you wouldn't enjoy some of the benefits we've shown here, like automatic integration tests.

WHY NOT DAOS?

The Roo team is perfectly justified in their stance against generating DAOs by default. The Roo team members went out of their way to explain their decision in their exceptional documentation. The following is quoted from *The Spring Roo - Reference Documentation*, Chapter 3. Application Architecture, Section 3.6. Goodbye DAOs (http://static.springsource.org/spring-roo/reference/html/architecture.html).

If we reflect for a moment on the main motivations for DAOs, it is easy to see why these are not applicable in Roo applications:

- Testing: In a normal application a DAO provides an interface that could be easily stubbed as part of unit testing. The interesting point about testing is that most people use mocking instead of stubbing in modern application, making it attractive to simply mock the persistence method or two that you actually require for a test (rather than the crudeness of stubbing an entire DAO interface). In Roo-based applications you simply mock the persistence-related methods that have been introduced to the entity. You can use normal mocking approaches for the instance methods on the Roo entity, and use Spring Aspect's @MockStaticEntityMethods support for the static finder methods.

- Separation of concern: One reason for having a DAO layer is that it allows a higher cohesion object-oriented design to be pursued. The high cohesion equates to a separation of concern that reduces the conceptual weight of implementing the system. In a Roo-based application separation of concern is achieved via the separate ITDs. The conceptual weight is also reduced because Roo handles the persistence methods rather than force the programmer to deal with them. Therefore separation of concern still exists in a Roo application without the requirement for a DAO layer.

- Pluggable implementations: A further benefit of DAOs is they simplify the switching from one persistence library to another. In modern applications this level of API abstraction is provided via JPA. As Roo uses JPA in its generated methods, the ability to plug in an alternate implementation is already fully supported despite there being no formal DAO layer. You can see this yourself by issuing the persistence setup command and specifying alternate implementations.

- Non-JPA persistence: It is possible that certain entities are stored using a technology that does not have a JPA provider. In this case Roo 1.0.0 does not support those entities out of the box. However, if only a small number of entities are effected [sic] by this consideration there is no reason one or more hand-written ITDs could not be provided by the user in order to maintain conceptual parity with the remainder of the Roo application (which probably does have some JPA). If a large number of entities are effected [sic], the project would probably benefit from the user writing a Roo add-on which will automatically manage the ITDs just as Roo does for JPA.

- Architectural reasons: Often people express a preference for a DAO because they've always done it that way. While maintaining a proven existing approach is generally desirable, adopting Roo for an application diminishes the value of a DAO layer to such an extent that it leaves little (if any) engineering-related reasons to preserve it.

It's also worth observing that most modern RAD frameworks avoid DAO layers and add persistence methods directly to entities. If you review similar technologies to Roo, you will see this is [sic] avoidance of a DAO layer is commonplace, mainstream and does not cause problems.

Now You See Me, Now You Don't—Removing Roo

One of our favorite aspects of Roo is that it's easy to remove it from a project. Since you can use Roo on existing legacy projects, and since it's easy to remove any trace of Roo from your source code, there's very little reason not to try it out. If you get any pushback from the team or your organization, you remove it in just a few moments, so there's very little risk involved.

Removing Roo is a task best undertaken from an IDE that understands AspectJ, such as Eclipse or STS. Here are the steps in Eclipse with AspectJ Development Tools (AJDT) installed:

1. Stop any Roo shells that might be running.

2. In Eclipse, within the Java Browsing perspective, right-click your project and choose Refactor ▶ Push In.

3. You will see a dialog box listing all of the ITDs. Select OK to push all of that code from your `.aj` source files into the appropriate `.java` source files.

4. Perform a recursive find and replace on the files in your project where you replace the regular expression `\n.*Roo.*\n` with `\n`. This will remove all of the Roo annotations and their import declarations.

5. Remove any Roo dependencies from your maven `pom.xml` file.

And that's it. Because there are no runtime dependencies and because Roo is built atop standard Java technologies, it's easy to walk away from the framework and not lose any of the work that you've done.

Summary

As you've seen in this chapter, although Roo isn't yet magical enough to put programmers out of work, it does give you an enormous jump-start in terms of raw development speed. It helps eliminate much of the tedium associated with developing enterprise Java applications by automatically generating boilerplate code into AspectJ ITDs and modifying your Spring application context configuration as your project grows.

Roo boasts a strong architecture based on OSGi and add-ons. With the backing of SpringSource, it's likely to evolve at a frantic pace as the Roo team strives to deliver more best-of-breed solutions that simplify the lives of developers around the globe.

One of the biggest hurdles for adopting most RAD frameworks on the JVM is that using them is a viable option only when writing a new application or in the rare circumstance that a total application rewrite is in order. But Roo can be introduced into an existing application without forcing any changes to the way other team members write their code. As the framework is proven in your environment, the productivity gains should be irrefutable, and your development team will likely embrace the positive change. We highly recommend that you try using it to implement a new feature on your existing Spring- and Hibernate-powered application.

Index

You Need the Companion eBook

Your purchase of this book entitles you to buy the companion PDF-version eBook for only $10. Take the weightless companion with you anywhere.

We believe this Apress title will prove so indispensable that you'll want to carry it with you everywhere, which is why we are offering the companion eBook (in PDF format) for $10 to customers who purchase this book now. Convenient and fully searchable, the PDF version of any content-rich, page-heavy Apress book makes a valuable addition to your programming library. You can easily find and copy code—or perform examples by quickly toggling between instructions and the application. Even simultaneously tackling a donut, diet soda, and complex code becomes simplified with hands-free eBooks!

Once you purchase your book, getting the $10 companion eBook is simple:

❶ Visit **www.apress.com/promo/tendollars/**.

❷ Complete a basic registration form to receive a randomly generated question about this title.

❸ Answer the question correctly in 60 seconds, and you will receive a promotional code to redeem for the $10.00 eBook.

eBookshop

Apress®
THE EXPERT'S VOICE™

233 Spring Street, New York, NY 10013

Offer valid through 2/11.